le besoin d'être aimé [...]
Des charmes féminins [...]
Des vertus d'homme et la franchise. [...] La ca
D'être tendres pour moi si leur personne est assez [...]
Ne pas savoir, ne pas pouvoir "Vouloir"
Aimer

J'ai peur qu'il ne soit pas assez élevé, je ne
et j'ai peur de le détruire en le disant
ne pas avoir [...] ma mère ni [...]
Moi, comme les gens que j'admire me voudraient
[celui] où certaines choses que je voudrais
[...] par un enchantement ——— et où les
[...] n'est pas dans les couleurs mais dans leur
La sienne — et après toutes

L'hirondelle

aujourd'hui Anatole France et Pierre Loti
Baudelaire et Alfred de Vigny
Hamlet

[...] Bérénice

THE PROUST PROJECT

EDITED BY ANDRÉ ACIMAN

THE Proust Project

FARRAR, STRAUS AND GIROUX

TURTLE POINT PRESS

BOOKS & CO.

HELEN MARX BOOKS

NEW YORK

Farrar, Straus and Giroux
19 Union Square West, New York 10003

Distributed in Canada by Douglas & McIntyre Ltd.
Printed in the United States of America
Published in association with Turtle Point Press Consortium:
Turtle Point Press, Books & Co., and Helen Marx Books
First edition, 2004

Library of Congress Cataloging-in-Publication Data
The Proust project / edited by André Aciman.
    p.   cm.
ISBN-13: 978-0-374-23832-2
ISBN-10: 0-374-23832-4 (hc : alk. paper)
1. Proust, Marcel, 1871–1922. A la recherche du temps perdu. I. Aciman, André.

PQ2631.R63A8624 2004
843'.912—dc22

                                            2004047060

Designed by Quemadura

www.fsgbooks.com

1 3 5 7 9 10 8 6 4 2

Frontispiece: Proust in Venice. Photographer unknown.
All rights reserved. Used with permission.

CONTENTS

That first time.

Most of us remember who we were, where we were, and what we were doing when we came face to face with Proust for the first time. Even passing by the neatly stacked volumes of *In Search of Lost Time* in a bookstore and deciding not to leaf through them, or not to buy any *just yet*, counts as a first time. Hearing grown-ups mention the name Proust while we paid him no mind, or thought he was someone else, or guessed his whole vision without so much as knowing a thing about him—these too, over time, go into making that first time when our mind encountered an illuminating consciousness called Proust. Sometimes, however, that undefined, primal moment is lost. We simply do not remember where, how, when . . . If only I could scale back in time and recover that first time and pin down its precise coordinates, then, for sure, I'll finally be able to hold on to my entire Marcel Proust experience, from first to the most recent. We do so with love when we go back to our first glance— why not with books? Besides, going back to nebulous, irretrievable beginnings is integral to the Proustian experience—not just because something pristine and authentic must have happened that first time, or because the book is about beginnings, but because, in retrospect, it seems there was never a time when we weren't already aware of Marcel Proust.

I do not remember exactly what happened late on a rainy weekday morning years ago in a bookstore called Gibert in the Latin Quarter, but I must have thought something along the following lines: I'm not sure whether I understand what I'm reading or whether I'm making it up. But I am almost certain that this writer, who I am ready to swear knows me better than I know myself and who is strange in just the way I know I am strange, will eventually turn out to be like all the others. All authors get close, sometimes very close, only to remind me that between them and

Preface

me there had scarcely been a thing in common. Except that I am on page three already and this about-face, which I've been dreading all along and which hovers like an unspoken threat while I'm reading this *Livre de Poche* edition, hasn't happened yet.

Not exactly this but something like it.

This is why reading Proust must have been quite uncanny the first time: it must have dawned on me—as it dawns on every reader of Proust—that this magical fusion of sensibilities that had so mesmerized me and made me want to hold on to it for fear it might any moment slip away was not incidental to the reading experience but, in Proust's case, irreducibly central to it. Without this fusion, the *Search* is a total fiasco. The novel is about intimacy, the miracle of intimacy—intimacy with others, intimacy with oneself, intimacy when we'd all but given up believing it existed—because there is also this about Proust that strikes an unmistakable chord: if intimacy is difficult to come by, it is because honesty is just as scarce, honesty with others and, above all, with oneself. One either feels this call to intimacy or one stops reading.

One of the reasons why Proust speaks so intimately is because he desperately sought and, by middle age, had finally developed a style, a vision, something like the "native air of a lost, forgotten, inner homeland" that was uniquely and exclusively his. It took the most painstaking skill and devotion to give this "homeland" its voice and to translate its timbre into everyone's language. The more exclusive this "native air," the more intimate it becomes. This is the paradox that underwrites every single sentence of the *Search*. How Proust closed the distance between one person and another person, or how he took his private, thoroughly idiosyncratic world and made us feel at home in it, is really a question of one thing only: art.

> [E]very reader is, while he is reading, the reader of his own self. The writer's work is merely a kind of optical instrument which he offers to the reader to enable him to discern what, without this book, he would perhaps never have perceived in himself. And the recognition by the reader in his own self of what the book says is the proof of its veracity, the contrary also being true . . .

Preface

Discovering Proust is like wandering through a totally unfamiliar land and finding it peopled with kindred spirits and sister souls and fellow countrymen and coreligionists. We grope and fumble awhile, but ultimately we see it: we have actually come home. Our *Landmänner* are all around us, and all we must do is reach out to them. They speak our language, our dialect, share our blind spots, and are awkward in exactly the same way we are, just as their manner of lacing every access of sorrow with slapstick reminds us so much of how we do it when we are sad and wish to hide it, that surely we are not alone and not as strange as we feared we were. The paradox again. So long as a writer tells us what he and only he can see, then surely he speaks our language.

That first time.

There are plenty of good reasons not to ask what we were doing, or who we were in love with, or what demons we were battling when we ran into Proust the first time. Such questions would tell us very little about ourselves, and less than nothing about Proust. Ask any literature majors in college and they will instantly remind you that the first two things to do when thinking *critically* about a work of literature is to banish all references to its author's life and all references to ours.

But this is precisely the problem with Proust. The *Search* is a novel about someone's past that allows us—indeed, invites us and ultimately compels us—to graft, to "bookmark" our own past onto his. Just change the characters, we say, alter their names, change the scenery, and you've captured my life. Indeed, we are so stitched into his life, and his is so woven into ours, that when rereading his novel we are just as likely to run into him revisiting his past as into ourselves having visited and revisited this or that passage . . . in the past. In Proust's own words: "A name read long ago in a book contains within its syllables the strong wind and the brilliant sunshine that prevailed while we were reading it."

And here is the tricky part: any attempt to avoid this necessary fusion between Proust and us is not to avoid a pitfall; it is to fall right into it.

Proust's novel may not be an incitement to play fast and loose with

Preface

literary criticism. But it does what great works normally do to criticism: it puts to shame all of our methodological devices and reminds us that our neat little prying tools are as obsolete and functionless as eighteenth-century pliers are to a modern neurosurgeon. The seductive power of a novel such as the *Search* lies in its personal invitation to each one of us to read Marcel's life as if we, and not Marcel, were its true subject. Marcel is the functional, the virtual, the shadow author; but—just as real copper was called *honest-to-god* copper during World War II when copper had become the code name for plutonium—it is we who are the novel's *honest-to-god* subject. There may be one Marcel, but he fails as a writer if he does not persuade his millions of readers that it is *they* who are the honest-to-god Marcel.

And that too is art.

If all of us have our primal moment with Proust, each has his or her primal scene as well. In my case, it is not the good-night kiss. Not the madeleine dunked in a lime-tree infusion. Not the three church steeples that beckon to the young Marcel, urging him to cast them down to paper, because their beauty had come to him, to use Joyce's words, "mirrored perfectly in lucid supple periodic prose."

For me, the primal scene takes place on a Saturday evening when the Proust family is out on a moonlit walk around the small country town of Combray, now renamed Illiers-Combray.

> [T]he next day being Sunday, with no need to be up and stirring before high mass, if it was a moonlight night and warm, then, instead of taking us home at once, my father, in his thirst for glory, instead of taking us home at once would lead us on a long walk round by the Cavalry, which my mother's utter incapacity for taking her bearings, or even for knowing which road she might be on, made her regard as a triumph of his strategic genius. Sometimes we would go as far as the viaduct, whose long stone strides began at the railway station, and to me typified all the wretchedness of exile beyond the last outposts of civilization, because every year, as we came down from Paris, we were warned to take special care when we got to Combray not to miss the station, to be ready before

Preface

the train stopped, since it would start again in two minutes and proceed across the viaduct, out of the lands of Christendom, of which Combray, to me, represented the farthest limit. We would return by the Boulevard de la Gare, which contained the most attractive villas in the town. In each of their gardens the moonlight, copying the art of Hubert Robert, scattered its broken staircases of white marble, its fountains, its iron gates temptingly ajar. Its beams had swept away the telegraph office. All that was left of it was a column, half shattered, but preserving the beauty of a ruin which endures for all time. I would by now be dragging my weary limbs, and ready to drop with sleep; the balmy scent of the lime-trees seemed a reward that could be won only at the price of great fatigue and not worth the effort. From gates far apart the watchdogs, awakened by our steps in the silence, would set up an antiphonal barking, as I still hear at times of the evenings, and among which the Boulevard de la Gare (when the public gardens of Combray were constructed on its site) must have taken refuge, for wherever I may be, as soon as they begin their alternate challenge and response, I can see it again with all its lime-trees, and its pavement glistening beneath the moon.

Because the evening is quite dark, Marcel is convinced that his parents have lost their way. Indeed, the sentences just quoted are themselves a touch awkward, labored, and lost. In describing the boy's desperate fatigue and the mystifying play of moonlight, Proust will do something that is familiar to his readers: he will pit the lyrical effusions of a dreamy, soulful, delicate, exhausted young sensibility against the hard brute facts of day-to-day, down-to-earth, latter-day reality: railway station, telegraph office, station boulevard, public garden. This, after all, is signature Proust: to capture the airy beauty of a moonlit evening, Proust must punctuate it with humdrum nuts-and-bolts facts; to gain access to poetry, he must pay tribute to prose; to find eternity in the moment, he must be too tired to see it. To exult in the timeless, he must feel totally time-bound. Ageless viaducts will always, always be offset by ordinary train stations, just as the visibly disoriented mother is always offset by the unflappable father, her tender helplessness foiled by his gruff, sobering exasperation.

Preface

In the play of light and dark, the boy spots a gate magically and mysteriously left ajar, almost inviting him to venture beyond. What world, what homes, what loves, what *paths unknown* await all around him if he only dared to heed their call. A beam of moonlight has touched the telegraph office and seemingly defaced it, so that the building suddenly looks like a vestige dating back to antiquity, and "[a]ll that was left of it was a column, half shattered, but preserving the beauty of a ruin which endures for all time." Now the ordinary has been touched—sanctioned—by antiquity, and from a menial turn-of-the-century telegraph office found everywhere in gray provincial towns like Combray has sprung miraculously something totally unsuspected, solemn and immemorial, transcending time and the small town square.

The question of time was already hovering over these sentences. During the family's walk, Marcel had allowed his mind to wander and muse on the viaduct and, by so doing, to go back to a not-so-distant time when the family had first arrived at Combray. But then, even after the mention of erstwhile ruins and the evocation of his family's arrival, the subject of time resurfaces yet again. The barking of the dogs along the station boulevard that night is now forever impressed in Marcel's memory; every time he will hear their antiphonal barking elsewhere in life, his mind will unavoidably go back to the moonlit boulevard with his parents in Combray. And here flickers yet a fourth suggestion of time. The barking of dogs will remind Marcel that the boulevard where dogs had once barked no longer exists, that it too, like buried antiquity, has disappeared and yielded its spot to municipal gardens.

The compulsive oscillations between imperfect, present perfect, simple past, and future anterior could have gone on forever if they were not interrupted by a very simple fact. The boy is really lost. It's very late. He is exhausted. There are grounds for worrying.

I know this scene too well. My father, my mother, the scant light on the streets, some barking dog following our footsteps from behind a dark fence, the gripping silence of the night signifying danger, the fear we might have missed the last metro and may never find a taxi anywhere.

Preface

"Do we really need a taxi? Or the metro?" asks my father finally pointing to our all-too-familiar Rue Greuze. *Change the characters, alter their names, change the scenery . . .*

> Suddenly my father would bring us to a standstill and ask my mother—"Where are we?" Exhausted by the walk but still proud of her husband, she would lovingly confess that she had not the least idea. He would shrug his shoulders and laugh. And then, as though he had produced *it* [italics mine] with his latchkey from his waistcoat pocket, he would point out to us, where it stood before our eyes, the back-gate of our own garden, which had come hand-in-hand with the familiar corner of the Rue du Saint-Esprit, to greet us at the end of our wanderings over paths unknown. My mother would murmur admiringly "You really are wonderful!"

Like every Proustian sentence, no matter how diffuse, the seemingly aimless walk in the dark did have a destination after all—but who knew? The pointless remarks about the moonlight and the dogs and their barking and the station square abutting the viaduct that marked the end of Christendom, and the boulevard that was eventually replaced by a municipal park, all had a purpose. Even the ambiguous "it" in the sentence just quoted had a purpose. The reader, like the boy Marcel a moment earlier, is totally lost, and has no idea what the pronoun *it* refers to, since it stands for a noun that hasn't been revealed yet, because the narrator, like the father, is also shrugging his shoulders and really having a good time of teasing and holding out on us, saving the key word "back-gate" until very last, forcing the reader to put all his faith on that "it" like a trapeze jumper whose life hangs on his wrist.

And perhaps this too had been the purpose all along: not to show how Marcel's tired mind meandered through different bends of time, but to string the reader along, to sidetrack the reader, to lose the reader, the way the writer has allowed himself to wander and to lose his bearings in such an impossibly long sentence, the better to savor the shock of seeing the family reach, of all places in the world, and against all expecta-

Preface

tions, the back-gate to a home that is none other than their very own. What could have been more natural, more obvious? Marcel may have been playing with danger to overcome it, to let his mind wander and take all manner of twists on this spooky nightwalk the better to be roused by the most welcome sight of all. Home.

And yet, what matters isn't just home or the back-gate. What matters is the sheer joy of revelation, of epiphany. The whole point of getting lost—and every sentence by Proust seems intentionally meant to get lost—is the sudden, bewildering luster that accompanies every form of homecoming. What one *comes home* to may be a back-gate, or the disclosure of one's artistic vocation, or the secret behind cooked asparagus, or the fact that, after all is said and done, one was never really in love with the woman who made us want to die for want of her love. What matters is the joy with which, after many, many turns, we find ourselves discovering things we've always known but didn't know we knew. The long walk, like Proust's long sentence, is simply an elaborate birthing—a painstaking, meticulous piece of midwifery that takes him from things apparently lost (*perdus*) to things finally recovered (*retrouvés*).

Perhaps we put off coming home to relish coming home. Or to find secret pathways and unforeseen shortcuts—and with them, perhaps, adventure, novelty, excitement. It is because we've lost our way and because our habits can no longer come to our rescue that we struggle to put our world back together again—and in the process catch glimpses of an ancillary, adjacent, undisclosed netherworld. The more time is wedged between loss and recovery, the more poignant and more luminous the homecoming. Who can forget Ulysses' return to his homeland after twenty long years. The Phaeacians have no sooner deposited his sleeping body on Ithacan soil than the "great Odysseus woke from sleep on native ground at last—he'd been away for years—but failed to know the land."*

But failed to know the land . . . Perhaps the boy Marcel and the writer Proust enjoy being lost. Perhaps what they love is deferral—not losing

*From the Robert Fagles translation of *The Odyssey*.

Preface

time, not recovering time, but opening a space all their own and making time. Or perhaps they wish to invent a new home but don't have the courage to go all the way and are only too glad to have toyed with the notion and gotten off lightly. Like an author who realizes that the best thing he could have done was to avoid ending his sentence and, on a whim almost, to keep going, he has suddenly entered a thrilling uncharted territory that turns out to be closer to his heart than anything he had previously set down to describe. It came to him by accident. But then the thing about these accidents is that they are intentionally deployed.

And here we're once again back to the question of art: art propitiates accidental homecomings. It sets up and invokes that privileged moment which the Greeks called *anagnorisis*: recognition. In the end it is seldom what is revealed that matters for Proust. For all he cares, it could be asparagus or roasted chicken or the metallic chime of a tiny bell or of a fallen spoon. It is revelation that matters.

Nothing pleases him more than to sense that something is hovering on the very tip of consciousness, at once beckoning and withdrawing and finally coaxed into the light of day. No wonder, then, that when Marcel hears Vinteuil's sonata in *The Captive*—the "soundtrack" to Swann and Odette's romance—the sonata does not lunge at him but, as it had done with Swann long before Marcel's birth, it gradually discloses which sonata it is. What a joy for Marcel finally to recognize it. What a joy for Proust to have wandered into the following passage. And what a joy for us to recognize that long-lost, familiar, primal scene.

> The concert began, I did not know what was being played; I found myself in a strange land. Where was I to place it? Who was the composer? I longed to know, and, seeing nobody near me whom I could ask, I should have liked to be a character in those *Arabian Nights* which I never tired of reading and in which, in moments of uncertainty, there appears a genie, or a maiden of ravishing beauty, invisible to everyone else but not to the perplexed hero to whom she reveals exactly what he wishes to learn. And indeed at that very moment I was favored with just such a magical apparition. *As when, in a stretch of country which one thinks one does not know and which in fact we have approached from a new direction, after*

Preface

turning a corner one finds oneself suddenly emerging on to a road every inch of which is familiar, but one had simply not been in the habit of approaching it that way, one suddenly says to oneself: "Why, this is the lane that leads to the garden gate of my friends the X——s; I am only two minutes from their house," and there, indeed, is their daughter who has come out to greet one as one goes by [italics mine]; so, all of a sudden, I found myself, in the midst of this music that was new to me, right in the heart of Vinteuil's sonata; and, more marvelous than any girl, the little phrase, sheathed, harnessed in silver, glittering with brilliant sonorities, as light and soft as silken scarves, came towards me, recognizable in this new guise. My joy at having rediscovered it . . .

Both the earlier passage from *Swann's Way* and the later one from *The Captive* tell the same tale with the same moral: we stray and get lost, and are almost ready to give up, but how wonderful that middle mist between premonition and certainty, between errancy and home. And how much more wonderful to see old things as if for the first time.

This, I wager, lies at the heart of Proust's vision.

A few pages later Marcel will listen to Vinteuil's septet and begin thinking of the vital role that art plays in the life of great artists. What are great artists? Great artists are individuals who are forever attuned "to a lost country" they do not necessarily remember, an "inner homeland" which they betray from time to time when they make concessions to workaday existence but are lucky to recover its "native air." Great artists delve into the better part of themselves which they cannot share with anyone, not even themselves, because they cannot know it unless they've objectified it and given it a form, and having given it a form, put it before the world and said—like a chemist finally discovering an element—This was it all along, wasn't it? And we turn to him as we would to a magician and we say, You really are wonderful.

[I]s it not true that . . . all the residuum of reality which we are obliged to keep to ourselves, which cannot be transmitted in talk, even from friend to friend, from master to disciple, from lover to mistress, that ineffable something which differentiates qualitatively what each of us has felt and what he is obliged to leave behind at the threshold of the phrases

Preface

in which he can communicate with others only by limiting himself to externals, common to us all and of no interest—are brought out by art, the art of a Vinteuil like that of an Elstir, which exteriorises in the colors of the spectrum the intimate composition of those worlds which we call individuals and which, but for art, we should never know?

Art does not only transcend time. The genius of an artist, as Marcel tells Albertine a while later, is his ability to reveal to others a world that is entirely unique to him.

The only true voyage, the only bath in the Fountain of Youth, would be not to visit strange lands but to possess other eyes, to see the universe through the eyes of another, of a hundred others, to see the hundred universes that each of them sees, that each of them is; and this we can contrive with an Elstir, with a Vinteuil; with men like these we do really fly from star to star.

Proust was an extraordinarily munificent writer. He loved nothing better than to discover, through the eyes of others, ways of seeing and of understanding life around him that he might never have otherwise imagined. Not all of us are as unselfish or as lucky. We would be plenty happy to know that others see what we see, not more, perhaps less, or that others are really like us, but not better, and that each of us, in the end, shares the same basic Proust. But as we read the pages of this volume, let us put our thoughts on hold and try to see Proust through the eyes of twenty-eight other pairs of eyes, each beckoning a Proust we never knew existed, a Proust we would never have thought possible until someone told us that their Proust was no less real than ours.

ANDRÉ ACIMAN
NEW YORK CITY

The English-language edition of Marcel Proust's *A la recherche du temps perdu* generally used in the book is D. J. Enright's *In Search of Lost Time*, published in 1993 by Random House. This edition is the latest revision of C. K. Scott Moncrieff's classic *Remembrance of Things Past*, which was published serially between 1922 and 1930, then revised by Terence Kilmartin in 1981.

In the essays by Lydia Davis and Richard Howard we have used the authors' own translations. Ms. Davis's excerpt is taken from the edition of *Swann's Way* published in 2003 by Viking Press. All other page references are to the Random House edition.

Plot précis connecting sections from *In Search of Lost Time* are by Noam Scheindlin.

It is with the deepest gratitude that I wish to thank Anne Skillion, whose judgment and devotion to *The Proust Project* remain a moving tribute to our friendship.

THE PROUST PROJECT

The little village of Combray, not far from Paris, is the country residence of a well-to-do bourgeois family. For Marcel, the young narrator, there are spring walks on flower-lined paths and summertime days spent luxuriously reading in his cool dark room. His grandmother likes to take evening strolls in the garden after dinner, her desire for fresh air knowing no bounds. His hypochondriacal invalid aunt, whose malady, she claims, prevents her from ever sleeping, "rests" in rooms forever fragrant with freshly baked brioches. There is a stern father, and a doting mother who comes every night before bed to give her son a good-night kiss, after which, and only after which, he can sleep.

When the family has a guest, it is generally Charles Swann, a man who, although a Jew and a bourgeois, is currently in fashion with the aristocratic dinner-party set and has made a name for himself in the society columns. When the bell rings at the garden gate, the theater of anticipation begins: the questioning looks, the admonitions not to whisper and make the guest uncomfortable. "A visitor! Who in the world could it be?" Someone goes to answer the door. A voice is heard approaching, and with that, Swann once again joins the family. Although he is married, Swann has the air of a bachelor; he is well aware that his wife is not highly regarded, so he conducts his social visits alone.

His visit is a pleasure to everyone but little Marcel. Because his parents are busy with their guest, for Marcel, Swann's visit spells banishment, loneliness, sleeplessness: the unavailability of his mother for her nightly kiss.

I never took my eyes off my mother. I knew that when they were at table I should not be permitted to stay there for the whole of dinner-time, and that Mamma, for fear of annoying my father, would not allow me to kiss her several times in public, as I would have done in my room. And so I promised myself that in the dining-room, as they began to eat and drink and as I felt the hour approach, I would put beforehand into this kiss, which was bound to be so brief and furtive, everything that my own efforts could muster, would carefully choose in advance the exact spot on her cheek where I would imprint it, and would so prepare my thoughts as to be able, thanks to these mental preliminaries, to consecrate the whole of the minute Mamma would grant me to the sensation of her cheek against my lips, as a painter who can have his subject for short sittings only prepares his palette, and from what he remembers and from rough notes does in advance everything which he possibly can do in the sitter's absence. But tonight, before the dinner-bell had sounded, my grandfather said with unconscious cruelty: "The little man looks tired; he'd better go up to bed. Besides, we're dining late tonight."

And my father, who was less scrupulous than my grandmother or my mother in observing the letter of a treaty, went on: "Yes; run along; off to bed."

I would have kissed Mamma then and there, but at that moment the dinner-bell rang.

"No, no, leave your mother alone. You've said good night to one another, that's enough. These exhibitions are absurd. Go on upstairs."

And so I must set forth without viaticum; must climb each step of the staircase "against my heart," as the saying is, climbing in opposition to my heart's desire, which was to return to my mother, since she had not, by kissing me, given my heart leave to accompany me. That hateful staircase, up which I always went so sadly, gave out a smell of varnish which had, as it were, absorbed and crystallised the special quality of sorrow that I felt each evening, and made it perhaps even crueller to my sensibility because, when it assumed this olfactory guise, my intellect was powerless to resist it. When we have gone to sleep with a raging toothache and are conscious of it only as of a little girl whom we attempt, time after time, to pull out of the water, or a line of Molière which we repeat incessantly to ourselves, it is a great relief to wake up, so that our intelligence can disentangle the idea of toothache from any artificial semblance of heroism or rhythmic cadence. It was the converse of this relief which I

Swann's Way

felt when my anguish at having to go up to my room invaded my consciousness in a manner infinitely more rapid, instantaneous almost, a manner at once insidious and brutal, through the inhalation—far more poisonous than moral penetration—of the smell of varnish peculiar to that staircase.

(*Swann's Way*, 35–36)

Judith Thurman

It is dinnertime at Combray, a mild spring evening, warm enough to take coffee in the garden, and Swann is expected. Marcel, the "little man" who has embarked upon his "puberty of sorrow," is fed early by the cook, Françoise, and sent to his room—up the staircase that smells so odiously of varnish (and it is Proust's intention that his narrator should strip away, layer by layer—as tenderly as a lover undressing his paramour— the lacquer of secrecy and decorum that overlays the rawness of the world). Meanwhile, his mamma passes a companionable evening in the "forbidden and unfriendly dining-room," "tasting of unknown pleasures," as her son waits, famished, for the "host" of her kiss. An infinitude of yearning is compressed into the restless and pathetic hours in which he listens for the rustle of her skirts, imagining how her lips will brush his cheek, and how his own will leave their imprint—their ephemeral mark of possession—upon hers.

Was any writer ever sexually more inquisitive, disillusioned, or rapacious than this fragile aesthete with exquisite manners who entombs himself in a cork-lined room? The *Search* is a novel that seethes not only with carnality but with candor about it. I had forgotten how shameless its opening scenes are, and my shock was not one of prudery but of gratitude for the example of so much brazen freedom. Proust sets the tone—the bar of audacity—with Marcel's first reverie. As he lies in bed, consoling himself under the covers, as the sleepless and pubescent do,

Judith Thurman

a woman—Eve—is born "during my sleep from some misplacing of my thigh. Conceived from the pleasure I was on the point of consummating, she it was, I imagined, who offered me that pleasure. My body, conscious that its own warmth was penetrating hers, would strive to become one with her, and I would awake. The rest of humanity seemed very remote in comparison with this woman whose company I had left but a moment ago; my cheek was still warm from her kiss, my body ached beneath the weight of hers." The identity of this delicious and pliant half-waking apparition will shortly be revealed, and it must be said that Marcel's desire for the true subject of his dream is no chaster, no more dignified, no less intense or incontinent than his lust for her stand-in. As he yearns and schemes obsessively to possess her—picturing their two merged bodies alone in Eden—he reformulates Genesis (the "Overture" to the *Search* is Proust's Genesis) so that the First Couple are not a man and a woman, but a mother and son.

When I was younger and green, I read the *Search* for what it could teach me about refinement. Now that I am seasoned, I read it for what it teaches me about voracity. Proust is the model of a great writer: a tenacious soul weak with hunger for experience and sensation, but above all for the milk of meaning to be sucked from them. Hunger, he suggests, not only exercises the faculty of imagination but generates it. The starving, like confectioners of fiction, gorge voluptuously on nothing. They are connoisseurs of all that has been promised, lost, withheld, cherished, discredited, and expended; of what lies beyond reach, in the past, may not exist, or is yet to come. In the form of hunger, a human infant waiting for the breast first experiences life-and-death suspense: narrative at its most primal. And narrative at its worldliest, like Proust's—a banquet that would be decadent and cloying in its excess of richness if it didn't appeal to our appetite for the sublime—teaches us not only to understand, and helps us not only to endure and to accept, but to savor the insatiable longings that define us.

A dreamy boy, young Marcel can stare for hours at the steeple of the Cathedral of Saint-Hilaire, which presides over all the business of Combray, and he can sit in the garden and read for hours while Françoise, the family housekeeper, prepares asparagus meal after meal (because the pregnant kitchen maid, whom she detests, is allergic to it). Eventually, however, Marcel grows frustrated with the stillness and predictability of life in Combray. He dreams of traveling to Italy, of encountering a young woman on his walks in the woods, of the Normandy resort town of Balbec.

When Marcel goes to visit his uncle in Paris against his parents' wishes, he is so charmed by a mysterious "lady in pink" whom he meets in his uncle's company that he kisses her hand, a precocious act that sends the flattered woman into peals of laughter. To Marcel, the lady in pink embodies an essential feminine mysteriousness, and she becomes, if not the object of his desire, something like the guardian angel of all the imagined women who dance through his increasingly unbearable solitude.

One day, on a walk with his father and grandfather, Marcel encounters a young girl with red hair, pink freckles, and black eyes who seems to appear magically from out of a hedge of flowers. She makes an obscene gesture. When she is called away by her mother we learn that she is Gilberte Swann, the daughter of Charles and the lady in pink. She will be the first of Marcel's great loves. The lady in pink, as it turns out, is Odette de Crécy. Swann's excruciating love for this woman will be the subject of Swann in Love.

Marcel's walks on what his family calls the "Guermantes way" along the banks of the river Vivonne take him in the direction of the village of Guermantes, the ancestral home of the celebrated family whose lineage descends from Geneviève de Brabant. Having seen a portrait of the current Duchesse de Guermantes, Marcel daydreams about her incessantly. In his fantasies, the great lady befriends him, walks with him through the ducal park, and stands side by side along the river with him fishing for trout. When one day during Mass the real

Swann's Way

Duchesse de Guermantes walks in, dressed in shiny mauve silk and bearing a little pimple on her nose, Marcel is hugely disappointed.

Marcel considers himself a writer, yet his career has not begun auspiciously; he is unable to get past imagining the great work that he will one day create. He does not know what to write about. His life contains no drama, his surroundings are mundane. He dreams of going to Venice, the city of gold and light, or to the savage beaches of Normandy. But one day on a walk along the pond at Montjouvain, the early spring plants thrusting up all around him, he sees the tiled roof of a hut cast a pink reflection onto the water so radiant and unimaginable that he can only exclaim, "Gosh, gosh, gosh, gosh!" (Zut, zut, zut, zut!) Shortly after, Marcel finds himself in a carriage driving in the country and, as he watches the distant church steeples move along the horizon, feels the urge to write.

How much more distressing still, after that day, during my walks along the Guermantes way, did it seem to me than it had seemed before to have no aptitude for literature, and to have to give up all hope of ever being a famous writer! The sorrow I felt over this, as I daydreamed alone, a little apart from the others, made me suffer so much that in order not to feel it anymore, my mind of its own accord, by a sort of inhibition in the face of pain, would stop thinking altogether about poems, novels, a poetic future on which my lack of talent forbade me to depend. Then, quite apart from all these literary preoccupations and not connected to them in any way, suddenly a roof, a glimmer of sun on a stone, the smell of the road would stop me because of a particular pleasure they gave me, and also because they seemed to be concealing, beyond what I could see, something which they were inviting me to come take and which despite my efforts I could not manage to discover. Since I felt that it could be found within them, I would stay there, motionless, looking, breathing, trying to go with my thoughts beyond the image or the smell. And if I had to catch up with my grandfather, continue on my way, I would try to find them again by closing my eyes; I would concentrate on recalling precisely the line of the roof, the shade of the stone which, without my being able to understand why, had seemed to me so full, so ready to open, to yield me the thing for which they themselves were merely a cover. Of course it was not impressions of this kind that could give me back the hope I had lost, of succeeding in becoming a writer and a poet some day, because they were always tied to a particular object with no intellectual value and no reference to any abstract truth. But at least they gave me an unreasoning pleasure, the illusion of a sort of fecundity, and so distracted me from the tedium, from the sense of my own impotence which I had felt each time I looked for a philosophical subject for a great literary work. But the moral duty imposed on me by the impressions I received from form, fragrance or colour was so arduous—to try to perceive what was concealed behind them—that I would soon look for excuses that would allow me to save myself from this effort and spare myself this fatigue. Fortunately, my parents would call me, I would feel I did not have the tranquillity I needed at the moment for pursuing my search in a useful way, and that it would be better not to think about it anymore until I was back at home, and not to fatigue myself beforehand to no purpose. And so I would stop concerning myself with this unknown thing that was enveloped in a form or a fragrance, feeling quite easy in my mind since I was bringing it back to the house protected by the covering of images under which I would find it alive, like the fish that, on days when I had been allowed to go fishing, I would carry home in my creel covered by a layer of grass that kept them fresh. Once I was back at the house I would think about other things, and so there would accumulate in my mind (as in my room the flowers I had gathered on my walks or objects I had been given) a stone on which a glimmer of light played, a roof, the sound of a bell, a smell of leaves, many different images beneath which the reality I sensed but did not have enough determination to discover had died long before. Once, however—when our walk had extended far beyond its usual duration and we were very happy to encounter halfway home, as the afternoon was ending, Dr Percepied, who, going past at full speed in his carriage, recognized us and invited us to climb in with him—I had an impression of this kind and did not abandon it without studying it a little. They had had me climb up next to the coachman, we were going like the wind because, before returning to Combray, the doctor still had to stop at Martinville-le-Sec to see a patient at whose door it had been agreed that we would wait for him. At the bend of a road I suddenly experienced that special pleasure which was unlike any other, when I saw the two steeples of Martinville, shining in the setting sun and appearing to change position with the motion of our carriage and the windings of the road, and then the steeple of Vieuxvicq, which, though separated from them by a hill and a valley and situated on a higher plateau in the distance, seemed to be right next to them.

As I observed, as I noted the shape of their spires, the shifting of their lines, the sunlight on their surfaces, I felt that I was not reaching the full depth of my impression, that something was behind that motion, that brightness, something which they seemed at once to contain and conceal.

The steeples appeared so distant, and we seemed to approach them so slowly, that I was surprised when we stopped a few moments later in front of the Martinville church. I did not know why I had taken such pleasure in the sight of them on the horizon, and the obligation to try to discover the reason seemed to me quite painful; I wanted to hold in reserve in my head those lines moving in the sun, and not think about them anymore now. And it is quite likely that had I done so, the two steeples would have gone forever to join the many trees, rooftops, fragrances, sounds, that I had distinguished from others because of the obscure pleasure they gave me which I never thoroughly studied. I got down to talk to my parents while we waited for the doctor. Then we set off again, I was back in my place on the seat, I turned my head to see the steeples again, a little later glimpsing them one last time at a bend in the road. Since the coachman, who did not seem inclined to talk, had hardly answered anything I said, I was obliged, for lack of other company, to fall back on my own and try to recall my steeples. Soon their lines and their sunlit surfaces split apart, as if they were a sort of bark, a little of what was hidden from me inside them appeared to me, I had a thought which had not existed a moment before, which took shape in words in my head, and the pleasure I had just recently experienced at the sight of them was so increased by this that, seized by a sort of drunkenness, I could no longer think of anything else. At that moment, as we were already far away from Martinville, turning my head I caught sight of them again, quite black this time, for the sun had already set. At moments the bends of the road would hide them from me, then they showed themselves one last time, and finally I did not see them again.

Without saying to myself that what was hidden behind the steeples of Martinville had to be something analogous to a pretty sentence, since it had appeared to me in the form of words that gave me pleasure, I asked the doctor for a pencil and some paper and I composed, despite the jolts of the carriage, and in order to ease my conscience and yield to my enthusiasm, the following little piece that I have since found again and that I have not had to submit to more than a few changes:

"Alone, rising from the level of the plain, and appearing lost in the open country, the two steeples of Martinville ascended toward the sky. Soon we saw three: wheeling around boldly to position itself opposite them, the laggard steeple of Vieuxvicq had come along to join them. The minutes were passing, we were going fast, and yet the three steeples were still far away ahead of us, like three birds poised on the plain, motionless, distinguishable in the sunlight. Then the steeple of Vieuxvicq moved away, receded into the distance, and the steeples of Martinville remained alone, illuminated by the light of the setting sun, which even at that distance I saw playing and smiling on their sloping sides. We had taken so long approaching them that I was thinking about the time we would still need in order to reach them, when suddenly the carriage turned and set us down at their feet; and they had flung themselves so roughly in front of us that we had only just time to stop in order not to run into the porch. We continued on our way; we had already left Martinville a little while before, and the village, after accompanying us for a few seconds, had disappeared, when, lingering alone on the horizon to watch us flee, its steeples and that of Vieuxvicq were still waving goodbye with their sunlit tops. At times one of them would draw aside so that the other two could glimpse us again for an instant; but the road changed direction, they swung round in the light like three golden pivots and disappeared from my gaze. But a little later, when we were already close to Combray, and the sun had set, I caught sight of them one last time from very far away, seeming now no more than three flowers painted on the sky above the low line of the fields. They reminded me, too, of the three young girls in a legend, abandoned in a solitary place where darkness was already falling; and while we moved off at a gallop, I saw them timidly seek their way and, after some awkward stumbling of their noble silhouettes, press against one another, slip behind one another, now forming, against the still pink sky, no more than a single black shape, charming and resigned, and fade away into the night." I never thought of this page again, but at that moment, when in the corner of the seat where the doctor's coachman usually placed in a basket the poultry he had bought at the market in Martinville, I had finished writing it, I was so happy, I felt it had so perfectly relieved me of those steeples and what they had been hiding behind them, that, as if I myself were a hen and had just laid an egg, I began to sing at the top of my voice.

(*Swann's Way*, 182–86)

Lydia Davis

A number of interesting thoughts are inspired by this passage. First is the curious (and amusing) observation that whereas many novels contain a child who wants to grow up to be famous, particularly a famous writer, or is sad that he will never be one, this is among the few novels in which the child in question will have his wish granted and will in fact grow up to be a famous writer. And as we read this, what is also interesting is our perspective: we the readers know that the child on whom this young narrator is based has indeed grown up to be a famous writer; yet neither the fictional nor the real child knows this; and even Proust the author, as he writes it, cannot be sure, though he may suspect it. So we the readers are the only ones who know—we know more than Proust himself, in this case.

Then there is the quoted passage that is presented as the young narrator's first piece of serious writing. For one thing, it is not very different from the description that preceded it, in the adult narrator's words, and the fact that it is not very different draws our attention to it more pointedly. In what ways is it different and why should Proust want to, in effect, duplicate a passage—write it twice over with only slight variations? Is he first presenting it as it "really" is, so that we can compare the reality to the child's depiction of it? Yet the adult narrator's description of it is no more "real" than the child's.

Lydia Davis

Which brings up at least two more questions. Do we worry about verisimilitude in this novel? Proust is such a master of convincing prose that we accept a great deal without question. How likely is it, really, in fact, that anyone could write such a lovely description with a pencil and scrap of paper in the fading daylight while seated on the hard seat of a carriage that is jolting at a fast clip not over a paved road but over the little stones and ruts of a dirt track?

And, further, how likely is it that a child could write such a sophisticated and polished description at all, even under more peaceful circumstances and even if, as Marcel says, he himself as an adult touched it up a bit before presenting it? Young Marcel's age is a constant puzzle, anyway, in the first volume of the novel: it seems, throughout, to be an amalgam of different ages. Would a child of thirteen or, say, seven do all of the following: wait for his mother's kiss in the hallway; enjoy his private lust in the little room that smelled of orrisroot; be allowed to sit with the adults at dinner for a short time only; read Bergotte and discuss him with his friend Bloch and with Swann; tearfully hug the hawthorns in his new jacket and rip the curlpapers out of his hair; write the description of the steeples; dread the approach of bedtime once again, and with it the separation from his mother?

Lastly—or not lastly, since there are surely many more interesting thoughts buried in these pages—there is the inherent interest of the central question Proust is addressing here: the mystery of how a written thing first begs to be written and then comes into being. How a simple object seems to call out to us (Proust's reiterates the examples of roof and stone); how we are urged to do something about our feeling, at first not knowing what; how a "pretty sentence" relieves us of that urge; how we feel exhilaration afterward; and how, more generally, our expressive reaction to the excitement of inspiration and creation may be the inarticulate *Zut, zut, zut, zut* of the adolescent striking the vegetation with his walking stick which we witnessed in an earlier passage; or, in this passage, the highly articulate written description; or, most primitive, age-old, and perhaps equally satisfying—song: "I began to sing." The boy

The Proust Project

himself does not yet see that his responsiveness to an ordinary object will make the "success" of the successful writer and that he need not be discouraged that he has not found an appropriately great subject for his future literary work.

After Marcel's sortie into the written word comes the end of part 1 of Swann's Way. Abruptly Marcel's childhood falls away; we shall not return to Combray again.

We have already been introduced to Swann through his friendship with Marcel's family and his interference with Marcel's good-night kiss. Now we enter into Charles Swann's world years earlier, before his marriage, when he is courting Odette and is a regular at a salon hosted by Madame Verdurin. She is a bourgeois social climber whose weekly salon, she fancies, is the most brilliant in Paris. The regulars at Madame Verdurin's gatherings include a bumbling doctor who is incapable of completing a joke, a professor who discourses endlessly on the etymologies of place-names, and an impoverished elderly Russian princess, all of whom come to hobnob with the painters, poets, and composers of the day. The "faithful" are treated to chamber music performances, although certain pieces are outlawed on account of the insalubrious effect they have on Madame, her heightened perceptive qualities making her vulnerable to headaches for days on end. Anything that falls outside the realm of art is not to be touched on in Madame Verdurin's rarefied aesthetic queendom, and when one of the faithful dies, the name is stricken from the salon's collective memory, never to be uttered again. Severe retribution, if not excommunication, awaits those who miss a Wednesday, even if the unfortunate friend died on the Tuesday before.

It is on these Wednesday evenings that Swann and Odette de Crécy first meet and conduct their courtship, sitting close to each other on an elaborately ornamented Beauvais settee, listening to music. Usually the music is by the composer Vinteuil. There is a sonata he has written, sacred to Swann, the pianist and violinist building up the theme slowly and rhythmically, hinting, balking, and finally yielding the "little phrase" that Swann loves, the phrase that is to become the "national anthem of their love."

The Proust Project

Odette had received him in a pink silk dressing-gown, which left her neck and arms bare. She had made him sit down beside her in one of the many mysterious little alcoves which had been contrived in the various recesses of the room, sheltered by enormous palms growing out of pots of Chinese porcelain, or by screens upon which were fastened photographs and fans and bows of ribbon. She had said at once, "You're not comfortable there; wait a minute, I'll arrange things for you," and with a little simpering laugh which implied that some special invention of her own was being brought into play, she had installed behind his head and beneath his feet great cushions of Japanese silk which she pummelled and buffeted as though to prove that she was prodigal of these riches, regardless of their value. But when her footman came into the room bringing, one after another, the innumerable lamps which (contained, mostly, in porcelain vases) burned singly or in pairs upon the different pieces of furniture as upon so many altars, rekindling in the twilight, already almost nocturnal, of this winter afternoon the glow of a sunset more lasting, more roseate, more human—filling, perhaps, with romantic wonder the thoughts of some solitary lover wandering in the street below and brought to a standstill before the mystery of the human presence which those lighted windows at once revealed and screened from sight—she had kept a sharp eye on the servant, to see that he set them down in their appointed places. She felt that if he were to put even one of them where it ought not to be the general effect of her drawing-room would be destroyed, and her portrait, which rested upon a sloping easel draped with plush, inadequately lit. And so she followed the man's clumsy movements with feverish impatience, scolding him severely when he passed too close to a pair of jardinières, which she made a point of always cleaning herself for fear that they might be damaged, and went across to examine now to make sure he had not chipped them.

Swann's Way

She found something "quaint" in the shape of each of her Chinese ornaments, and also in her orchids, the cattleyas especially—these being, with chrysanthemums, her favourite flowers, because they had the supreme merit of not looking like flowers, but of being made, apparently, of silk or satin. "This one looks just as though it had been cut out of the lining of my cloak," she said to Swann, pointing to an orchid, with a shade of respect in her voice for so "chic" a flower, for this elegant, unexpected sister whom nature had bestowed upon her, so far removed from her in the scale of existence, and yet so delicate, so refined, so much more worthy than many real women of admission to her drawing-room. As she drew his attention, now to the fiery-tongued dragons painted on a bowl or stitched on a screen, now to a fleshy cluster of orchids, now to a dromedary of inlaid silverwork with ruby eyes which kept company, upon her mantelpiece, with a toad carved in jade, she would pretend now to be shrinking from the ferocity of the monsters or laughing at their absurdity, now blushing at the indecency of the flowers, now carried away by an irresistible desire to run across and kiss the toad and dromedary, calling them "darlings." And these affectations were in sharp contrast to the sincerity of some of her attitudes, notably her devotion to Our Lady of Laghet, who had once, when Odette was living at Nice, cured her of a mortal illness, and whose medal, in gold, she always carried on her person, attributing to it unlimited powers. She poured out Swann's tea, inquired "Lemon or cream?" and, on his answering "Cream, please," said to him with a laugh: "A cloud!" And as he pronounced it excellent, "You see, I know just how you like it." This tea had indeed seemed to Swann, just as it seemed to her, something precious, and love has such a need to find some justification for itself, some guarantee of duration, in pleasures which without it would have no existence and must cease with its passing, that when he left her at seven o'clock to go and dress for the evening, all the way home in his brougham, unable to repress the happiness with which the afternoon's adventure had filled him, he kept repeating to himself: "How nice it would be to have a little woman like that in whose house one could always be certain of finding, what one never can be certain of finding, a really good cup of tea." An hour or so later he received a note from Odette, and at once recognised that large hand-writing in which an affectation of British stiffness imposed an apparent discipline upon ill-formed characters, suggestive, perhaps, to less biased eyes than his, of an untidiness of mind, a fragmentary education, a want of sincerity and will-power. Swann had left his cigarette-case at her house. "If only," she wrote, "you had also forgotten your heart! I should never have let you have that back."

More important, perhaps, was a second visit which he paid her a lit-tle later. On his way to the house, as always when he knew that they were to meet, he formed a picture of her in his mind; and the necessity, if he was to find any beauty in her face, of concentrating on the fresh and rosy cheekbones to the exclusion of the rest of her cheeks which were so often drawn and sallow, and sometimes mottled with little red spots, distressed him as proving that the ideal is unattainable and happiness mediocre. He was bringing her an engraving which she had asked to see. She was not very well, and received him in a dressing-gown of mauve crêpe de Chine, drawing its richly embroidered material over her bosom like a cloak. Standing there beside him, her loosened hair flowing down her cheeks, bending one knee in a slightly balletic pose in order to be able to lean without effort over the picture at which she was gazing, her head on one side, with those great eyes of hers which seemed so tired and sullen when there was nothing to animate her, she struck Swann by her resemblance to the figure of Zipporah, Jethro's daughter, which is to be seen in one of the Sistine frescoes. He had always found a peculiar fascination in trac-ing in the paintings of the old masters not merely the general character-istics of the people whom he encountered in his daily life, but rather what seems least susceptible of generalisation, the individual features of men and women whom he knew: as, for instance, in a bust of the Doge Lore-dan by Antonio Rizzo, the prominent cheekbones, the slanting eyebrows, in short, a speaking likeness to his own coachman Rémi; in the colouring of a Ghirlandaio, the nose of M. de Palancy; in a portrait by Tintoretto, the invasion of the cheek by an outcrop of whisker, the broken nose, the penetrating stare, the swollen eyelids of Dr du Boulbon. Perhaps, hav-ing always regretted, in his heart, that he had confined his attention to the social side of life, had talked, always, rather than acted, he imagined a sort of indulgence bestowed upon him by those great artists in the fact that they also had regarded with pleasure and had introduced into their works such types of physiognomy as give those works the strongest possible certificate of reality and truth to life, a modern, almost a topical savour; perhaps, also, he had so far succumbed to the prevailing frivolity of the world of fashion that he felt the need to find in an old masterpiece some such anticipatory and rejuvenating allusion to personalities of today. Perhaps, on the other hand, he had retained enough of the artistic temperament to be able to find a genuine satisfaction in watching these individual characteristics take on a more general significance when he saw them, uprooted and disembodied, in the resemblance between an historic portrait and a modern original whom it was not intended to represent. However that might be—and perhaps because the abundance of impressions which he had been receiving for some time past, even though they had come to him rather through the channel of his appreciation of music, had enriched his appetite for painting as well—it was with an unusual intensity of pleasure, a pleasure destined to have a lasting effect upon him, that Swann remarked Odette's resemblance to the Zipporah of that Alessandro de Mariano to whom people more willingly give his popular surname, Botticelli, now that it suggests not so much the actual work of the Master as that false and banal conception of it which has of late obtained common currency. He no longer based his estimate of the merit of Odette's face on the doubtful quality of her cheeks and the purely fleshy softness which he supposed would greet his lips there should he ever hazard a kiss, but regarded it rather as a skein of beautiful, delicate lines which his eyes unravelled, following their curves and convolutions, relating the rhythm of the neck to the effusion of the hair and the droop of the eyelids, as though in a portrait of her in which her type was made clearly intelligible.

He stood gazing at her; traces of the old fresco were apparent in her face and her body, and these he tried incessantly to recapture thereafter, both when he was with Odette and when he was only thinking of her in her absence; and, although his admiration for the Florentine master-

piece was doubtless based upon his discovery that it had been repro-
duced in her, the similarity enhanced her beauty also, and made her
more precious. Swann reproached himself with his failure, hitherto, to
estimate at her true worth a creature whom the great Sandro would have
adored, and was gratified that his pleasure in seeing Odette should have
found a justification in his own aesthetic culture. He told himself that in
associating the thought of Odette with his dreams of ideal happiness he
had not resigned himself to a stopgap as inadequate as he had hitherto
supposed, since she satisfied his most refined predilections in matters of
art. He failed to observe that this quality would not naturally avail to
bring Odette into the category of women whom he found desirable, since,
as it happened, his desires had always run counter to his aesthetic taste.
The words "Florentine painting" were invaluable to Swann. They enabled him, like a title, to introduce the image of Odette into a world of
dreams and fancies which, until then, she had been debarred from entering, and where she assumed a new and nobler form. And whereas the
mere sight of her in the flesh, by perpetually reviving his misgivings as
to the quality of her face, her body, the whole of her beauty, cooled
the ardour of his love, those misgivings were swept away and that love
confirmed now that he could re-erect his estimate of her on the sure
foundations of aesthetic principle; while the kiss, the physical possession which would have seemed natural and but moderately attractive
had they been granted him by a creature of somewhat blemished flesh
and sluggish blood, coming, as they now came, to crown his adoration
of a masterpiece in a gallery, must, it seemed, prove supernaturally
delicious.

(*Swann's Way*, 310–17)

Olivier Bernier

Reality, how we see it, feel it, distort it, insert it into the flow of time: obviously, that is the theme of Proust's masterpiece. And who among us, having read him, has not gained a new understanding which changes the way we contemplate the passing of our lives?

Within that great revelation, however, embedded in that dazzlingly complex style, many other new ideas catch our attention. The most civilized, the most cultured of men, Proust understood literature, architecture, music, art, better than most professionals. He looked at paintings, and analyzed them more acutely. He deciphered their message more precisely, more thoroughly, and as he did so, he pointed the way toward a new relationship with art.

Paintings, after all, are not just rectangles of color on the wall: they are the way in which artists broaden our view of the world, the way in which they make us *see*. No haystack will ever look as it did before Monet; Vermeer has made us delight in a little piece of yellow wall which we would never otherwise have noticed. Artists give us permission to look: they remove the thick veil of habit; they transmute the stale into the thrillingly new.

When it was a question of decoding the world, Proust was always ready, and his revelations carry new understandings. "I myself was," he writes on the very first page of the *Search*, "the immediate subject of a book: a church, a quartet, the rivalry between François I and Charles V," the subject, in other words, of the book he had been reading, the music he had heard before falling asleep. This integration of art and reality with the unconscious is one of the great gifts I have received from Proust.

With it goes a new freedom. Art history is all about knowledge: tracing pedigrees, influences, provenances, showing what came from where, setting precise dates. On rare occasions, for rare persons, it involves connoisseurship, the ability to discriminate between the good and the great, between the worthwhile and the imitative.

To make these distinctions in a fiercely, and often mindlessly, egalitarian world requires courage, the courage born of example. We may find that courage in Proust's description of the church in Combray, of Vinteuil's sonata. He shows us that we are free to judge, that some works are better than others, and as we read him, we understand that we should, if we can, follow his example. He allows us to have an individual relationship to art, one in which our personality, our experience, enrich our judgment. And that judgment is, as it should be, a manifestation of preference. Art is not neutral.

When, on the stage of a museum auditorium, I tell an audience why this building is great, and that other mediocre, I go far beyond what graduate schools teach, or even allow. The value judgments I make, in defiance of the widely cherished belief that nothing is *better* than anything else, I make, in part, because Proust has allowed me to do so.

All this is evident in the depiction of Odette's salon, in the irony with which her execrable taste is described, in the silver dromedary and the jade toad. That, however, is only a beginning. Because painters teach us to look at the world, we see the world in terms of paintings. I know I am coming near Venice when I see the pines so often painted by Giambattista Tiepolo; the tree at the bottom of the garden seems more worth contemplating because it reminds me of Courbet.

Swann, like his maker, is a connoisseur, prompt to discern in Odette the likeness to Zipporah in the Vatican Botticelli fresco. "He stood gazing at her; traces of the old fresco were apparent in her face and her body . . . [T]he similarity . . . made her more precious . . . When he had

Olivier Bernier

looked for a long time at [his photograph of the] Botticelli, he thought of his own Botticelli," of Odette. Only then does Swann fall in love with this woman about whom he famously exclaims, at the end of *Swann in Love*, that she was not his type.

Reality, it seems, is often not where we expect to find it. What matters, in the end, is not the world of contingencies, but that of permanence. Works of art, unchanging and masterly, give shape to those fleeting phenomena that surround us; and it is only when we discern (or sometimes imagine) a coincidence between the two that we can fall in love—with an idea, a woman or a sight.

One night Swann arrives late at Madame Verdurin's, having first kept a rendezvous with a buxom young seamstress, enjoying this tryst all the more in the knowledge that Odette would be waiting for him later. By the time Swann reaches the Verdurins', however, Odette has already left. All at once he realizes that he cannot live without her. Odette is a mystery now; she is a stranger; her behavior cannot be controlled, and Swann must have her. *He spends the rest of the evening chasing her shadow through the streets of Paris, stopping at every café, every restaurant where she may have been, and circling back again. She is not at the Maison Dorée, not at Tortoni's or Prévost's. Every place in which she is not increases the excruciating mystery of Odette-without-Swann. In despair, Swann walks toward his carriage, after checking at one last café, turns, and bumps into her. There was no room at Prévost's; she was in a little alcove in the Maison Dorée; he must have failed to see her there. Together, they enter into Odette's carriage, Swann instructing the driver of his own carriage to follow behind.*

Ｓhe had so little expected to see him that she started back in alarm. As for him, he had ransacked the streets of Paris not because he supposed it possible that he should find her, but because it was too painful for him to abandon the attempt. But this happiness which his reason had never ceased to regard as unattainable, that evening at least, now seemed doubly real; for, since he himself had contributed nothing to it by anticipating probabilities, it remained external to himself; there was no need for him to think it into existence— it was from itself that there emanated, it was itself that projected towards him, that truth whose radiance dispelled like a bad dream the loneliness he had so dreaded, that truth on which his happy musings now dwelt unthinkingly. So will a traveller, arriving in glorious weather at the Mediterranean shore, no longer certain of the existence of the lands he has left behind, let his eyes be dazzled by the radiance streaming towards him from the luminous and unfading azure of the sea.

He climbed after her into the carriage which she had kept waiting, and ordered his own to follow.

She was holding in her hand a bunch of cattleyas, and Swann could see, beneath the film of lace that covered her head, more of the same flowers fastened to a swansdown plume. She was dressed, beneath her cloak, in a flowing gown of black velvet, caught up on one side to reveal a large triangle of white silk skirt, and with a yoke, also of white silk, in the cleft of the low-necked bodice, in which were fastened a few more cattleyas. She had scarcely recovered from the shock which the sight of Swann had given her, when some obstacle made the horse start to one side. They were thrown forward in their seats; she uttered a cry, and fell back quivering and breathless.

"It's all right," he assured her, "don't be frightened." And he slipped his arm round her shoulder, supporting her body against his own. Then he went on: "Whatever you do, don't utter a word; just make a sign, yes or no, or you'll be out of breath again. You won't mind if I straighten the flowers on your bodice? The jolt has disarranged them. I'm afraid of their dropping out, so I'd just like to fasten them a little more securely."

She was not used to being made so much fuss of by men, and she smiled as she answered: "No, not at all; I don't mind in the least."

But he, daunted a little by her answer, and also, perhaps, to bear out the pretence that he had been sincere in adopting the stratagem, or even because he was already beginning to believe that he had been, exclaimed, "No, no, you mustn't speak. You'll get out of breath again. You can easily answer in signs; I shall understand. Really and truly now, you don't mind my doing this? Look, there's a little—I think it must be pollen, spilt over your dress. Do you mind if I brush it off with my hand? That's not too hard? I'm not hurting you, am I? Perhaps I'm tickling you a bit? I don't want to touch the velvet in case I crease it. But you see, I really had to fasten the flowers; they would have fallen out if I hadn't. Like that, now; if I just tuck them a little further down . . . Seriously, I'm not annoying you, am I? And if I just sniff them to see whether they've really got no scent? I don't believe I ever smelt any before. May I? Tell the truth, now."

Still smiling, she shrugged her shoulders ever so slightly, as who should say, "You're quite mad; you know very well that I like it."

He ran his other hand upwards along Odette's cheek; she gazed at him fixedly, with that languishing and solemn air which marks the women of the Florentine master in whose faces he had found a resemblance with hers; swimming at the brink of the eyelids, her brilliant eyes, wide and slender like theirs, seemed on the verge of welling out like two great tears. She bent her neck, as all their necks may be seen to bend, in the pagan scenes as well as in the religious pictures. And in an attitude that was doubtless habitual to her, one which she knew to be appropriate to such moments and was careful not to forget to assume, she seemed to need all her strength to hold her face back, as though some invisible force were drawing it towards Swann's. And it was Swann who, before she allowed it, as though in spite of herself, to fall upon his lips, held it back for a moment longer, at a little distance, between his hands. He had wanted to leave time for his mind to catch up with him, to recognise the dream which it had so long cherished and to assist at its realisation, like a relative invited as a spectator when a prize is given to a child of whom she has been especially fond. Perhaps, too, he was fixing upon the face of an Odette not yet possessed, nor even kissed by him, which he was seeing for the last time, the comprehensive gaze with which, on the day of his departure, a traveller hopes to bear away with him in memory a landscape he is leaving for ever.

But he was so shy in approaching her that, after this evening which had begun by his arranging her cattleyas and had ended in her complete surrender, whether from fear of offending her, or from reluctance to appear retrospectively to have lied, or perhaps because he lacked the audacity to formulate a more urgent requirement than this (which could always be repeated, since it had not annoyed her on the first occasion), he resorted to the same pretext on the following days. If she had cattleyas pinned to her bodice, he would say: "It's most unfortunate; the cattleyas don't need tucking in this evening; they've not been disturbed as they were the other night. I think, though, that this one isn't quite straight. May I see if they have more scent than the others?" Or else, if she had none: "Oh! no cattleyas this evening; then there's no chance of my indulging in my little rearrangements." So that for some time there was no change in the procedure which he had followed on that first evening, starting with fumblings with fingers and lips at Odette's bosom, and it was thus that his caresses still began. And long afterwards, when the rearrangement (or, rather, the ritual pretence of a rearrangement) of her cattleyas had quite fallen into desuetude, the metaphor "Do a cattleya," transmuted into a simple verb which they would employ without thinking when they wished to refer to the act of physical possession (in which, paradoxically, the possessor possesses nothing), survived to commemorate in their vocabulary the long-forgotten custom from which it sprang. And perhaps this particular manner of saying "to make love" did not mean exactly the same thing as its synonyms. However jaded we may be about women, however much we may regard the possession of the most divergent types as a repetitive and predictable experience, it none the less becomes a fresh and stimulating pleasure if the women concerned are—or are thought by us to be—so difficult as to oblige us to make it spring from some unrehearsed incident in our relations with them, as had originally been for Swann the arrangement of the cattleyas. He tremblingly hoped, that evening (but Odette, he told himself, if she was deceived by his stratagem, could not guess his intention), that it was the possession of this woman that would emerge for him from their large mauve petals; and the pleasure which he had already felt and which Odette tolerated, he thought, perhaps only because she had not recognised it, seemed to him for that reason—as it might have seemed to the first man when he enjoyed it amid the flowers of the earthly paradise— a pleasure which had never before existed, which he was striving now to create, a pleasure—as the special name he gave it was to certify— entirely individual and new.

(*Swann's Way*, 328–32)

Lara Vapnyar

Here they are in the carriage. Both "quivering and breathless." He is reaching for her, mumbling about the cattleyas with the naïve slyness of a schoolboy. She is bending her neck with the exquisite precision of a veteran prostitute—bringing her face close enough to Swann's lips, but doing so as if against her will. The kiss is about to happen and as a result it will be lost.

It doesn't happen—not quite yet.

Just as Odette's face is "falling" upon Swann's lips, his hands slow her down as if to freeze the frame. What follows is a breathtaking process of saving the moment.

"Perhaps, too, he was fixing upon the face of an Odette not yet possessed, nor even kissed by him, which he was seeing for the last time, the comprehensive gaze with which, on the day of his departure, a traveller hopes to bear away with him in memory a landscape he is leaving for ever."

The beauty of this sentence is in Proust's ability to move from past to future, and back, and back again, never quite touching the present. In the words "not yet possessed" there is a glimpse of the future, where Odette would already be possessed by Swann and what's happening now in the carriage would inevitably be looked upon as the past. The metaphoric traveler is making a similar time journey: he is looking at the place he is about to depart from (the act of leaving is still in the future) as if it had already slipped into the past and he had memories of it.

The only thing that is missing is the present . . .

Once, many years ago, I had a crush on a boy who didn't pay much attention to me. Every time I saw him I hoped for a kiss. One kiss, I thought. Even a rushed, accidental, businesslike kiss. After a while I stopped hoping. And when the boy kissed me at last—pecked me on a cheek, as he and I were both putting our shoes on after a school party—I didn't notice it at all! It was only later, walking home, that I thought: Wait, wait, wait, didn't he just kiss me? I struggled to bring back the memory of the kiss, the sensation, the smell, the taste, but all I could remember was the smell of shoe polish, and the muffled sounds of the dying party.

The kiss was missed. The moment lost. Lost and simultaneously added to the whole sequence of lost moments that constitute almost in its entirety a human life.

But, of course, I didn't realize any of that until years later when I read the *Search*, a book that like no other book is devoted to chasing, capturing, and "regaining" lost or bound-to-be-lost moments.

Swann and Odette don't kiss in the carriage scene.

The moment of the kiss, like many other moments in Proust, is captured while dashing between the future (anticipation), and the past (memories), and also in the strange tangle of the past and the future together (anticipation of the memories and memories of anticipation).

The question that arises when reading Proust is whether we can get ahold of the present at all, except in our anticipation and memories of it. What if the present simply doesn't exist? Not even as a transition between the past and the future, because there is no such transition in the Proustian universe. The past is already tainted by the future, and the future is always looking back.

The feeling of horror that Swann felt the night Odette skipped out on their rendezvous at the Verdurins' is quick to return. Swann's haphazard attendance on Wednesdays is earning him demerits, and he soon becomes the rival of a newcomer to Madame Verdurin's, a certain Comte de Forcheville. Why Odette would be attracted to a man so unintelligent, so lacking in subtlety, is a mystery to Swann.

Meanwhile Swann realizes that he knows nothing about Odette. Everywhere he hears rumors of a sordid past involving both male and female lovers. One day Swann receives an anonymous letter confirming everything.

By this time, however, he has stopped caring. His love for Odette is fading. The details of her past mean nothing to him. They will soon marry.

The Normandy town of Balbec is a place of savage mystery in Marcel's imagination: a wind-whipped raging surf, leathered fishermen riding the waves, the steeple of Balbec cathedral piercing the roiling clouds, the bells. But Marcel, with his sensitive physique and nervous temperament, cannot go there; he cannot go anywhere, and must content himself with looking at the train schedule, letting the strange names of the towns along the rail route fill him with the stark immensity of these faraway places, places that would be available to him if only his parents would let him take the 1:22 train out of Paris.

For Marcel, there is the Champs-Elysées, where his grandmother takes him daily. There he finds something else to make his heart race: Gilberte Swann. They play together. When she calls him by his Christian name for the first time, Marcel has the sensation that he is being held in her mouth, naked.

When New Year's Day came, I first of all paid a round of family visits with Mamma who, so as not to tire me, had planned them beforehand (with the aid of an itinerary drawn up

Within a Budding Grove

by my father) according to district rather than degree of kinship. But no sooner had we entered the drawing-room of the distant cousin whose claim to being visited first was that her house was at no distance from ours, than my mother was horrified to see standing there, his present of marrons glacés or déguisés in his hand, the bosom friend of the most sensitive of all my uncles, to whom he would at once go and report that we had not begun our round with him. And this uncle would certainly be hurt; he would have thought it quite natural that we should go from the Madeleine to the Jardin des Plantes, where he lived, before stopping at Saint-Augustin, on our way to the Rue de l'Ecole de Médecine.

Our visits ended (my grandmother had dispensed us from the duty of calling on her, since we were to dine there that evening), I ran all the way to the Champs-Elysées to give to our own special stall-keeper, with instructions to hand it over to the person who came to her several times a week from the Swanns to buy gingerbread, the letter which, on the day when my beloved had caused me so much pain, I had decided to send her at the New Year, and in which I told her that our old friendship was vanishing with the old year, that I would now forget my grievances and disappointments, and that, from this first day of January, it was a new friendship that we were going to build, so solid that nothing could destroy it, so wonderful that I hoped Gilberte would go out of her way to preserve it in all its beauty and to warn me in time, as I promised to warn her, should either of us detect the least sign of a peril that might endanger it.

On the way home Françoise made me stop at the corner of the Rue Royale, before an open-air stall from which she selected for her own stock of presents photographs of Pius IX and Raspail, while for myself I purchased one of Berma. The wholesale admiration which that artist excited gave an air of slight impoverishment to this one face that she had to respond with, immutable and precarious like the garments of people who have none to "spare," this face on which she must continually expose to view only the tiny dimple upon her upper lip, the arch of her eyebrows, and a few other physical characteristics, always the same, which, after all, were at the mercy of a burn or a blow. This face, moreover, would not in itself have seemed to me beautiful, but gave me the idea and consequently the desire to kiss it, by reason of all the kisses that it must have sustained and for which, from its page in the album, it seemed still to be appealing with that coquettishly tender gaze, that artfully ingenuous smile. For Berma must indeed have felt for many young men those desires which she confessed under cover of the character of Phèdre, desires which everything, even the glamour of her name which enhanced her beauty and prolonged her youth, must make it so easy for her to appease. Night was falling; I stopped before a column of playbills, on which was posted the performance in which she was to appear on January 1. A moist and gentle breeze was blowing. It was a weather with which I was familiar; I suddenly had a feeling and a presentiment that New Year's Day was not a day different from the rest, that it was not the first day of a new world in which I might, by a chance that was still intact, have made Gilberte's acquaintance anew as at the time of the Creation, as though the past did not yet exist, as though, together with the lessons I could have drawn from them for my future guidance, the disappointments which she had sometimes brought me had been obliterated; a new world in which nothing should subsist from the old—save one thing, my desire that Gilberte should love me. I realised that if my heart hoped for such a regeneration all around it of a universe that had not satisfied it before, it was because it, my heart, had not altered, and I told myself that there was no reason to suppose that Gilberte's had altered either; I felt that this new friendship was the same, just as there is no boundary ditch between their fore-runners and those new years which our desire, without being able to reach and so to modify them, invests, unknown to themselves, with a different name. For all that I might dedicate this new year to Gilberte, and, as one superimposes a religion on the blind laws of nature, endeavor to stamp New Year's Day with the particular image that I had formed of it, it was in vain. I felt that it was not aware that people called it New Year's Day, that it was passing in a wintry dusk in a manner that was not new to me: in the gentle breeze that blew around the column of playbills, I had recognised, had sensed the reappearance of, the eternal common substance, the familiar moisture, the unheeding fluidity of the old days and years.

Within a Budding Grove

I returned home. I had just spent the New Year's Day of old men, who differ on that day from their juniors, not because people have ceased to give them presents but because they themselves have ceased to believe in the New Year. Presents I had indeed received, but not that present which alone could bring me pleasure, namely a line from Gilberte. I was nevertheless still young, since I had been able to write her one, by means of which I hoped, in telling her of my solitary dreams of love and longing, to arouse similar dreams in her. The sadness of men who have grown old lies in their no longer even thinking of writing such letters, the futility of which their experience has shown.

When I was in bed, the noises of the street, unduly prolonged on this festive evening, kept me awake. I thought of all the people who would end the night in pleasure, of the lover, the troop of debauchees perhaps, who would be going to meet Berma at the stage-door after the performance that I had seen announced for this evening. I was not even able, to calm the agitation which this idea engendered in me during my sleepless night, to assure myself that Berma was not, perhaps, thinking about love, since the lines that she recited, which she had long and carefully rehearsed, reminded her at every moment that love is an exquisite thing, as of course she already knew, and knew so well that she displayed its familiar pangs— only enriched with a new violence and an unsuspected sweetness—to her astonished audience, each member of which had felt them for himself. I lighted my candle again, to look at her face once more. At the thought that it was no doubt at that very moment being caressed by those men whom I could not prevent from giving to Berma and receiving from her joys superhuman but vague, I felt an emotion more cruel than voluptuous, a longing that was presently intensified by the sound of the horn, as one hears it on the nights of the mid-Lent festival and often of other public holidays, which, because it then lacks all poetry, is more saddening, coming from a tavern, than "at evening, in the depths of the woods." At that moment, a message from Gilberte would perhaps not have been what I wanted. Our desires cut across one another, and in this confused existence it is rare for happiness to coincide with the desire that clamoured for it.

(*Within a Budding Grove*, 73–84)

Colm Tóibín

"It's high, it's high again," Dr. French, slightly irritated by the need for speech, disentangled himself from the contraption with which he had measured my blood pressure, and then, to the lovely painless sound of the ripping of Gor-Tex, he disentangled me.

"Are you free today? From work?" he asked.

"I don't work, you know that," I said, fastening the sleeve of my shirt. "I write sometimes. It's hardly work."

He glanced at me in disapproval, not because of what I had said— he harbored a deep respect for writing and writers—but because the attempt at flippancy had failed and had disclosed for a moment the deepest mixture of insecurity and self-regard. It had also been a failure of style and that seemed to worry him more than the possibility of cardiac arrest. He dialed a number on the internal hospital telephone system.

"Yes," he said, when he had replaced the receiver, "they can strap the machine on you and you can wear it for the rest of the day. It's over in the cardiac unit. You can go there now."

It was my birthday.

Not telling him this offered me a radiant and private moment of real power over him. I knew the machine tucked inside my shirt would be uncomfortable and swell to take my blood pressure every twenty minutes. Anybody else, I was sure, would have waited a day. I loved how free I was to feel that the beginning of a new, yearlong age, a fresh digit to place beside the old one, deserved nothing but mockery. I was moving toward the grave. Soon I would be the age my father was when he

Colm Tóibín

died, and I was suffering from the same disease. I grinned to myself at the idea as the nurse strapped on the machine. I was, she said, once I left the hospital, to spend the day as I normally would.

Neither doctor nor nurse warned me of the strange erotics of this birthday present tightening on my arm, purring its sound, holding me, and then unloosening like a long breath exhaled. I walked the city in its thrall. It was like love.

The day must be ordinary, they had said. Margaret Atwood was to read at the Municipal Gallery. I would go, as planned, with my friend June Levine, carrying a bottle of wine which I would take with me then to the party afterward at Anthony Glavin's in Whitehall.

I would, I knew, in any case, have told no one it was my birthday. Now I would not tell them either that I was more oddly content, more deeply at ease with myself, happier than someone blowing out candles on a cake, because I had a lovely machine wrapped around me, which would graph how the blood coursed through me, the blood pounding too hard against the fragile walls of arteries and veins, kidneys and heart muscles, my deepest instincts, as my father's blood did once, and maybe his father's too, until it would, unless I took the available medication, kill me. I was forty-eight. That day.

I crossed the city to see Margaret Atwood. Her fierce intelligence and sharp bond with the times, the dark fearless style of her, caused a hundred seriously intelligent-looking women and a few dozen men to sit listening to her with awe and silence and attention. In one second, however, as she stopped to turn a page, my new friend, my own grave private birthday present, began to swell and stiffen and whirr. Before I came here I did not think it would be heard, but I was wrong. It was almost loud.

No one moved. June Levine stared ahead. I watched the five women in front make fists of their hands and then turn.

Had, their angry faces seemed to ask, a mobile phone with a new low groaning sound been left on? As their heroine, suddenly so small and vulnerable against this intrusion, stopped and looked around in curious, almost distant surprise, their faces appeared to ask me why was it

The Proust Project

not being turned off? Fifteen seconds of my birthday were becoming an eternity, and then ten more seconds as the sound died down. I counted each one. When they were over, Atwood could resume, the oracle come from Canada. But, I knew, if she read for twenty more minutes, if she were one of those authors who could not stop, who thought one more passage would help bring her news, then it would rise again, my sound. And I would be forced once more to stare ahead as though none of me, least of all my blood being measured, belonged to me.

Later, when the author signed my book, she looked briefly into my soul.

At the party in Anthony Glavin's there was the noise made by friends; there was a garden; drinks were poured. There were smiles all around that night, as the day I was born came softly, whirringly, to an end, enticing me toward a future that only the graph of my blood pressure gathering pace, making marks, could see.

One day Gilberte tells Marcel that her parents do not approve of him and would prefer that the two have no more to do with each other. Marcel is devastated and writes a passionate defense of himself to Swann in the form of a sixteen-page letter, which he entrusts to Gilberte. But Gilberte brings the letter back to him the next day; her father had been unimpressed, she says; there is nothing that can possibly change his opinion of him. Gilberte hands the letter back to him, but Marcel has another idea: he wants her to try to stop him from getting it, and they begin to wrestle until pleasure overwhelms Marcel and he lets go. The letter now in Marcel's hands, Gilberte says to him, "You know, if you like, we might go on wrestling a bit longer."

Shortly after, perhaps from overexertion, the already frail Marcel falls ill. When Gilberte sends him an adoring letter, Marcel treasures it, kisses it, and feels, he says, "finally happy."

During his convalescence, things seem indeed to change. Marcel is welcomed into the home of the Swanns, where Gilberte has a miniature version of one of her mother's "at-homes."

Marcel has a friend, a Jew named Bloch, who excels in parodies of Homeric diction; he talks his way through life in similes and epithets. It is he who takes Marcel to his first brothel, where the madam tries to tempt Marcel with a young woman named Rachel: "Think of that, my boy, a Jewess! Wouldn't that be thrilling? Rrrr!" By this time Marcel's invalid aunt Léonie, she who offered him madeleines and teas, is dead, and the young boy becomes the possessor of all her furnishings. He donates her sofa to the brothel.

Gilberte, meanwhile, continues to run hot and cold. Marcel is a frequent visitor to her house now, but Gilberte avoids him when he is there, and he spends much more time with Odette, who does seem to genuinely like him. Still, he sends Gilberte flowers daily, and finding himself short of money, he takes a Chinese vase of his aunt Léonie's to an antiques dealer. Expecting a thousand francs, he receives ten thousand, all of which he plans to spend on flowers. On his way to pay Gilberte a surprise visit, he glimpses her walking with a man, on the

The Proust Project

Champs-Elysées. He ends up spending the ten thousand francs rap-
idly, very rapidly, at the brothel.

Ultimately his love for Gilberte wanes; he knows that he will soon
forget her, that she will become nothing to him. Indeed this is what
happens. They will meet again when they are much older but they will
never again be close. New desires are on the horizon. Marcel is finally
allowed to go to his dreamt-of Balbec. He leaves with his grandmother
on the 1:22.

When, that evening, after having accompanied my grandmother to her destination and spent some hours in her friend's house, I had returned by myself to the train, at any rate I found nothing to distress me in the night which followed; this was because I did not have to spend it imprisoned in a room whose somnolence would have kept me awake; I was surrounded by the soothing activity of all those movements of the train which kept me company, offered to stay and talk to me if I could not sleep, lulled me with their sounds which I combined—like the chime of the Combray bells—now in one rhythm, now in another (hearing as the whim took me first four equal semi-quavers, then one semi-quaver furiously dashing against a crotchet); they neutralised the centrifugal force of my insomnia by exerting on it contrary pressures which kept me in equilibrium and on which my immobility and presently my drowsiness seemed to be borne with the same sense of relaxation that I should have felt had I been resting under the protecting vigilance of powerful forces in the heart of nature and of life, had I been able for a moment to metamorphose myself into a fish that sleeps in the sea, carried along in its slumber by the currents and the waves, or an eagle outstretched upon the buoyant air of the storm.

Sunrise is a necessary concomitant of long railway journeys, like hard-boiled eggs, illustrated papers, packs of cards, rivers upon which boats strain but make no progress. At a certain moment, when I was counting over the thoughts that had filled my mind during the preceding minutes,

Within a Budding Grove

so as to discover whether I had just been asleep or not (and when the very uncertainty which made me ask myself the question was about to furnish me with an affirmative answer), in the pale square of the window, above a small black wood, I saw some ragged clouds whose fleecy edges were of a fixed, dead pink, not liable to change, like the colour that dyes the feathers of a wing that has assimilated it or a pastel on which it has been deposited by the artist's whim. But I felt that, unlike them, this colour was neither inertia nor caprice, but necessity and life. Presently there gathered behind it reserves of light. It brightened; the sky turned to a glowing pink which I strove, glueing my eyes to the window, to see more clearly, for I felt that it was related somehow to the most intimate life of Nature, but, the course of the line altering, the train turned, the morning scene gave place in the frame of the window to a nocturnal village, its roofs still blue with moonlight, its pond encrusted with the opalescent sheen of night, beneath a firmament still spangled with all its stars, and I was lamenting the loss of my strip of pink sky when I caught sight of it anew, but red this time, in the opposite window which it left at a second bend in the line; so that I spent my time running from one window to the other to reassemble, to collect on a single canvas the intermittent, antipodean fragments of my fine, scarlet, ever-changing morning, and to obtain a comprehensive view and a continuous picture of it.

(*Within a Budding Grove*, 315–17)

Alain de Botton

If one loves Proust, finding another "Proustian" is normally understood to mean that one has landed on a kindred spirit. And yet, it's a symptom of how multifaceted Proust's work is that, more than any other great author, he's capable of generating wildly different reasons to appreciate him. There's the Proust who likes to describe social life, another who talks about ideas, a third fixated on sexual relations, and so on.

The Proust that has always most appealed to me is the "intimate" Proust, by which I mean the Proust who describes small, unheroic aspects of experience that other authors rush past in their hurry to construct a plot: the sensation of linen against your cheek, the smell of hotel corridors, the appearance of the sky by the seashore. Pages are lavished on these small moments. Proust is often thought of as a quintessentially nineteenth-century author, but I enjoy the number of modern experiences he describes: the sound of car gears changing, the sight of a plane in the sky, a conversation with a phone operator. Going on a train is something that all of us do, but that most novelists have sketched it only in the broadest strokes. We've all heard the train wheels beat against the rails, but it takes Proust to rescue the sound from our customary inattention and to pin it down in words that carry over the emotional charge of the original experience. The value of Proust's novel is not limited to its depiction of emotions and people akin to those in our own life, it stretches to an ability to describe these *far better* than we would have been able, to put a finger on perceptions that we recognize *as our own* but could not have formulated *on our own*. An effect of reading a book that has devoted attention to noticing such faint yet vital tremors is that once we've put the volume down and resumed our own life, we may attend to precisely the things which the author would have responded to had he or she been in our company. Our mind will be like a radar newly attuned to pick up certain objects floating through consciousness. The book will have *sensitized* us, stimulated our dormant antennae by evidence of its own developed sensitivity.

Arriving at Balbec, Marcel excitedly leaves the railway station in search of the cathedral and the sea. He finds the cathedral, but though he had imagined crashing waves heaving themselves against its algaed façade, as it turns out, the sea is twelve miles away and the church sits in a square amid unremarkable houses and a billiards hall. It is a terrible disappointment.

They take rooms at the Grand Hotel by the sea. Marcel finds his waking and sleeping, however, disrupted by the change in his accustomed rituals. He falls prey to anxiety and homesickness and relies for comfort on his grandmother, who communicates with him by knocking on the wall between their rooms. In the morning, she comes into his room and opens the shutter, letting in the day's rendition of the sea, sometimes dark as a mountain range, sometimes as smooth as an alpine pasture.

There are young women at Balbec who haunt Marcel's imagination: a solitary girl on a walk, or a waitress he must helplessly let pass out of his life into oblivion. He meets the eye of a pretty milkmaid one day as she is delivering cream. When, the next day, Françoise hands him a letter, he is sure it is from her, and is disappointed when it turns out to be from the famous author Bergotte.

One day, Marcel and his grandmother are invited for a ride in Madame de Villeparisis's carriage.

We came down towards Hudimesnil; and suddenly I was overwhelmed with that profound happiness which I had not often felt since Combray, a happiness analogous to that which had been given me by—among other things—the steeples of Martinville. But this time it remained incomplete. I had just seen, standing a little way back from the hog's-back road along which we were travelling, three trees which probably marked the entry to a covered driveway and formed a pattern which I was not seeing for the first time. I could not succeed in reconstructing the place from which they had been as it were de-

Within a Budding Grove

tached, but I felt that it had been familiar to me once; so that, my mind having wavered between some distant year and the present moment, Balbec and its surroundings began to dissolve and I wondered whether the whole of this drive were not a make-believe, Balbec a place to which I had never gone except in imagination, Mme de Villeparisis a character in a story and the three old trees the reality which one recaptures on raising one's eyes from the book which one has been reading and which describes an environment into which one has come to believe that one has been bodily transported.

I looked at the three trees; I could see them plainly, but my mind felt that they were concealing something which it could not grasp, as when an object is placed out of our reach, so that our fingers, stretched out at arm's-length, can only touch for a moment its outer surface, without managing to take hold of anything. Then we rest for a little while before thrusting out our arm with renewed momentum, and trying to reach an inch or two further. But if my mind was thus to collect itself, to gather momentum, I should have to be alone. What would I not have given to be able to draw aside as I used to do on those walks along the Guermantes way, when I detached myself from my parents! I felt indeed that I ought to do so. I recognised that kind of pleasure which requires, it is true, a certain effort on the part of the mind, but in comparison with which the attractions of the indolence which inclines us to renounce that pleasure seem very slight. That pleasure, the object of which I could only dimly feel, which I must create for myself, I experienced only on rare occasions, but on each of these it seemed to me that the things that had happened in the meantime were of little importance, and that in attaching myself to the reality of that pleasure alone could I at length begin to lead a true life. I put my hand for a moment across my eyes, so as to be able to shut them without Mme de Villeparisis's noticing. I sat there thinking of nothing, then with my thoughts collected, compressed and strengthened I sprang further forward in the direction of the trees, or rather in that inner direction at the end of which I could see them inside myself. I felt again behind them the same object, known to me and yet vague, which I could not bring nearer. And yet all three of them, as the carriage moved on, I could see coming towards me. Where had I looked at them before? There was no place near Combray where an avenue opened off the road like that. Nor was there room for the site which they recalled to me in the scenery of the place in Germany where I had gone one year with my grandmother to take the waters. Was I to suppose, then, that they came from years already so remote in my life that the landscape which surrounded them had been entirely obliterated from my memory and that, like the pages which, with a sudden thrill, we recognise in a book that we imagined we had never read, they alone survived from the forgotten book of my earliest childhood? Were they not rather to be numbered among those dream landscapes, always the same, at least for me in whom their strange aspect was only the objectivation in my sleeping mind of the effort I made while awake either to penetrate the mystery of a place beneath the outward appearance of which I was dimly conscious of there being something more, as had so often happened to me on the Guermantes way, or to try to put mystery back into a place which I had longed to know and which, from the day when I had come to know it, had seemed to me to be wholly superficial, like Balbec? Or were they merely an image freshly extracted from a dream of the night before, but already so worn, so faded that it seemed to me to come from somewhere far more distant? Or had I indeed never seen them before, and did they conceal beneath their surface, like certain trees on tufts of grass that I had seen beside the Guermantes way, a meaning as obscure, as hard to grasp, as is a distant past, so that, whereas they were inviting me to probe a new thought, I imagined that I had to identify an old memory? Or again, were they concealing no hidden thought, and was it simply visual fatigue that made me see them double in time as one sometimes sees double in space? I could not tell. And meanwhile they were coming towards me; perhaps some fabulous apparition, a ring of witches or of Norns who would propound their oracles to me. I chose rather to believe that they were phantoms of the past, dear companions of my childhood, vanished friends who were invoking our common memories. Like ghosts they seemed to be appealing to me to take them with me, to bring them back to life. In their simple and passionate gesticulation I could discern the helpless anguish

Within a Budding Grove

of a beloved person who has lost the power of speech, and feels that he will never be able to say to us what he wishes to say and we can never guess. Presently, at a cross-roads, the carriage left them. It was bearing me away from what alone I believed to be true, what would have made me truly happy; it was like my life.

I watched the trees gradually recede, waving their despairing arms, seeming to say to me: "What you fail to learn from us today, you will never know. If you allow us to drop back into the hollow of this road from which we sought to raise ourselves up to you, a whole part of yourself which we were bringing to you will vanish for ever into thin air." And indeed if, in the course of time, I did discover the kind of pleasure and disquiet which I had just felt once again, and if one evening—too late, but then for all time—I fastened myself to it, of those trees themselves I was never to know what they had been trying to give me nor where else I had seen them. And when, the road having forked and the carriage with it, I turned my back on them and ceased to see them, while Mme de Villeparisis asked me what I was dreaming about, I was as wretched as if I had just lost a friend, had died myself, had broken faith with the dead or repudiated a god.

(*Within a Budding Grove*, 404–408)

Geoffrey O'Brien

The passage—already marked off by an ellipsis from what precedes it—
kicks in with the starkness of an episode in a medieval chanson de geste:

> We came down towards Hudimesnil

and with equal abruptness—a semicolon the only buffer—"suddenly I
was overwhelmed with that profound happiness which I had not often
felt again since Combray, a happiness analogous to that which had been
given me by—among other things—the steeples of Martinville." The
steeples had imparted, through Marcel's verbal formulation of the experience of seeing them, a full realization of the pleasure of the act of
writing: a pleasure so intense and unexpected that he burst into song.
In this present instance, however—which occurs as Marcel is driving
in a carriage on an excursion into the countryside near Balbec with his
grandmother and Madame de Villeparisis—the happiness "remained
incomplete." The passage which describes it is therefore itself a fragment, a detached although perfectly shaped shard.

The happiness comes from his noticing three trees that presumably
serve as an entrance to a covered alley; they make a pattern he has seen
before in a place he can no longer identify. (Neither the nature of the
pattern nor the genus of the trees is sufficiently relevant to be noted.) A
fissure opens between the place he is in and the unidentifiable place in
which he once was, and in that instant his immediate surroundings and

all the people attached to them become less real than those in other and remote times. It's as if he had roused himself from a book he was reading (the book that is his life in the present, and the people who are part of it) to be brought back into the real world evoked by the three trees. This figure of the reader looking up from a book reenacts in minute and stunningly casual fashion the whole metaphysical machinery for whose expression Calderón, for example, required dungeons, palaces, ancient curses, and dispossessed dynasties. As easily as looking away from the page you are reading, the universe is redefined and disassembled.

Marcel will never grasp what the three trees connect him to, perhaps only because circumstances—the carriage moving irresistibly onward, the company he cannot escape from—deny him the possibility of pausing and retreating into himself. The trees function as a kind of indecipherable Symbolist poem—anticipating the Imagism that Pound has not yet formulated—containing a single line, consisting finally only of the words "three trees": an opaque ideogram marking the limits of consciousness. What cannot be doubted is their power over him, a power that (given the incompleteness of the experience) he can approach only through questions, a series of what-ifs that lay out, to no real avail, possible definitions of what his perception of the trees might amount to.

It might be a memory of so remote a period of childhood that he cannot even locate its geographic context; it might belong to a dream landscape (with the proviso that for Marcel a dream landscape is itself a distillation of the mystery underlying a landscape seen in waking life); it might be something dreamt the night before and forgotten, thus acquiring an illusory aura of remoteness in time; it might on the contrary be something so entirely new that the shock of its unfamiliarity is indistinguishable from the effect of a half-forgotten memory. Or maybe Marcel is just tired and experiencing a fatigue-induced double vision—not of space but of time. "I couldn't tell." The baldness of the sentence again marks the absolute closure that can only pertain to an incomplete experience.

And at this point—with the failure of knowledge—all hell, metaphorically, breaks loose: we are dealing no longer with trees but with

The Proust Project

Norns, witches, prophetesses, ghosts demanding resurrection. But their gesticulations are those of an invalid who has lost the use of his voice and despairs, knowing that his friends will never grasp what he intends to say. It is too late in any case, because the carriage has moved and taken Marcel not only from the trees but from "everything that would have made me truly happy." The trees, sounding now truly like the chorus from some mythological drama of the fin de siècle, chant to him: "What you fail to learn from us today, you will never know." In fact he will never know: and by not knowing will lose some crucial part of himself, even if—"one evening—too late, but then for all time"—he will recover in the spiritual and erotic bondage of his relationship with Albertine an analogue of what he lost.

The carriage turns a corner and the trees vanish for all time: an act (not the passive fact of being carried away but the act of turning his back on them) so harsh that Proust can liken it only to grief, death, betrayal, or apostasy. The party will return from its outing precisely as if nothing had happened.

An elegant, self-assured young man appears at the Grand Hotel one afternoon: the Marquis de Saint-Loup-en-Bray, a nephew of the Duchesse de Guermantes. He is cold and aloof upon meeting Marcel. Improbably, he and Marcel become intimate friends; their friendship is so intense that Saint-Loup calls it "the great joy of his life"—apart from the love he has for his mistress, Rachel, formerly of the brothel.

But Marcel's attention is also drawn elsewhere: to the band of athletic young girls who seem to rule the beach and the town. They swing their hips as they walk and speak in slang, and Marcel surmises that they are "mistresses of racing cyclists."

Marcel soon devotes all his thought and energy to this little band and does anything he can to be near them. At a party, Marcel meets one of them, a girl with long dark hair and plump cheeks. Her name is Albertine, and he is charmed by her mellifluous small talk.

From this time on, Marcel spends his days with the little band, playing games, walking along the beach, suffering Albertine's occasional rejections, doing anything he can to remain by her side.

Back in Paris, Marcel develops a new love interest in his family's new next-door neighbor, the Duchesse de Guermantes. Every day at the time she leaves the house, he stands on the street just so he can greet her as she goes by in her carriage. Any further contact between the two would seem out of the question, but under the pretense of a friendly visit to the town of Doncières where his friend Saint-Loup is stationed, Marcel tries in vain to secure a photograph of the duchesse.

Now, every morning, long before the hour at which she left her house, I went by a devious route to post myself at the corner of the street along which she generally came, and, when the moment of her arrival seemed imminent, I strolled back with an air of being absorbed in something else, looking the other way, and raised my eyes to her face as I drew level with her, but as though I had not in the least expected to see her. Indeed, for the first few mornings, so as to be sure of not missing her, I waited in front of the house. And every time the carriage gate opened (letting out one after another so many people who were not the one for whom I was waiting) its grinding rattle prolonged itself in my heart in a series of oscillations which took a long time to subside. For never was devotee of a famous actress whom he does not know, kicking his heels outside the stage door, never was angry or idolatrous crowd, gathered to insult or to carry in triumph through the streets the condemned assassin or the national hero whom it believes to be on the point of coming whenever a sound is heard from the inside of the prison or the palace, never were these so stirred by emotion as I was, awaiting the emergence of this great lady who in her simple attire was able, by the grace of her movements (quite different from the gait she affected on entering a drawing-room or a box), to make of her morning walk—and for me there was no one in the world but she out walking— a whole poem of elegant refinement and the loveliest ornament, the rarest flower of the season. But after the third day, so that the porter should not discover my strategem, I betook myself much further afield, to some point upon the Duchess's usual route. Often before that evening at the theatre I had made similar little excursions before lunch, when the weather was fine; if it had been raining, at the first gleam of sunshine I would hasten downstairs to take a stroll, and if, suddenly, coming towards me along the still wet pavement, changed by the sun into a golden lacquer, in the transformation scene of a crossroads powdered with mist which the sun tanned and bleached, I caught sight of a schoolgirl followed by her governess or of a dairy-maid with her white sleeves, I stood motionless, my hand pressed to my heart which was already leaping towards an unexplored life; I tried to bear in mind the street, the time, the number of the door through which the girl (whom I followed sometimes) had vanished and failed to reappear. Fortunately the fleeting nature of these cherished images, which I promised myself that I would make an effort to see again, prevented them from fixing themselves with any vividness in my memory. No matter, I was less depressed now at the thought of my own ill health, of my never having summoned up the en-

ergy to set to work, to begin a book, for the world appeared to me a pleas-
anter place to live in, life a more interesting experience to go through,
now that I had learned that the streets of Paris, like the roads round Balbec, were in bloom with those unknown beauties whom I had so often
sought to conjure from the woods of Méséglise, each of whom aroused a
voluptuous longing which she alone seemed capable of assuaging.

On coming home from the Opéra, I had added for the following morning, to those whom for some days past I had been hoping to meet again,
the image of Mme de Guermantes, tall, with her high-piled crown of
silky, golden hair, with the tenderness promised by the smile which she
had directed at me from her cousin's box. I would follow the route which
Françoise had told me that the Duchess generally took, and I would try
at the same time, in the hope of meeting two girls whom I had seen a few
days earlier, not to miss the coming out of a class or a catechism. But
meanwhile, from time to time, the scintillating smile of Mme de Guermantes, and the warm feeling it had engendered, came back to me. And
without exactly knowing what I was doing, I tried to find a place for them
(as a woman studies the effect a certain kind of jewelled buttons that have
just been given her might have on a dress) beside the romantic ideas
which I had long held and which Albertine's coldness, Gisèle's prema-
ture departure, and before them my deliberate and too long sustained
separation from Gilberte had set free (the idea for instance of being loved
by a woman, of having a life in common with her); then it was the image
of one or other of the two girls seen in the street that I coupled with those
ideas, to which immediately afterwards I tried to adapt my memory of
the Duchess. Compared with those ideas, the memory of Mme de Guermantes at the Opéra was a very insignificant thing, a tiny star twinkling
beside the long tail of a blazing comet; moreover I had been quite familiar with the ideas long before I came to know Mme de Guermantes;
whereas the memory of her I possessed but imperfectly; at moments it es-
caped me; it was during the hours when, from floating vaguely in my
mind in the same way as the images of various other pretty women, it
gradually developed into a unique and definitive association—exclusive
of every other feminine image—with those romantic ideas of mine which

were of so much longer standing than itself, it was during those few hours in which I remembered it most clearly, that I ought to have taken steps to find out exactly what it was; but I did not then know the importance it was to assume for me; I cherished it simply as a first private meeting with Mme de Guermantes inside myself; it was the first, the only accurate sketch, the only one made from life, the only one that was really Mme de Guermantes; during the few hours in which I was fortunate enough to retain it without giving it any conscious thought, it must have been charming, though, that memory, since it was always to it, freely still at that moment, without haste, without strain, without the slightest compulsion or anxiety, that my ideas of love returned; then, as gradually those ideas fixed it more permanently, it acquired from them a greater strength but itself became more vague; presently I could no longer recapture it; and in my dreams I no doubt distorted it completely, for whenever I saw Mme de Guermantes I realised the disparity—always, as it happened, different—between what I had imagined and what I saw. True, every morning now, at the moment when Mme de Guermantes emerged from her doorway at the top of the street, I saw again her tall figure, her face with its bright eyes and crown of silken hair—all the things for which I was waiting there; but, on the other hand, a minute or two later, when, having first turned my eyes away so as to appear not to be expecting this encounter which I had come to seek, I raised them to look at the Duchess at the moment in which we converged, what I saw then were red patches (as to which I did not know whether they were due to the fresh air or to a blotchy skin) on a sullen face which with the curtest of nods, a long way removed from the affability of the *Phèdre* evening, acknowledged the greeting which I addressed to her daily with an air of surprise and which did not seem to please her. And yet, after a few days during which the memory of the two girls fought against heavy odds for the mastery of my amorous feelings with that of Mme de Guermantes, it was in the end the latter which, as though of its own accord, generally prevailed while its competitors withdrew; it was to it that I finally found myself, on the whole voluntarily still and as though from choice and with pleasure, to have transferred all my thoughts of love. I had ceased to dream of the little girls coming from their catechism, or of a certain dairy-maid; and yet I had also lost all hope of encountering in the street what I had come to seek, either the affection promised to me at the theatre in a smile, or the profile, the bright face beneath its pile of golden hair which were so only when seen from afar. Now I should not even have been able to say what Mme de Guermantes was like, what I recognised her by, for every day, in the picture which she presented as a whole, the face was as different as were the dress and the hat.

Why, on such and such a morning, when I saw advancing towards me beneath a violet hood a sweet, smooth face whose charms were symmetrically arranged about a pair of blue eyes and into which the curve of the nose seemed to have been absorbed, did I gauge from a joyous commotion in my breast that I was not going to return home without having caught a glimpse of Mme de Guermantes? Why did I feel the same perturbation, affect the same indifference, turn away my eyes with the same abstracted air as on the day before, at the appearance in profile in a side street, beneath a navy-blue toque, of a beak-like nose alongside a red cheek with a piercing eye, like some Egyptian deity? Once it was not merely a woman with a bird's beak that I saw but almost the bird itself; Mme de Guermantes's outer garments, even her toque, were of fur, and since she thus left no cloth visible, she seemed naturally furred, like certain vultures whose thick, smooth, tawny, soft plumage looks like a sort of animal's coat. In the midst of this natural plumage, the tiny head arched out its beak and the bulging eyes were piercing and blue.

One day I would be pacing up and down the street for hours on end without seeing Mme de Guermantes when suddenly, inside a dairy shop tucked in between two of the mansions of this aristocratic and plebeian quarter, there would emerge the vague and unfamiliar face of a fashionably dressed woman who was asking to see some *petits suisses*, and before I had had time to distinguish her I would be struck, as by a flash of light reaching me sooner than the rest of the image, by the glance of the Duchess; another time, having failed to meet her and hearing midday strike, realising that it was not worth my while to wait for her any longer, I would be mournfully making my way homewards absorbed in my disappointment and gazing absent-mindedly at a receding carriage, when suddenly I realised that the nod which a lady had given through the carriage window was meant for me, and that this lady, whose features, relaxed and pale, or alternatively tense and vivid, composed, beneath a round hat or a towering plume, the face of a stranger whom I had supposed that I did not know, was Mme de Guermantes, by whom I had let myself be greeted without so much as an acknowledgement. And sometimes I would come upon her as I entered the carriage gate, standing outside the lodge where the detestable porter whose inquisitive eyes I loathed was in the act of making her a profound obeisance and also, no doubt, his daily report. For the entire staff of the Guermantes household, hidden behind the window curtains, would tremble with fear as they watched a conversation which they were unable to overhear, but which meant as they very well knew that one or other of them would certainly have his day off stopped by the Duchess to whom this Cerberus had betrayed him.

In view of the succession of different faces which Mme de Guermantes displayed thus one after another, faces that occupied a relative and varying expanse, sometimes narrow, sometimes large, in her person and attire as a whole, my love was not attached to any particular one of those changeable elements of flesh and fabric which replaced one another as day followed day, and which she could modify and renew almost entirely without tempering my agitation because beneath them, beneath the new collar and the strange cheek, I felt that it was still Mme de Guermantes. What I loved was the invisible person who set all this outward show in motion, the woman whose hostility so distressed me, whose approach threw me into a turmoil, whose life I should have liked to make my own, chasing away her friends. She might flaunt a blue feather or reveal an inflamed complexion, and her actions would still lose none of their importance for me.

(*The Guermantes Way*, 69–76)

Wayne Koestenbaum

Adoration, complicated, takes a few thousand pages to explain. Proust, describing Marcel's momentary infatuation with the Duchesse de Guermantes, who waves at him from an opera box and who nods to him, later, from her carriage, proves that idol worship is not a dead end. Sometimes, the idol smiles back. Reciprocation, however, can kill ardor.

Mirror-minded, Marcel worships the Duchesse de Guermantes, mostly because of her storied name. Voyeur, he sees her enter an opera box; her white chiffon dress dominates the eye. With a white-gloved hand, she waves at him; singled out from the anonymous crowd, he receives the individuating shower of her gaze. The next day, he starts stalking her; he follows her while she does errands around town. Unflattering detail: he notices red blotches on her face.

And then a woman in a carriage nods at him. Only after a moment does he realize that this respectful stranger is the Duchesse de Guermantes, but now her carriage has already passed, and he has failed to acknowledge her greeting. Does she secretly reciprocate his passion? Or is she irritated at his shadowing obsequiousness?

When I first read Proust, in the summer of 1986 or 1987, these duchess-besotted passages reinforced my own love for upper-class mavens with imposing, stiff hairdos (Jacqueline Onassis) and for sopranos (Anna Moffo). Proust gave me leave to pursue infatuation as a calling: he legitimated fandom, and made it appear poetic, not pathetic. Anatomizing adoration, subjecting it to detailed analysis, seemed, Proust's example suggested, not merely a solipsistic exercise but a high-toned quest, an act of self-ethnography. Joseph Cornell practiced it. So did

The Proust Project

Gide, Genet, and Leiris. They treated their abject crushes (on stars, ballerinas, aristocrats, shopgirls, convicts, sailors) with exegetical intensity.

It's not so much that Marcel loves the duchess. He loves what she does to his mind: she rearranges perception. She is a walking piece of installation art *avant la lettre*. Her ineffability paralyzes him; she conveniently epitomizes a milieu. Marcel's extreme consciousness requires the ballast of a motionless, heraldic, feminine object. The duchess could be Vivien Leigh, or Arletty, or Catherine Deneuve, or Kim Novak in *Vertigo*, a figment one never stops searching for; the duchess is any woman you have idealized for reasons that sensible people would call silly or superficial. Proust's *Search* is full of love objects, and the duchess is not the central one. And yet, in my biased estimation, Marcel's brief love for the duchess—her name, her remoteness, her station, her beauty, her nose, her pronunciation, her chiffon—stands out as the most poignant.

Once upon a time, a famous woman said to me, "Give me a call." I gave her a call. Nothing happened. She'd lost interest in me. Just as well. I can't bear nearness to fame: overmuch eminence humiliates the glare-blinded bystander. And yet when this famous woman, my Duchesse de Guermantes, said "Give me a call," futurity opened its counterfeit gates, and, like Marcel, I believed that I had stumbled upon immanence.

The duchess's thaw—suddenly acknowledging Marcel's existence—epitomizes certain sublime aesthetic experiences: recall how a difficult piece of music (Schoenberg?) eventually unlocks its latent melody and yields a thwarted warmth. Such temperature oscillations—the duchess's quick shift from indifference to interest—remind us that, when packing for a trip to the Proustian uncanny, we should bring bathing suits *and* parkas.

Marcel's sojourn in Doncières revives his senses, and he takes pleasure in the life of the garrison and in Saint-Loup's solicitude. All this changes, however, when he places a telephone call to his grandmother. When he hears her frail voice, he realizes that he must return home. Indeed, this is a premonition of things to come.

I went upstairs, and found my grandmother not at all well. For some time past, without knowing exactly what was wrong, she had been complaining of her health. It is in sickness that we are compelled to recognise that we do not live alone but are chained to a being from a different realm, from whom we are worlds apart, who has no knowledge of us and by whom it is impossible to make ourselves understood: our body. Were we to meet a brigand on the road, we might perhaps succeed in making him sensible of his own personal interest if not of our plight. But to ask pity of our body is like discoursing in front of an octopus, for which our words can have no more meaning than the sound of the tides, and with which we should be appalled to find ourselves condemned to live. My grandmother's ailments often passed unnoticed by her attention, which was always directed towards us. When they gave her too much pain, in the hope of curing them she tried in vain to understand them. If the morbid phenomena of which her body was the theatre remained obscure and beyond the reach of her mind, they were clear and intelligible to certain beings belonging to the same natural kingdom as themselves, beings to whom the human mind has learned gradually to have recourse in order to understand what its body is saying to it, as when a foreigner addresses us we try to find someone of his country who will act as interpreter. These can talk to our body, can tell us if its anger is serious or will soon be appeased. Cottard, who had been called in to examine my grandmother—and who had infuriated us by asking with a subtle smile, the moment we told him she was ill: "Ill? You're sure it's not what they call a diplomatic illness?"—tried to soothe his patient's restlessness by a milk diet. But incessant bowls of milk soup gave her no relief, because my grandmother sprinkled them liberally with salt, the injurious effects of which were then unknown (Widal not yet having made his discoveries). For, medicine being a compendium of the successive and contradictory mistakes of medical practitioners, when we summon the wisest of them to our aid the chances are that we may be relying on a scientific truth the error of which will be recognised in a few years' time. So that to believe in medicine would be the height of folly, if not to believe in it were not a greater folly still, for from this mass of errors a few truths have in the long run emerged. Cottard had told us to take her temperature. A thermometer was fetched. Almost throughout its entire length the tube was empty of mercury. One could scarcely make out, nestling at the bottom of its trough, the silver salamander. It seemed dead. The little glass pipe was slipped into my grandmother's mouth. We had no need to leave it there for long; the little sorceress had not been slow in casting her horoscope. We found her motionless, perched halfway up her tower and declining to move, showing us with precision the figure that we had asked of her, a figure with which all the most careful thought that my grandmother's mind might have devoted to herself would have been incapable of furnishing her: 101°. For the first time we felt some anxiety. We shook the thermometer well, to erase the ominous sign, as though we were able thus to reduce the patient's fever simultaneously with the temperature indicated. Alas, it was only too clear that the little sibyl, bereft of reason though she was, had not pronounced judgment arbitrarily, for the next day, scarcely had the thermometer been inserted between my grandmother's lips when almost at once, as though with a single bound, exulting in her certainty and in her intuition of a fact that to us was imperceptible, the little prophetess had come to a halt at the same point, in an implacable immobility, and pointed once again to that figure 101 with the tip of her gleaming wand. She said nothing else; in vain had we longed, wished, prayed, she was deaf to our entreaties; it seemed as though this were her final word, a warning and a threat.

Then, in an attempt to constrain her to modify her response, we had recourse to another creature of the same kingdom, but more potent, a creature not content with questioning the body but capable of commanding it, a febrifuge of the same order as the modern aspirin, which had not then come into use. We had not brought the thermometer down below 99.5°, in the hope that it would not have to rise from there. We made my grandmother swallow this drug and then replaced the thermometer in her mouth. Like an implacable warder to whom one presents a permit signed by a higher authority whose patronage one enjoys, and who, finding it to be in order, replies: "All right, I've nothing to say; if that's how it is you may pass," this time the vigilant out-sister did not move. But sullenly she seemed to be saying: "What good will it do you? Since you know quinine, she may give me the order not to go up once, ten times, twenty times. And then she'll grow tired of telling me, I know her, believe me. This won't last for ever. And then where will it have got you?"

Thereupon my grandmother felt the presence within her of a being who knew the human body better than she; the presence of a contemporary of the races that have vanished from the earth, the presence of earth's first inhabitant—far earlier than the creation of thinking man; she felt that primeval ally probing in her head, her heart, her elbow; he was reconnoitring the ground, organising everything for the prehistoric combat which began at once to be fought. In a moment, a crushed Python, the fever was vanquished by the potent chemical element to which my grandmother, across all the kingdoms, reaching out beyond all animal and vegetable life, would have liked to be able to give thanks. And she remained moved by this glimpse which she had caught, through the mists of so many centuries, of an element anterior to the creation even of plants. Meanwhile the thermometer, like one of the Parcae momentarily vanquished by a more ancient god, held its silver spindle motionless. Alas! other inferior creatures which man has trained to hunt the mysterious quarry which he himself is incapable of pursuing in the depths of his being, reported cruelly to us every day a certain quantity of albumin, not large, but constant enough for it also to appear to be related to some persistent malady which we could not detect. Bergotte had shaken that scrupulous instinct in me which made me subordinate my intellect when he spoke to me of Dr du Boulbon as of a physician who would not bore

The Proust Project

me, who would discover methods of treatment which, however strange they might appear, would adapt themselves to the singularity of my intelligence. But ideas transform themselves in us, overcome the resistance we put up to them at first, and feed upon rich intellectual reserves which were ready-made for them without our realising it. So, as happens whenever remarks we have heard made about someone we do not know have had the faculty of awakening in us the idea of great talent, of a sort of genius, in my inmost mind I now gave Dr du Boulbon the benefit of that unlimited confidence which is inspired in us by the man who, with an eye more penetrating than other men's, perceives the truth. I knew indeed that he was more of a specialist in nervous diseases, the man to whom Charcot before his death had predicted that he would reign supreme in neurology and psychiatry. "Ah, I don't know about that. It's quite possible," put in Françoise, who was in the room and who was hearing Charcot's name, as indeed du Boulbon's, for the first time. But this in no way prevented her from saying "It's possible." Her "possibles," her "perhapses," her "I don't knows" were peculiarly irritating at such moments. One wanted to say to her: "Naturally you didn't know, since you haven't the faintest idea what we are talking about. How can you even say whether it's possible or not, since you know nothing about it? Anyhow, you can't say now that you don't know what Charcot said to du Boulbon. You do know because we've just told you, and your 'perhapses' and 'possibles' are out of place, because it's a fact."

(*The Guermantes Way*, 403–406)

Andrew Solomon

Illness of the mind is terrifying because it affects the organ that perceives it, but illness of the body terrifies because what perceives and what is perceived lie so far apart. Descartes did us no favors when he split the human, but for those of his heirs who experience the world more through analysis than through physical experience, alienation from the physical self is the most urgent reality. Without our minds, we may still be bodies, but without our bodies we are no minds. The body is a trap of partition: while our minds may tangle entirely in other minds, our bodies, even in the most intimate acts, remain discrete. There is no greater loneliness than that of the isolate body. The senses seem to mediate between mind and body, but in fact what we see, even what we feel and touch, do not unite; they pass in sequence from the physical to the mental. The unmediated life neither exists nor is profound.

In illness one is overwhelmed by pain and fear which are rooted in the bewildering fact of corporeal dysfunction. Surely it should be possible to exercise will on our bodies, to force them to the service of a triumphal mind? We try this, over and over, and sometimes it works briefly. At last, however, we find that our very self, which in health seems inviolable, is only a by-product of the physical. At the whim of the body, the spirit dissolves. We defend ourselves from this unwelcome knowledge by speaking of a soul that lives forever, because to think of the person as fully contingent on the body runs contrary to internal experience, logic, and hope. We are humiliated by our bodies, which have the last word—and without reference to a self that seems, in health, to be more essential. This, as it turns out, is true for mental illness as well as physical illness: the painful revelation of brain science is that even the most abstract and glorious parts of the mind may be described in a vocabulary of the physical, can be expressed as, if not reduced to, anatomy.

To discourse in front of an octopus is not deeply satisfying, but to realize that you are the octopus is ghastly.

Already in fifth-century Athens there was an open debate about whether illness was a purely physical or also a philosophical problem. Hippocrates argued that all illness was the result of organic dysfunction. "All that philosophers have written on natural science no more pertains to medicine than to painting," he wrote. Aristotle, on the other hand, said that "the brain is a residue lacking any sensitive faculty," and argued for a study of illness based in the human heart—a philosophical heart, albeit with a specific location in the body. The very nature of illness was to be debated ever onward, with some thinkers feeling the self alienated from the body and some finding the self inseparable from the body. No fine print here—without the body, there is no self that we can discern. Our perpetual mission is the union of opposites—mind and body—which should not have been divorced from each other in the first place.

When we speak of the octopus, we also, inevitably, look at a Christian notion of the sinful body united with a pure spirit. Somehow this octopus is the flawed part of us. It is the part the insufferable needs of which so weigh down the characters in Proust, leading them into damage and despair. To love purely and freely, without the encumbrance of desire or illness—this ascetic goal seems to preoccupy Marcel even as he writes of human weakness, sensual despair, and the alien body. This body—will no one rid me of its pleasures and its pain? And yet, one does not even have the language with which to address the monstrous thing within which one is imprisoned and without which one is gone.

During an expedition to the Champs-Elysées, Marcel's grandmother seems to have felt unwell. "She smiled at me sorrowfully and gripped my hand. She had realized that there was no need to hide from me what I had at once guessed, that she had had a slight stroke."

We made our way back along the Avenue Gabriel through the strolling crowds. I left my grandmother to rest on a bench and went in search of a cab. She, in whose heart I always placed myself in order to form an opinion of the most insignificant person, she was now closed to me, had become part of the external world, and, more than from any casual passer-by, I was obliged to keep from her what I thought of her condition, to betray no sign of my anxiety. I could not have spoken of it to her with any more confidence than to a stranger. She had suddenly returned to me the thoughts, the griefs which, from my earliest childhood, I had entrusted to her for all time. She was not yet dead. But I was already alone. And even those allusions which she had made to the Guermantes, to Molière, to our conversations about the little clan, assumed a baseless, adventitious, fantastical air, because they sprang from this same being who tomorrow perhaps would have ceased to exist, for whom they would no longer have any meaning, from the non-being—incapable of conceiving them—which my grandmother would shortly be.

"Monsieur, I don't like to say no, but you have not made an appointment, you haven't a number. Besides, this is not my day for seeing patients. You surely have a doctor of your own. I cannot stand in for him, unless he calls me in for consultation. It's a question of professional etiquette . . ."

Just as I was signalling to a cabman, I had caught sight of the famous Professor E——, almost a friend of my father and grandfather, acquainted at any rate with them both, who lived in the Avenue Gabriel, and, on a sudden inspiration, had stopped him just as he was entering his house, thinking that he would perhaps be the very person to examine my grandmother. But, being evidently in a hurry, after collecting his letters he seemed anxious to get rid of me, and I could only speak to him by going up with him in the lift, of which he begged me to allow him to press the buttons himself, this being an idiosyncrasy of his.

"But Doctor, I'm not asking you to see my grandmother here; you will realise when I've explained to you that she isn't in a fit state; what I'm asking is that you should call at our house in half an hour's time, when I've taken her home."

"Call at your house! Really, Monsieur, you can't mean such a thing. I'm dining with the Minister of Commerce. I have a call to pay first. I must change at once, and to make matters worse my tail-coat is torn and the other one has no buttonhole for my decorations. Would you please oblige me by not touching the lift-buttons. You don't know how the lift works; one can't be too careful. Getting that buttonhole made means more delay. However, out of friendship for your family, if your grandmother comes here at once I'll see her. But I warn you I shan't be able to give her more than a quarter of an hour."

I had set off again at once, without even getting out of the lift, which Professor E—— had himself set in motion to take me down again, eyeing me distrustfully as he did so.

We may, indeed, say that the hour of death is uncertain, but when we say this we think of that hour as situated in a vague and remote expanse of time; it does not occur to us that it can have any connexion with the day that has already dawned and can mean that death—or its first assault and partial possession of us, after which it will never leave hold of us again—may occur this very afternoon, so far from uncertain, this afternoon whose time-table, hour by hour, has been settled in advance. One insists on one's daily outing so that in a month's time one will have had the necessary ration of fresh air; one has hesitated over which coat to take, which cabman to call; one is in the cab, the whole day lies before one, short because one must be back home early, as a friend is coming to see one; one hopes that it will be as fine again tomorrow; and one has no suspicion that death, which has been advancing within one on another plane, has chosen precisely this particular day to make its appearance, in a few minutes' time, more or less at the moment when the carriage reaches the Champs-Elysées. Perhaps those who are habitually haunted by the fear of the utter strangeness of death will find something reassuring in this kind of death—in this kind of first contact with death—because death thus assumes a known, familiar, everyday guise. A good lunch has preceded it, and the same outing that people take who are in perfect health. A drive home in an open carriage comes on top of its first onslaught; ill as my grandmother was, there were, after all, several people who could testify that at six o'clock, as we came home from the Champs-Elysées, they had bowed to her as she drove past in an open carriage, in perfect weather. Legrandin, making his way towards the Place de la Concorde, raised his hat to us, stopping to look after us with an air of surprise. I, who was not yet detached from life, asked my grandmother if she had acknowledged his greeting, reminding her of his touchiness. My grandmother, thinking me no doubt very frivolous, raised her hand in the air as though to say: "What does it matter? It's of no importance."

Yes, it might have been said that a few minutes earlier, while I was looking for a cab, my grandmother was resting on a bench in the Avenue Gabriel, and that a little later she had driven past in an open carriage. But would it have been really true? A bench, in order to maintain its position at the side of an avenue—although it may also be subject to certain conditions of equilibrium—has no need of energy. But in order for a living being to be stable, even when supported by a bench or in a carriage, there must be a tension of forces which we do not ordinarily perceive, any more than we perceive (because its action is multi-dimensional) atmospheric pressure. Perhaps if a vacuum were created within us and we were left to bear the pressure of the air, we should feel, in the moment that preceded our extinction, the terrible weight which there was now nothing else to neutralise. Similarly, when the abyss of sickness and death opens up within us, and we have nothing left to oppose to the tumult with which the world and our own body rush upon us, then to sustain even the thought of our muscles, even the shudder that pierces us to the marrow, then even to keep ourselves still, in what we ordinarily regard as no more than the simple negative position of a thing, demands, if one wants one's head to remain erect and one's demeanour calm, an expense of vital energy and becomes the object of an exhausting struggle.

And if Legrandin had looked back at us with that air of astonishment, it was because to him, as to the other people who passed us then, in the cab in which my grandmother was apparently sitting on the back seat, she had seemed to be foundering, slithering into the abyss, clinging desperately to the cushions which could scarcely hold back the headlong plunge of her body, her hair dishevelled, her eyes wild, no longer capable of facing the assault of the images which their pupils no longer had the strength to bear. She had appeared, although I was beside her, to be plunged in that unknown world in the heart of which she had already received the blows of which she bore the marks when I had looked up at her in the Champs-Elysées, her hat, her face, her coat deranged by the hand of the invisible angel with whom she had wrestled.

I have thought, since, that this moment of her stroke cannot have altogether surprised my grandmother, that indeed she had perhaps foreseen it a long time back, had lived in expectation of it. She had not known, naturally, when this fatal moment would come, had never been certain, any more than those lovers whom a similar doubt leads alternately to found unreasonable hopes and unjustified suspicions on the fidelity of their mistresses. But it is rare for these grave illnesses, such as that which now at last had struck her full in the face, not to take up residence in a sick person a long time before killing him, during which period they hasten, like a "sociable" neighbour or tenant, to make themselves known to him. A terrible acquaintance, not so much for the sufferings that it causes as for the strange novelty of the terminal restrictions which it imposes upon life. We see ourselves dying, in these cases, not at the actual moment of death but months, sometimes years before, when death has hideously come to dwell in us. We make the acquaintance of the Stranger whom we hear coming and going in our brain. True, we do not know him by sight, but from the sounds we hear him regularly make we can form an idea of his habits. Is he a malefactor? One morning, we can no longer hear him. He has gone. Ah! if only it were for ever! In the evening he has returned. What are his plans? The consultant, put to the question, like an adored mistress, replies with avowals that one day are believed, another day questioned. Or rather it is not the mistress's role but that of interrogated servants that the doctor plays. They are only third parties. The person whom we press for an answer, whom we suspect of being about to play us false, is Life itself, and although we feel it to be no longer the same, we believe in it still, or at least remain undecided until the day on which it finally abandons us.

I helped my grandmother into Professor E——'s lift and a moment later he came to us and took us into his consulting room. But there, pressed for time though he was, his offensive manner changed, such is the force of habit, and his habit was to be friendly, not to say playful, with his patients. Since he knew that my grandmother was a great reader, and was himself one, he devoted the first few minutes to quoting various favourite passages of poetry appropriate to the glorious summer weather. He had placed her in an armchair and himself with his back to the light so as to have a good view of her. His examination was minute and thorough, even obliging me to leave the room for a moment. He continued it after my return, then, having finished, went on, although the quarter of an hour was almost at an end, repeating various quotations to my grandmother. He even made a few jokes, which were witty enough, though I should have preferred to hear them on some other occasion, but which completely reassured me by the tone of amusement in which he uttered them. I then remembered that M. Fallières, the President of the Senate, had, many years earlier, had a false seizure, and that to the consternation of his political rivals he had taken up his duties again a few days later and had begun, it was said, to prepare an eventual candidature for the Presidency of the Republic. My confidence in my grandmother's prompt recovery was all the more complete in that, just as I was recalling the example of M. Fallières, I was distracted from pursuing the parallel by a shout of laughter which served as conclusion to one of the Professor's jokes. After which he took out his watch, frowned feverishly on seeing that he was five minutes late, and while he bade us good-bye rang for his dress clothes to be brought to him at once. I waited until my grandmother had left the room, closed the door and asked him to tell me the truth.

The Proust Project

"Your grandmother is doomed," he said to me. "It is a stroke brought on by uraemia. In itself, uraemia is not necessarily fatal, but this case seems to me hopeless. I need not tell you that I hope I am mistaken. At all events, with Cottard you're in excellent hands. Excuse me," he broke off as a maid came into the room with his tail-coat over her arm. "As I told you, I'm dining with the Minister of Commerce, and I have a call to pay first. Ah! life is not all a bed of roses, as one is apt to think at your age."

And he graciously offered me his hand. I had shut the door behind me, and a footman was ushering us into the hall, when my grandmother and I heard a great shout of rage. The maid had forgotten to cut and hem the buttonhole for the decorations. This would take another ten minutes. The Professor continued to storm while I stood on the landing gazing at my grandmother who was doomed. Each of us is indeed alone. We set off homewards.

(*The Guermantes Way*, 425–32)

J. D. McClatchy

For all the several times I have *read* the novel, the once I *listened* to it was the most telling. Admittedly, it was in English and abridged to a mere forty compact discs, but what it lacked in authenticity it made up for in narrative power. Read aloud to, one feels like the young, febrile Marcel tucked under the sheets, listening to the longest imaginable bedtime story. Experienced in this way, the novel's subtleties fade before its story line. For all the sweep of its speculations, the buoyant eddies of intellectual retrieval and clarifying trope, one clings to the novel's more basic melodramatic appeal. The story opens, after all, in a mood of suspense, and the neurotic child's panic amid the little Oedipal struggle foretells so many later competitions for favor. Moments of crisis—confrontation, flight, revelation, heartache—finally rivet this novel together. And to my mind, the most stark and wrenching of these moments is the death of Marcel's grandmother. Not only are we losing one of the book's most beloved characters (in a book where, we are led to believe, nothing is ever lost), but the episode reminds us that of all the great themes animating *In Search of Lost Time*, death is paramount. Underlying both memory and desire is death. We want to raise the dead or fill the heart's voids, but must first acknowledge the emptiness, the ghost, before our eyes. What better description of death is there, after all, than *lost time*?

(Time surges forward, memory swerves backward . . . Of all my round birthdays, only the thirtieth occasioned tears. That was in 1975, in the midst of a desultory family celebration. Suddenly, mid-sentence, I started weeping. Undoubtedly it was caused by the mortal shadow passing over the moment. But it was occasioned by a casual reference to my grandmother. I had known only one of my grandmothers, and as the firstborn of her only child, I was her pet. In my turn, I adored *her*, was never so happy as in the chair opposite hers at high tea in a swank seaside hotel, or beside her at Technicolor movie musicals, or sitting in the back seat of her silk-upholstered Buick. I was eleven when she died. I remember being taken to the hospital for her last birthday. My parents and I sat by her bed—I was forced to wear a silly party hat—while she tried to swallow, through an angled straw, a bitter, stinging mouthful of champagne. She died a week later. It was the custom of the day, in my family's circle at least, not to allow children to attend funerals—for fear of wounding their sensibilities? So I was left at home, staring out the window as my parents left for the church, and only years later came the tears that had been welling all along.)

The passage I've highlighted, in fact, is a calm in the middle of more tumultuous scenes. There is the moment, months and pages earlier, when Marcel, returned from barracks life and discovering his grandmother reading in her drawing room, realizes for the first time that hitherto he had only seen her through love's animating lens, so that the woman had been indistinguishable from his idea of her: "I, for whom my grandmother was still myself, I who had never seen her save in my own soul, always in the same place in the past, through the transparency of contiguous and overlapping memories, suddenly [saw] . . . an overburdened old woman whom I did not know." Time has a life of its own, and mortality—relentless in its course of change and meaninglessness, uncontrollable by desire or habit—has forced a renunciation and isolated both Marcel and his grandmother into lives that will end. From this moment on, the mirror having been shattered, the old woman sickens, and the physical overwhelms the emotional. "It is in sickness," Marcel now eerily realizes (and who better to write of this than Proust himself?), "that we are compelled to recognise that we do not live alone but are chained to a being from a different realm, from whom we are worlds apart, who has no knowledge of us and by whom it is impossible to make ourselves understood: our body."

(My friend the writer and Proustian Patrick Giles, when I mentioned

J. D. McClatchy

to him that I was writing on this subject, remarked that in the novel death always enslaves Marcel "with the same combination of sexual excitement and metaphysical amplitude we associate with Emily Dickinson." And then he doubled back to the author: "Proust was a beloved memorialist. Even casual acquaintances cherished the long, patient, searching, understanding letters of condolence he sent them in the wake of a mortal loss. Unlike Dickinson, who derived her most intense sensual contact with death by touching [at least through words] those whom death had most recently scalded in its vicinity, Proust wrote from a compassionate sense of agency. He understood death and its place in every moment of life so thoroughly, he could share the burden of death and lighten it with sympathy and his own deeper powers of illumination— there is no time without death and, thus, no life.")

Proust knew well the grotesque low comedy of the physical. Scenes just before and a while after this episode with Dr. E—— testify to his unsparing attention to the farce of flesh. The grandmother's stroke in the public lavatory (the attendant "Marquise" a character like the porter in *Macbeth*) or the leeches later applied to her body all have a grisly fascination, eliciting from any reader the weak grin of suppressed horror. And throughout, as in the scene above, the "red shoes" syndrome is heartlessly at work. We all have something better to do than die, no? In the doctor's palaver, language is all lies, all mercy; memory is a routine and a surgical instrument; literature is a ruse and a comfort. No matter by choice or fate, each of us is alone.

Other deaths follow, of course—most dramatically, Albertine's— until in the last volume "the idea of death took up occupancy in me." But from the start, death swells in prominence, more ominous, more ruminated upon in each book. Every choice is a tragic one because none of us can fully disclose himself to others. There may be moments of truth along the way to death, and for a fleeting moment the masks of selfishness and custom and inhibition may be dropped. But because of its final cruelty, none of us can be "together." Death sees to that. Each of us is a boy at the window, watching his mother leave for *her* mother's funeral. Each of us is alone indeed. We set off homewards.

Mary Ann Caws

Above all the other figures in Proust's novel, the grandmother—based on Proust's own mother—is the one I'd most like to take a stroll with. She's the one who turns up her face to the rain, who can't bear reproductions of things, and whose death is as heartrending as anything in Proust's work. I'd have loved to walk with her on Belle-Ile in Brittany, where Proust went in the hopes of meeting Sarah Bernhardt, who might be sitting on her favorite rock. Or in Cabourg ("Balbec"), where my children went to camp, or just about anywhere else. She's the real one.

Walking together. In Proust, many contraries do just this. Cover-up and revelation walk side by side, as do guilt and spite, blindness and insight. The entire passage describing the grandmother's death balances the hidden with the clear, the overlooked with the unsuspected, and, above all, piercing love with seeming indifference.

If, initially, Marcel has to keep from his grandmother his anxiety over her sudden illness, she has no less a desire to veil it over, thus concealing from him the signs of her stroke in her disheveled appearance, all the while clenching her teeth so as not to vomit. He has lived inside her mind, and so her perishing deprives him of place and benchmark, abandoning him to his own living solitude.

Dying, the grandmother will try not to fail her daughter in her hour of greatest need before their eternal separation, and so will pretend that her own intense pain is only indigestion, even as her daughter will promise to cure her of it. This is, says Proust, one of "those false promises we swear but are unable to keep," thus drawing us all, by the simple collective pronoun, into the emotion of the excruciating moment. Truth-telling has no place here, in the home of such ardent love. Yet, like the spectators in Bernini's unforgettable sculpture of Saint Teresa stabbed by the dart of the angel, Françoise as truth-seeing onlooker fastens on the grandmother a "dumbfounded, indiscreet and ominous" gaze. Such high drama deserves such terrible tribute.

Other instances of social witness against individual truth abound: "[I]t might have been said" that the grandmother rested on a bench, that she rode past, in fine weather, at six o'clock, or then that she was—against her custom—sliding down in her seat and clinging to the cushions, while Marcel, still attached to life, is mindful of Legrandin's sensitivity and the courtesies owed to any passerby. The grandmother knows, as always, what matters. During the examination, the doctor will quote poetry, make a few jokes at which he will laugh loudly, and will rage at his maid for forgetting to cut and hem the buttonhole for his decoration even as Marcel gazes at his doomed grandmother.

The mortal scene is now cast in black shadow on the wall against the rust of sunset, as all ages and places are summoned into a historic background for the tragic truth: the carriage is "like a hearse on some Pompeian terra-cotta."

Yet even to the end, both life and death can walk together, can play a role more gentle than honest. "Life, in withdrawing from her, had taken with it the disillusionments of life. A smile seemed to be hovering on my grandmother's lips. On that funeral couch, death, like a sculptor of the Middle Ages, had laid her down in the form of a young girl." And since in Proust's great work, things true and untrue coexist in the complexity of mutual completeness, this ending resounds in perfect pitch.

After Marcel's desire for the duchesse has begun to decline, he meets her at the home of Madame Villeparisis, an old friend of his grandmother. She is charmed by Marcel and invites him to her home for a dinner party the following week. It is the beginning of a long friendship. Marcel will spend many evenings at the home of the Duc and Duchesse de Guermantes, but the duchesse will never again be the object of his desire.

Through the Guermantes, Marcel is introduced to Monsieur de Charlus, the duc's intimidating, volatile brother. One day Marcel sees Charlus enter the tailor's shop below Marcel's house. Spying, he hears grunts of sexual pleasure, followed by cheeky, flirtatious dialogue between the two.

I now understood, moreover, why earlier, when I had seen him coming away from Mme de Villeparisis's, I had managed to arrive at the conclusion that M. de Charlus looked like a woman: he was one! He belonged to that race of beings, less paradoxical than they appear, whose ideal is manly precisely because their temperament is feminine, and who in ordinary life resemble other men in appearance only; there where each of us carries, inscribed in those eyes through which he beholds everything in the universe, a human form engraved on the surface of the pupil, for them it is not that of a nymph but that of an ephebe. A race upon which a curse is laid and which must live in falsehood and perjury because it knows that its desire, that which constitutes life's dearest pleasure, is held to be punishable, shameful, an inadmissible thing; which must deny its God, since its members, even when Christians, when at the bar of justice they appear and are arraigned, must before Christ and in his name refute as a calumny what is their very life; sons without a mother, to whom they are obliged to lie even in the hour when they close her dying eyes; friends without friendships, despite

Sodom and Gomorrah

all those which their frequently acknowledged charm inspires and their often generous hearts would gladly feel—but can we describe as friendships those relationships which flourish only by virtue of a lie and from which the first impulse of trust and sincerity to which they might be tempted to yield would cause them to be rejected with disgust, unless they are dealing with an impartial or perhaps even sympathetic spirit, who however in that case, misled with regard to them by a conventional psychology, will attribute to the vice confessed the very affection that is most alien to it, just as certain judges assume and are more inclined to pardon murder in inverts and treason in Jews for reasons derived from original sin and racial predestination? And lastly—according at least to the first theory which I sketched in outline at the time, which we shall see subjected to some modification in the sequel, and in which, had the paradox not been hidden from their eyes by the very illusion that made them see and live, this would have angered them above all else—lovers who are almost precluded from the possibility of that love the hope of which gives them the strength to endure so many risks and so much loneliness, since they are enamoured of precisely the type of man who has nothing feminine about him, who is not an invert and consequently cannot love them in return; with the result that their desire would be for ever unappeased did not their money procure for them real men, and their imagination end by making them take for real men the inverts to whom they have prostituted themselves. Their honour precarious, their liberty provisional, lasting only until the discovery of their crime; their position unstable, like that of the poet one day fêted in every drawing-room and applauded in every theatre in London, and the next driven from every lodging, unable to find a pillow upon which to lay his head, turning the mill like Samson and saying like him: "The two sexes shall die, each in a place apart!"; excluded even, except on the days of general misfortune when the majority rally round the victim as the Jews round Dreyfus, from the sympathy—at times from the society—of their fellows, in whom they inspire only disgust at seeing themselves as they are, portrayed in a mirror which, ceasing to flatter them, accentuates every blemish that they have refused to observe in themselves, and makes them understand that what they have been calling their love (and to which, playing upon the word, they have by association annexed all that poetry, painting, music, chivalry, asceticism have contrived to add to love) springs not from an ideal of beauty which they have chosen but from an incurable disease; like the Jews again (save some who will associate only with those of their race and have always on their lips the ritual words and the accepted pleasantries), shunning one another, seeking out those who are most directly their opposite, who do not want their company, forgiving their rebuffs, enraptured by their condescensions; but also brought into the company of their own kind by the ostracism to which they are subjected, the opprobrium into which they have fallen, having finally been invested, by a persecution similar to that of Israel, with the physical and moral characteristics of a race, sometimes beautiful, often hideous, finding (in spite of all the mockery with which one who, more closely integrated with, better assimilated to the opposing race, is in appearance relatively less inverted, heaps upon one who has remained more so) a relief in frequenting the society of their kind, and even some support in their existence, so much so that, while steadfastly denying that they are a race (the name of which is the vilest of insults), they readily unmask those who succeed in concealing the fact that they belong to it, with a view less to injuring them, though they have no scruple about that, than to excusing themselves, and seeking out (as a doctor seeks out cases of appendicitis) cases of inversion in history, taking pleasure in recalling that Socrates was one of themselves, as the Jews claim that Jesus was one of them, without reflecting that there were no abnormal people when homosexuality was the norm, no anti-Christians before Christ, that the opprobrium alone makes the crime because it has allowed to survive only those who remained obdurate to every warning, to every example, to every punishment, by virtue of an innate disposition so peculiar that it is more repugnant to other men (even though it may be accompanied by high moral qualities) than certain other vices which exclude those qualities, such as theft, cruelty, breach of faith, vices better understood and

Sodom and Gomorrah

so more readily excused by the generality of men; forming a freemasonry far more extensive, more effective and less suspected than that of the Lodges, for it rests upon an identity of tastes, needs, habits, dangers, apprenticeship, knowledge, traffic, vocabulary, and one in which even members who do not wish to know one another recognise one another immediately by natural or conventional, involuntary or deliberate signs which indicate one of his kind to the beggar in the person of the nobleman whose carriage door he is shutting, to the father in the person of his daughter's suitor, to the man who has sought healing, absolution, or legal defence in the doctor, the priest, or the barrister to whom he has had recourse; all of them obliged to protect their own secret but sharing with the others a secret which the rest of humanity does not suspect and which means that to them the most wildly improbable tales of adventure seem true, for in this life of anachronistic fiction the ambassador is a bosom friend of the felon, the prince, with a certain insolent aplomb born of his aristocratic breeding which the timorous bourgeois lacks, on leaving the duchess's party goes off to confer in private with the ruffian; a reprobate section of the human collectivity, but an important one, suspected where it does not exist, flaunting itself, insolent and immune, where its existence is never guessed; numbering its adherents everywhere, among the people, in the army, in the church, in prison, on the throne; living, in short, at least to a great extent, in an affectionate and perilous intimacy with the men of the other race, provoking them, playing with them by speaking of its vice as of something alien to it—a game that is rendered easy by the blindness or duplicity of the others, a game that may be kept up for years until the day of the scandal when these lion-tamers are devoured; obliged until then to make a secret of their lives, to avert their eyes from the direction in which they would wish to stray, to fasten them on what they would naturally turn away from, to change the gender of many of the adjectives in their vocabulary, a social constraint that is slight in comparison with the inward constraint imposed upon them by their vice, or what is improperly so called, not so much in relation to others as to themselves, and in such a way that to themselves it does not ap-

The Proust Project

pear a vice. But certain among them, more practical, busier men who have not the time to go and drive their bargains, or to dispense with the simplification of life and the saving of time which may result from co-operation, have formed two societies of which the second is composed exclusively of persons similar to themselves.

(*Sodom and Gomorrah*, 19–24)

Edmund White

In these pages Proust alludes to so many conflicting theories of homosexuality that they end up by casting doubt on one another—and on all such theories. In fact they suggest, finally, that only the conventions of a few cultures (but not all or even most cultures) determine the definition of normality; mere convention and nothing more absolute defines the status of homosexuality.

On the face of it nothing could seem further from the Proustian position. He starts out with the most extreme (and the most offensive) theory: that male homosexuals are inverts, i.e., women disguised as men. This whole initial disquisition on homosexuality is triggered by Marcel's realization that Charlus's face in repose is that of a woman since "he was one." This is the theory of "the soul of a woman enclosed in the body of a man" first worked out by the German sexologist Karl Heinrich Ulrichs in 1868.

As Elisabeth Ladenson, a contemporary American Proust critic, has put it, "According to this paradigm, to which Proust largely adheres in his depiction of male inverts," a man who desires another man does so insofar as he is himself in some essential way a woman. Desire even for a member of the same biological sex is thus seen as inherently heterosexual, as it were, and it is at least in part for this reason that Proust eschews the term "homosexuality," preferring "inversion."

But Proust, so often given to classicizing, discussed "inversion" not in contemporary medical terms but rather by citing the neo-Platonic notion that the desired form, male or female, is inscribed at birth on a facet of the pupil of the eye—in this case an "ephebe" rather than a "nymph." Since this very duality harks back to a very long tradition of Greek and Roman boy-love, often enjoyed in alternation with the love of women, the nineteenth-century medicalization of homosexuality is already undermined by classical tolerance, just as it is in the deliberately anticlimactic series of shock words: "punishable, shameful, an inadmissible thing" (*pour punissable et honteux, pour inavouable*).

Before the beginning of gay liberation in 1969, even the most staunch defenders of homosexuality (and there weren't many) were forced to define it as a sickness or a crime or a sin (thereby introducing three other etiologies—medical, judicial, and religious). Proust in this passage has already employed the pseudomedical term "invert"; now in elaborate and venomous and confusing sentences he invokes the judge as well as God and Christ (law and religion).

But these invocations are embedded in a comparison of inverts to Jews, disobliging to both. These pages were ones that Proust had had many years to think over. He had first written in 1909 a chapter on "The Accursed Race" ("La Race maudite"), which was part of what was eventually published posthumously in the 1950s as *Contre Sainte-Beuve*. These old pages were recycled almost intact here in *Cities of the Plain* (first published in 1921). Proust sets out to show the similarities between the self-hating homosexual and the anti-Semitic Jew. Just as the Jew who has converted to Christianity must deny his original faith before the bar of justice (the Inquisition), in the same way the male homosexual can enjoy the love of his parents and the camaraderie of his friends only by denying "his very life," i.e., his real desires.

Although Proust takes an abstract, generic stance in this passage, it coincides with the dismissal of friendship as worthless found throughout the *Search* and a strange ambivalence toward his parents. In his vast novel, which he began only after his parents' death, he devotes hundreds of pages to the theme of male homosexuality and even more to les-

Edmund White

bianism. Just as Vinteuil's daughter and her girlfriend profane her father's photograph, in the same way Proust in real life installed his parents' furniture in a male brothel (and gave his father's clothes to a servant). Was this frankness about the shocking subject of homosexuality in his novel, were these acts of profanation in real life Proust's ways of avenging himself on parents to whom he could never reveal the truth about his sexual identity? Is he one of those "sons without a mother, to whom they are obliged to lie even in the hour when they close her dying eyes"? Perhaps to divert attention from his own *parti pris*, Proust rendered loathsome most of the male homosexual characters in his book while carefully preserving the heterosexuality of Marcel; it was this grotesquerie that André Gide complained about to Proust himself.

Proust's apparent homophobia is matched by his apparent anti-Semitism. Proust may have made fun of the Bloch family by showing how venal and vulgar its members were, but he was also the man who stood by Dreyfus and who would ask his friends to curb anti-Semitic jibes in his presence, because his mother was Jewish. Homosexuals, however, are even more self-hating in Proust's account. He says that whereas Jews in an extreme case (the Dreyfus Affair) will band together, homosexuals are so self-hating they will not close ranks around one of their pariahs (Oscar Wilde). If these parallels and contrasts that Proust establishes are negative, they conceal a hidden suggestion that homosexuality is not really a sickness after all but that inverts constitute something like a minority.

The nastiness and despair inherent in these paragraphs camouflage the radical notion that homosexuals constitute a "race"; only a step away is the idea that to reject homosexuals is to be guilty of "racism." While Proust overtly subscribes to the prejudices of his day, he covertly undermines them. In an early short story a Proustian character argues that homosexuality might be due to an artistic hypersensitivity to beauty. Now in this passage he drops that defense in favor of a more potent one: "[T]here were no abnormal people when homosexuality was the norm, no anti-Christians before Christ," since "the opprobrium alone makes the crime." This is Proust's most extreme idea, that the triumph of Christianity has engendered two accursed races, Jews and homosexuals.

As if dismayed by the implications of his own words, Proust immediately goes on to argue, in effect, and rather unconvincingly, that if homosexuals were beyond reproach in pagan times, they are reprehensible now since only the most hardened cases persist in practicing their vice in such unfriendly Christian times.

Even this thought, however, is instantly softened by the next reflection: those who persist in homosexuality do so because of their "innate disposition." They have no choice—and Proust has come full circle to a theory of biological determinism that only the most irrational bigot could possibly stigmatize. This stigma exists, however, and, as in old-fashioned "anachronistic" adventure stories, in Proust's novel nobles fraternize across class lines with felons, made complicit by their shared sexual tastes. The notion of such a queer freemasonry had been popularized during the various trials of Philipp von Eulenberg, a German diplomat and friend to the kaiser. This trial—which suggested that the kaiser was surrounded by homosexuals in high places— occurred shortly before Proust wrote the original 1909 version of these pages.

Proust's ambivalence about homosexuality and its causes is very rich and productive. As Luc Fraisse writes in *Sodome et Gomorrhe de Marcel Proust*, "To dissect a vice and to reveal a sickness remain linked in his attitude: inversion is a sickness, he asserts in a sketch, a nervous taint, says the final text, an innate vice, since the last paragraph of the novel observes in Albertine 'the predisposition of vice,' the first term canceling out the second. Although normal in antiquity, inversion would lead to a reproach which is a cultural invention; a cause for guilt in human beings, it exists in a state of innocence in plants: such is the role of the vegetable metaphor in the first part of *Cities of the Plain*, as Gilles Deleuze has underlined. In another passage inversion is reduced to a subcategory in the most general laws of desire; or, on the contrary, it allows the study of passion to be pushed to an extreme and accentuates

Edmund White

the alienation of the beloved and proves that love is an illness." In other words, it's not just homosexuality that is an illness in Proust but love itself in all its forms. Homosexuality is a rich, ambiguous subject for Proust to investigate precisely because it is as open to interpretation as love (or life) itself.

Marcel has returned to Balbec. Back in the Grand Hotel, his bed against the wall, the curtains drawn, he remembers his grandmother, who would tap against the wall to comfort him and who would open the curtains for him in the morning. He realizes that it is only now that he can experience his grandmother's absence, and his grieving begins.

Upheaval of my entire being. On the first night, as I was suffering from cardiac fatigue, I bent down slowly and cautiously to take off my boots, trying to master my pain. But scarcely had I touched the topmost button than my chest swelled, filled with an unknown, a divine presence, I was shaken with sobs, tears streamed from my eyes. The being who had come to my rescue, saving me from barrenness of spirit, was the same who, years before, in a moment of identical distress and loneliness, in a moment when I had nothing left of myself, had come in and had restored me to myself, for that being was myself and something more than me (the container that is greater than the contained and was bringing it to me). I had just perceived, in my memory, stooping over my fatigue, the tender, preoccupied, disappointed face of my grandmother, as she had been on that first evening of our arrival, the face not of that grandmother whom I had been astonished and remorseful at having so little missed, and who had nothing in comon with her save her name, but of my real grandmother, of whom, for the first time since the afternoon of her stroke in the Champs-Elysées, I now recaptured the living reality in a complete and involuntary recollection. This reality does not exist for us so long as it has not been re-created by our thought (otherwise men who have been engaged in a titanic struggle would all of them be great epic poets); and thus, in my wild desire to fling myself into her arms, it was only at that moment—more than a year after her burial, because of the anachronism which so often prevents the calendar of facts from corresponding to the calendar of feelings—that I became conscious that she was dead. I had often spoken about her since then, and thought of her also, but behind my words and thoughts, those

Sodom and Gomorrah

of an ungrateful, selfish, cruel young man, there had never been anything that resembled my grandmother, because, in my frivolity, my love
of pleasure, my familiarity with the spectacle of her ill health, I retained
within me only in a potential state the memory of what she had been. No
matter at what moment we consider it, our total soul has only a more or
less fictitious value, in spite of the rich inventory of its assets, for now
some, now others are unrealisable, whether they are real riches or those
of the imagination—in my own case, for example, not only of the ancient
name of Guermantes but those, immeasurably graver, of the true memory of my grandmother. For with the perturbations of memory are linked
the intermittencies of the heart. It is, no doubt, the existence of our body,
which we may compare to a vase enclosing our spiritual nature, that in-
duces us to suppose that all our inner wealth, our past joys, all our sorrows, are perpetually in our possession. Perhaps it is equally inexact to
suppose that they escape or return. In any case if they remain within us,
for most of the time it is in an unknown region where they are of no use
to us, and where even the most ordinary are crowded out by memories
of a different kind, which preclude any simultaneous occurrence of them
in our consciousness. But if the context of sensations in which they are
preserved is recaptured, they acquire in turn the same power of expelling everything that is incompatible with them, of installing alone in
us the self that originally lived them. Now, inasmuch as the self that I had
just suddenly become once again had not existed since that evening long
ago when my grandmother had undressed me after my arrival at Balbec,
it was quite naturally, not at the end of the day that had just passed, of
which that self knew nothing, but—as though Time were to consist of a
series of different and parallel lines—without any solution of continuity,
immediately after the first evening at Balbec long ago, that I clung to the
minute in which my grandmother had stooped over me. The self that I
then was, that had disappeared for so long, was once again so close to me
that I seemed still to hear the words that had just been spoken, although
they were now no more than a phantasm, as a man who is half awake
thinks he can still make out, close by, the sound of his receding dream. I
was now solely the person who had sought a refuge in his grandmother's

arms, had sought to obliterate the traces of his sorrow by smothering her with kisses, that person whom I should have had as much difficulty in imagining when I was one or other of those that for some time past I had successively been as now I should have had in making the sterile effort to experience the desires and joys of one of those that for a time at least I no longer was. I remembered how, an hour before the moment when my grandmother had stooped in her dressing-gown to unfasten my boots, as I wandered along the stiflingly hot street, past the pastry-cook's, I had felt that I could never, in my need to feel her arms round me, live through the hour that I had still to spend without her. And now that this same need had reawakened, I knew that I might wait hour after hour, that she would never again be by my side. I had only just discovered this because I had only just, on feeling her for the first time alive, real, making my heart swell to the breaking-point, on finding her at last, learned that I had lost her for ever. Lost for ever; I could not understand, and I struggled to endure the anguish of this contradiction: on the one hand an existence, a tenderness, surviving in me as I had known them, that is to say created for me, a love which found in me so totally its complement, its goal, its constant lodestar, that the genius of great men, all the genius that might have existed from the beginning of the world, would have been less precious to my grandmother than a single one of my defects; and on the other hand, as soon as I had relived that bliss, as though it were present, feeling it shot through by the certainty, throbbing like a recurrent pain, of an annihilation that had effaced my image of that tenderness, had destroyed that existence, retrospectively abolished our mutual predestination, made of my grandmother, at the moment when I had found her again as in a mirror, a mere stranger whom chance had allowed to spend a few years with me, as she might have done with anyone else, but to whom, before and after those years, I was and would be nothing.

Instead of the pleasures that I had been experiencing of late, the only pleasure that it would have been possible for me to enjoy at that moment would have been, by touching up the past, to diminish the sorrows and

Sodom and Gomorrah

sufferings of my grandmother's life. But I did not remember her only in that dressing-gown, a garment so appropriate as to have become almost symbolic of the pains, unhealthy no doubt but comforting too, which she took for me; gradually I began to remember all the opportunities that I had seized, by letting her see my sufferings and exaggerating them if necessary, to cause her a grief which I imagined as being obliterated immediately by my kisses, as though my tenderness had been as capable as my happiness of making her happy; and, worse than that, I who could conceive of no other happiness now but that of finding happiness shed in my memory over the contours of that face, moulded and bowed by tenderness, had striven with such insensate frenzy to expunge from it even the smallest pleasures, as on the day when Saint-Loup had taken my grandmother's photograph and I, unable to conceal from her what I thought of the childish, almost ridiculous vanity with which she posed for him, with her wide-brimmed hat, in a flattering half light, had allowed myself to mutter a few impatient, wounding words, which, I had sensed from a contraction of her features, had struck home; it was I whose heart they were rending, now that the consolation of countless kisses was for ever impossible.

But never again would I be able to erase that tightening of her face, that anguish of her heart, or rather of mine; for as the dead exist only in us, it is ourselves that we strike without respite when we persist in recalling the blows that we have dealt them. I clung to this pain, cruel as it was, with all my strength, for I realised that it was the effect of the memory I had of my grandmother, the proof that this memory was indeed present within me. I felt that I did not really remember her except through pain, and I longed for the nails that riveted her to my consciousness to be driven yet deeper. I did not try to mitigate my suffering, to embellish it, to pretend that my grandmother was only somewhere else and momentarily invisible, by addressing to her photograph (the one taken by Saint-Loup, which I had with me) words and entreaties as to a person who is separated from us but, retaining his personality, knows us and remains bound to us by an indissoluble harmony. Never did I do this,

The Proust Project

for I was determined not merely to suffer, but to respect the original form of my suffering as it had suddenly come upon me unawares, and I wanted to continue to feel it, following its own laws, whenever that contradiction of survival and annihilation, so strangely intertwined within me, returned.

(*Sodom and Gomorrah*, 210–20)

John Jeremiah Sullivan

It took me over a year to believe that my father was dead. Not that I denied it, or even actively disbelieved it; I simply had not yet learned it was true. I was washing dishes in my apartment in New York when my mother called to tell me that the dog of my youth—a gigantic piebald semiretarded mutt, half Great Dane and half Labrador, with paws the size of dessert plates and a ridiculous black mask across his eyes—had been, as she put it, "put down" at the age of fifteen. She had come downstairs to let him outside for his morning devoir and found him unable to stand. She looked into his eyes and for the first time, in his long senescence, saw pain. "I'm sorry," she said, "I wish I could have told you first. But . . . we owed it to him, you know."

We were always dog people. Tippy was the first—my brother's dog. She was about 75 percent black Lab, one of those preternaturally intelligent mongrels that at birthday parties herd children away from the street. My little sister and I got off the bus one day after school and found her dead in her favorite spot in the front yard, under a giant maple tree that covered our house in shadow. We rubbed her head frantically, calling her name, but a black fly landed on her lip, to no response, and we knew that something was off. We burst into the house, screaming for my father. Normally, when you woke him from a nap, he would emerge from the bedroom enraged, his hand raised in preparation for one of his mock slaps, which seemed like actual pain-inflicters until they got to about six inches of your arm, at which point they would sort of flutter out, ending in a tap—then he would stomp away. But something about the pitch of our voices warned him, and he came into the hallway with a dazed and worried look. There followed one of those irretrievably pure child-hood moments, from before decorum and shame have tamed our re-sponses: I ran to him, threw my arms around his waist, and, looking up, called out, "Why? Why?"

Within a month we had bought another Lab-like female from a man in Louisville who had seven puppies to sell. My father named her Rug-gles (after his favorite film comedian, Charlie Ruggles) and gave her to my sister, who was still crying every night over the shock of that first death. Ruggles was sweet but intensely stupid: her slobber defined her. She was athletic, however—a real jumper, with powerful haunches—and when her first heat came on, we found it impossible to keep her gated. She would bound over the four-and-a-half-foot chain-link fence that surrounded our backyard, her fore and back paws bunching to-gether just at the crest of her arc, and touch down already sprinting like mad. Every male dog in the neighborhood still in possession of his equipment, it seemed, had a go at her, and she turned up heavily pregnant.

Her seven puppies—when she had them at four o'clock in the morn-ing, in a cutout refrigerator box, on the Fourth of July—were every size and color. In most cases, we could trace each one to a neighborhood stud. The last to be born was the biggest, and we recognized him imme-diately as the bastard son of a harlequin Dane who lived on the other side of the hill from our house and stood almost to my shoulders. This son looked like a huge potato that had sprouted a head, white with black spots all over, and pads on his paws that were the exact pink of a brand-new pencil eraser. My father named him Remnant (because he was Rug-gles' last puppy: the end of the rug is the remnant), and when his mother rolled wearily onto her flank to offer her teats, he would casually push the others aside, swimming through them almost, until he had estab-lished himself at the center of the pack. Whatever the opposite of the runt is called, he was that.

Six weeks later, when the time came to give them away, we made up our minds that we would simply keep the one that was left, after the other six had been adopted. This would be my dog. But we noticed immediately that when the prospective owners would show up, and most of the litter would go running to them, jumping up onto their legs, Remnant would sneak off and hide in a boxwood by the back door, as if he knew what was going on and wanted no part of it. I asked my parents if I could keep him.

That little show of intelligence turned out to be a ruse, or more likely an illusion. He soon revealed himself to be every bit as stupid as his mother. I should say, though, that with Ruggles and Remnant both, we were never certain if they had been born brain-damaged, or if we had accidentally made them that way by allowing them to eat whatever they wanted. You could never keep food away from them. They could get things down from the top of the refrigerator, out from under the bed, from inside boxes and bags. They ate loaves of bread, a large bottle full of heartworm pills, a packet of raw hot dogs, Shakespeare (my sister's gerbil), carpeting, grass, bulbs from my mother's gardens, our scary and demented cat Skipper's turds, and, once, an entire unopened box of big chunky chocolate bars, the kind they make you sell to raise money for school-related causes. I remember the next night, when my father sent me into the backyard with a plastic bag to do "poo patrol," there was a full moon, and the many prodigious piles that mother and son had been leaving throughout the day were glinting in the silvery light: flecks of the foil wrappers that the chocolate bars had been wrapped in.

We loved our fat, stupid dogs, even when the neighbors complained about them and our friends made fun of them. My father had contempt for the whole pukka-suburban philosophy of pet-rearing, with thousand-dollar bills from obedience school and harsh commands issued in public for the admiration of other owners. To him—and to the rest of us, by training—dogs were *meant* to be like Remnant and Ruggles, large idiotic creatures who ran around and did as they pleased until you screamed at them, who terrified strangers but would never hurt one, who gave and craved unconditional affection in outsized doses and agreed to live with you until one of you died.

Remnant, who kept growing through even his second year and was, in the end, positively enormous, with a bark like a shotgun going off, seemed the archetype of the big dumb mutt, and my father especially loved him. He would call me over to the window in the family room to watch Remnant (who had become an ever better jumper than his mother) getting ready to go over the fence. The dog would trot to the middle of the lawn and turn, gathering speed as he approached the obstacle, finally soaring into the air; he did all this in a manner somehow leisurely, with his tongue hanging out. "He runs like a pony," my father said, shaking his head.

When we moved to Ohio, our house had an identical fence around the backyard, but the neighbors immediately let us know that they would not put up with our dogs getting loose. So we had to chain them, for the first time in their lives. After a couple of months, however, my father realized that if you simply shook the chain at Remnant, made clinking sounds in the general area of his faded red collar, and said, "Now you're chained, Remmy," he would believe that he had been restrained and not even attempt the jump. For five years the chain sat coiled by the sliding patio door, never again used, totally effective. My father named it the Great Chain of Nonbeing.

After my parents divorced, when my father would stop by the house to pick up me and my sister or drop off some piece of legal paperwork, Remnant would hear his master's voice and come pounding down the stairs. There was something sad about their little reunions in the foyer; even Remnant, trembling with emotion, could sense it. He would turn and head back upstairs after only a minute or two, casting an uncertain glance at my mother, as if he had been caught doing something bad. And my father held back, too: he would only bend to pet the dog, not squat, as he used to do, till their faces were level. The respective displays were muted; it was like two old friends saying hello in a courtroom or at a funeral.

It did not surprise me when Remnant outlived my father. I could never think of the dog as old. Even after Ruggles died, when I would come home for Christmas or Easter to find him much reduced—with a dog diaper on (at one point), and the black around his mouth gone gray, his hearing and eyesight lost (you had to stomp on the floor to get his attention, a summons he responded to when he felt like it), his back legs trembling as he climbed the stairs, and then his refusal to climb the stairs at all—it seemed to me that these were more of his antics. And indeed, when my mother had a scare a full year before the end (she heard him whimpering one night and called the vet, who said it was "probably time"), she was at the point of loading him into the station wagon for his final voyage when he suddenly called on mysterious reserves and began to prance around, looking five years younger. "It's like when he was a puppy and people were coming to adopt them," my mother said. "He knows when somebody wants to take him away."

But the second time, he failed; he had nothing left. He allowed himself to be carried by my mother and her new husband in a bedsheet to the backseat of the car. He was silent all the way to the vet. And my mother came home with his ashes (there were a lot of them) in a Tupperware container.

I was not prepared for my reaction to this news; the call, after all, was one that if anything I was surprised hadn't come much sooner. But when I pictured Remnant (I at first saw a Polaroid of myself holding him under the swing set when he was small enough to fit in my hands, his black-and-white face still pinched and fetal), I thought suddenly of my father, fourteen months dead, who had loved and been loved by this dim-witted dog, and I saw the two of them rubbing their faces together furiously, as they loved equally to do, saw Remnant sitting impatiently by my father's desk while he wrote, the great tail going nonstop like a windshield wiper on the dusty concrete floor until my father would finally finish and rise and mount the steps, crying, "Does Remnant want a bone? Does he want a bone?" and I saw my father out driving in the car after Remnant had gotten away, which he did all the time in the days before the Chain, when he would turn up at a strip mall somewhere, with some old lady cornered, and my father when he found him would always say, "It's all right, it's all right; he only wants to lick you," and I understood suddenly that Remnant's tremendous head, even at the end when he could neither hear nor see, had been this repository, a link, that he had preserved in the recesses of his memory these strands of my father's being, perhaps

The Proust Project

only a scent or a certain word, but I knew too that our being consists in these strands, as much as it does in our bodies, that we draw our existence from a kind of web that is always eaten away at from the outside yet never disappears, while we do; it was as though Remnant had come back to teach me how death does its work, and that life is this slow amassing of a company of shades who build up around us until we are suffered to join them ("The dead annex the quick as surely as the Kingdom of France annexes the Duchy of Orléans," said Beckett); I saw man following dog into the darkness, the dog—like us—unaware of his place in the chain, the man my father, whom I had not really grieved, not yet, the reality of whose death had so far failed, like the news of a foreign catastrophe, to impinge on my deepest self, the fundamental datum of whose death I was now for the first time hearing about, learning about, for it was not until that moment, more than a year after his burial, because of that anachronism which so often prevents the calendar of facts from corresponding to that of our feelings, that I became conscious that he was dead. And I shook with sobs.

Richard Howard

We are nothing without one another
yet between us is utter abyss.

PAUL VALÉRY

No favorite character, no phylactery of psychological insight; instead, the consecrated feature of Proustian textuality: the sentence. Of course, not just any sentence in the *Search* but those—they are frequent, even endemic—which occur when Proust flexes his rhetorical muscles (the reader can feel the discourse tighten and release) in preparation for the binding effort, the intentional and uniting articulation of continuous prose.

Pythonically draped upon conclusive syntactic trusses to form a mesmeric design, *la phrase* is my cynosure. It is not the remarkable range of character studies, nor what Henry James proleptically called portraits of places which ultimately and indeed initially deserve the adjective *Proustian*, but the structural characteristic of the sentence, the signal unit of this writer's behavior, which I would instance as a preferential index. Let me offer a (comparatively) wieldy example which, in the middle of the first chapter of *Sodom and Gomorrah* 2, introduces the crucial notion—a conception even more deeply rooted than "involuntary memory," to which of course it is related—of the *intermittencies of the heart*. Herewith:

> Considered in its entirety at any given moment, the human soul has no
> more than an almost fictitious value for all its array of riches, since now

The Proust Project

some of these, now others, whether actual or imaginary, are inaccessible—
in my own case, for example, not only the ancient name Guermantes, but
the much graver instance of the true memory of my grandmother. For to
memory's flaws are linked the intermittences of the heart.

It is the coiling elaboration of that first sentence which readies us, which
works us up, as we say nowadays, for the ten words which follow, and for
the famous phrase which Proust once thought to use as the comprehensive title of his entire work. The metaphorical and psychological meaning of the medical term *intermittence* occurs in Maeterlinck's essay on
immortality (in *L'Intelligence des fleurs*) which Proust had consulted for
an application, in *Sodom and Gomorrah* 1, of a botanical metaphor for
homosexual love: "As if the functions of that organ by which we delight
in life were intermittent; as if our very presence, except in pain, were no
more than a perpetual series of withdrawals and returns." But what I
want to emphasize here is not the interesting derivation of the concept
itself, but the way Proust's long(ish) sentence about various kinds of
loss—not only of the snobbish association with the noble Guermantes
but of Marcel's authentic love for his grandmother—is articulated in the
relentless twists and turns, the grammatical feints and dodges analo-
gizing the structure of consciousness itself, whereupon he can deliver
the knockout, the pith and vinegar of the tiny aphorism consequent
upon such serpentine speculation.

It is hardly surprising that I should respond to the question of "favorite phenomenon in Proust" by choosing the sentence, a rhetorical
stratagem, rather than fetishizing a character, a situation, or a scene. For
Proust is famous, even notorious, for his sentences, some the longest in
literature, others like the one I have chosen shapely enough (though
ominously extensive), all concerned to unite our experience of the physical world to our interpretation, our understanding, our interior possession of that world in a grammatical reticulation of limitless resource.

Poetry—or at least verse—cannot accomplish this enterprise, it
must be the prose sentence, for prose, the past participle of the Latin
verb *provertere*, means "having moved forward"; whereas verse is what
turns, what returns in a ceremonial of recurrence. Of all writers I know,

Richard Howard

Proust persists, continues, divagates—he does go on. As my epigraph from Valéry suggests, it is perhaps because of all writers Proust has the wracking consciousness of separation, of division, of severance that he is so desperate to unite, to unify, to join.

It is of more than incidental interest to observe, in my characteristic but by no means particular choice of a Proustian sentence, how readily this writer associates the intermittencies of the heart with involuntary memory. As early as 1913 he remarks in a letter: "[W]e think we no longer love our dead, but that is because we don't remember them; suddenly we catch sight of an old glove and we burst into tears." The remark precedes the composition of the sentence I have instanced by some years, and it is remarkable to discover how loyal Proust's imagination is to his casually reported experience. The entire passage about the discovery of the "true memory" of Marcel's grandmother, from which I have violently extracted my capital sentence(s), should be considered closely—chapter 1 of part 2 of *Sodom and Gomorrah*, about thirty pages on.

André Aciman

The little phrase I am thinking of is conjured by Marcel when he is suddenly reminded of his grandmother during his second stay in Balbec. He had stayed at the same beach resort in Balbec with her once, but now, more than a year after her death, he is back to the very same hotel. What he finds, as Proustian characters always find when they expect maximum emotion, is minimum sensation. He encounters more or less what he experienced at the time of her death: a sense of surprise at feeling so singularly numb, almost indifferent, blasé. All of it is colored by Marcel's overloaded feeling of not feeling enough and by the hope that this shamed admission of emotional inadequacy might itself pass for genuine emotion.

Now, surrounded by the "indolent charm" of the Grand Hotel, what the young adult Marcel thinks of as he arrives at Balbec is not his grandmother, but the social life awaiting him, the band of young girls he had met there once before, and that vague, tantalizing thing Marcel always longs for: something exotic, someone new, unexpected, different who might ultimately lure him out of his humdrum bookish cocoon into what Proust calls a new life. As for his grandmother—well, if bereavement is the toll the living must pay for the loss of a loved one, then, clearly, Marcel, to use Jane Austen's words, "has been let off easily."

But we are, of course, being set up. For as soon as Marcel is in his hotel room and bends down to undo one of his boot buttons—something his grandmother had helped him with in this very same room—he suddenly bursts out sobbing, vehemently. What hits him is not just that he misses her terribly but that he will never, ever see her again, because

André Aciman

for the first time in his life, and in a manner that totally devastates Marcel the arch-premeditator, it finally sinks in, long after it happened, that his grandmother is dead.

Yet, come to think of it, this shouldn't be surprising. Emotion, as every reader of Proust knows after about thirty pages, always comes unannounced, obliquely, inadvertently, just as it does, say, in Freud. The more unexpected and less rehearsed, the more genuine and more poignant it is. This is how life works in Proust. Conversely, one may bump into the right people, but never when one wants to; one may get what one wants, but only after giving up on it or wanting something else instead. We reach out to seize precious moments not as they're happening but once we know we've lost them.

So far so good. The setup is familiar enough. Proust, this cross between Freud, Woody Allen, and Murphy of Murphy's Law is one of us; how well we know him and how well he knows us. How well he understands repression. And how simple and direct that outburst of earnest grief, and how admirable his knowledge that it is always better to feel something, anything, than to feel nothing at all, that human beings should and want to feel things, and that we are each of us heat-seeking subjects starved for feeling, which is why, even at the risk of getting hurt or making tremendous fools of ourselves, we will not shirk from being drawn to certain places, to certain objects, certain odors, to art, to tears, to plants, to writing, to memory, to music, to vice, and, of course, to other human beings, because by so doing each of us finds a secret, private conduit to an inner life that is not just our *new* life but our true life.

How magnificently and . . . predictably modern Proust is. So, for the sake of argument, let me overturn everything I've been saying and ask: What if this true, inner life is nothing more than a life made to be lost, but lost before it was ever possessed, or even glimpsed, though it seems to have been lived because it claims to be remembered? What if this true, inner life hovers on the horizon like a ghost ship that never materializes but never vanishes either? What if this other life were an ancillary life called . . . *paper*: an unlived life made on paper, lived for paper, by a man raised and fed on paper, who has learned that life itself can be

The Proust Project

so drearily unimaginative sometimes that, by a sort of miracle that jus-
tifies his lifelong confinement to paper, life will mimic what could only
have happened on paper? Where else but on paper does a man, desperately seeking a woman among millions in Paris, actually bump into
her on the streets very late at night? Proust's bookish eye is transfixed
by those moments in life that are stunning, not because of their inherent beauty, but because they cry out to be committed—i.e., returned—
to paper, to literature, to fiction, the ultimate seat of the inner life.

Small wonder that Proust put so much stock in style. The Proustian
sentence, which personifies procrastination, allows him to sink into paper and never to come up for air, to pile up metaphors and clauses, and
take all sorts of sinuous turns, the better to take sorrow and pain and
spread them out, like gold, into a cadence, just cadence, because cadence is like feeling, and cadence is like breathing, and cadence is desire, and if cadence doesn't reinvent everything we would like our life
to have been or to become, then just the act of searching, and probing
in that particularly cadenced way, becomes a way of feeling and of being in the world.

And yet, having built such a paper world, Proust can suddenly overturn everything I've been suggesting and jolts out like someone waking
from a dream, sputtering things as randomly and inchoately as a man
who's barely learned to speak. No reader of Montaigne can forget that
stunning moment when, after probing why he loved his deceased friend
so much, the author of the *Essays*, this master stylist of baroque prose,
breaks down and scrawls one of the most beautiful sentences penned in
French. You ask me, why I loved him, Montaigne says. I don't know. All
I can say is: *Parce que c'estoit luy, parce que c'estoit moy*—because it
was he, because it was I. Proust, too, knows how to cut through layer after layer of searching and probing prose and write as brief a sentence if
only because it, like his sudden outburst, wells up in him and erupts on
something that is more than just paper now. You ask me why I loved my
grandmother, he says, I don't know. All I know is this—and here is the
little sentence I mentioned at the beginning: *Elle était ma grand'mère
et j'étais son petit-fils*, She was my grandmother, and I was her grandson,

ponders Marcel after his emotional upheaval. And if that's not enough, a few lines down, Proust will say it again, more forcefully, because, while staring at her photograph in his hotel room, he will say it in yet more guileless terms: *C'est grand'mère, je suis son petit fils*, It's grandmother, I am her grandson.

It's grandmother, I'm her grandson.

Anyone can write this. But of course it's what's around it that makes it so eloquent. More to the point, life can't compete with this. Life doesn't even come close. And come to think of it, perhaps no one alive can.

The Verdurins take a house for the summer near Balbec and continue to hold their salons there. Monsieur de Charlus has become, improbably, one of the most faithful members of the "faithful." Though keeping such society is well below a man of his stature, there is, in regular attendance, a young violinist named Charlie Morel, whom he cannot live without. Morel, aware of this, takes his money and his gifts and torments him.

Albertine has begun to fade as a love object for Marcel, and he is only waiting for the right moment to make the final rupture. He is about to break things off when, as they sit on the train together, Albertine casually informs him that she has been invited to spend time with Mademoiselle Vinteuil, a notorious lesbian and the daughter of the composer of the "little phrase." Imagining the pleasure she will have without him, Marcel is unable to end the relationship. To his mother's chagrin, he declares, "I absolutely must marry Albertine."

Albertine has come to live in Marcel's house in Paris. His parents are in Combray. It is just Albertine and Marcel, and the maid Françoise. There is a familiar evening ritual: "every night, before leaving me, she used to slide her tongue between my lips like a portion of daily bread." Rapt, Marcel watches Albertine sleep.

B y shutting her eyes, by losing consciousness, Albertine had stripped off, one after another, the different human personalities with which she had deceived me ever since the day when I had first made her acquaintance. She was animated now only by the unconscious life of plants, of trees, a life more different from my own, more alien, and yet one that belonged more to me. Her personality was not constantly escaping, as when we talked, by the outlets of her unacknowledged thoughts and of her eyes. She had called back into herself everything of her that lay outside, had withdrawn, enclosed, reabsorbed herself into her body. In keeping her in front of my eyes, in my hands, I

The Captive

had an impression of possessing her entirely which I never had when she was awake. Her life was submitted to me, exhaled towards me its gentle breath.

I listened to this murmuring, mysterious emanation, soft as a sea breeze, magical as a gleam of moonlight, that was her sleep. So long as it lasted, I was free to dream about her and yet at the same time to look at her, and, when that sleep grew deeper, to touch, to kiss her. What I felt then was a love as pure, as immaterial, as mysterious, as if I had been in the presence of those inanimate creatures which are the beauties of nature. And indeed, as soon as her sleep became at all deep, she ceased to be merely the plant that she had been; her sleep, on the margin of which I remained musing, with a fresh delight of which I never tired, which I could have gone on enjoying indefinitely, was to me a whole landscape. Her sleep brought within my reach something as serene, as sensually delicious as those nights of full moon on the bay of Balbec, calm as a lake over which the branches barely stir, where, stretched out upon the sand, one could listen for hours on end to the surf breaking and receding.

On entering the room, I would remain standing in the doorway, not venturing to make a sound, and hearing none but that of her breath rising to expire upon her lips at regular intervals, like the reflux of the sea, but drowsier and softer. And at the moment when my ear absorbed that divine sound, I felt that there was condensed in it the whole person, the whole life of the charming captive outstretched there before my eyes. Carriages went rattling past in the street, but her brow remained as smooth and untroubled, her breath as light, reduced to the simple expulsion of the necessary quantity of air. Then, seeing that her sleep would not be disturbed, I would advance cautiously, sit down on the chair that stood by the bedside, then on the bed itself.

I spent many a charming evening talking and playing with Albertine, but none so sweet as when I was watching her sleep. Granted that she had, as she chatted with me, or played cards, a naturalness that no actress could have imitated; it was a more profound naturalness, as it were at one remove, that was offered me by her sleep. Her hair, falling along her pink cheek, was spread out beside her on the bed, and here and there

The Proust Project

an isolated straight tress gave the same effect of perspective as those moonlit trees, lank and pale, which one sees standing erect and stiff in the backgrounds of Elstir's Raphaelesque pictures. If Albertine's lips were closed, her eyelids, on the other hand, seen from where I was placed, seemed so loosely joined that I might almost have questioned whether she really was asleep. At the same time those lowered lids gave her face that perfect continuity which is unbroken by the eyes. There are people whose faces assume an unaccustomed beauty and majesty the moment they cease to look out of their eyes.

I would run my eyes over her, stretched out below me. From time to time a slight, unaccountable tremor ran through her, as the leaves of a tree are shaken for a few moments by a sudden breath of wind. She would touch her hair and then, not having arranged it to her liking, would raise her hand to it again with motions so consecutive, so deliberate, that I was convinced that she was about to wake. Not at all; she grew calm again in the sleep from which she had not emerged. Thereafter she lay motionless. She had laid her hand on her breast, the limpness of the arm so artlessly childlike that I was obliged, as I gazed at her, to suppress the smile that is provoked in us by the solemnity, the innocence and the grace of little children.

I, who was acquainted with many Albertines in one person, seemed now to see many more again reposing by my side. Her eyebrows, arched as I had never noticed them, encircled the globes of her eyelids like a halcyon's downy nest. Races, atavisms, vices reposed upon her face. Whenever she moved her head, she created a different woman, often one whose existence I had never suspected. I seemed to possess not one but countless girls. Her breathing, as it became gradually deeper, made her breast rise and fall in a regular rhythm, and above it her folded hands and her pearls, displaced in a different way by the same movement, like boats and mooring chains set swaying by the movement of the tide. Then, feeling that the tide of her sleep was full, that I should not run aground on reefs of consciousness covered now by the high water of profound slumber, I would climb deliberately and noiselessly on to the bed, lie down by her side, clasp her waist in one arm, and place my lips upon her

The Captive

cheek and my free hand on her heart and then on every part of her body in turn, so that it too was raised, like the pearls, by her breathing; I myself was gently rocked by its regular motion: I had embarked upon the tide of Albertine's sleep.

Sometimes it afforded me a pleasure that was less pure. For this I had no need to make any movement, but allowed my leg to dangle against hers, like an oar which one trails in the water, imparting to it now and again a gentle oscillation like the intermittent wing-beat of a bird asleep in the air. I chose, in gazing at her, the aspect of her face which one never saw and which was so beautiful. It is I suppose comprehensible that the letters which we receive from a person should be more or less similar to one another and combine to trace an image of the writer sufficiently different from the person we know to constitute a second personality. But how much stranger is it that a woman should be conjoined, like Radica with Doodica, with another woman whose different beauty makes us infer another character, and that in order to see them we must look at one of them in profile and the other in full face. The sound of her breathing, which had grown louder, might have given the illusion of the panting of sexual pleasure, and when mine was at its climax, I could kiss her without having interrupted her sleep. I felt at such moments that I had possessed her more completely, like an unconscious and unresisting object of dumb nature. I was not troubled by the words that she murmured from time to time in her sleep; their meaning was closed to me, and besides, whoever the unknown person to whom they referred, it was upon my hand, upon my cheek that her hand, stirred by an occasional faint tremor, tightened for an instant. I savoured her sleep with a disinterested, soothing love, just as I would remain for hours listening to the unfurling of the waves.

Perhaps people must be capable of making us suffer intensely before they can procure for us, in the hours of remission, the same soothing calm as nature does. I did not have to answer her as when we were engaged in conversation, and even if I could have remained silent, as for that matter I did when it was she who was talking, still while listening to her I did not penetrate so far into the depths of her being. As I continued to hear, to capture from moment to moment, the murmur, soothing as a barely perceptible breeze, of her pure breath, it was a whole physiological existence that was spread out before me, at my disposal; just as I used to remain for hours lying on the beach, in the moonlight, so long could I have remained there gazing at her, listening to her. Sometimes it was as though the sea was beginning to swell, as though the storm was making itself felt even inside the bay, and I would press myself against her and listen to the gathering roar of her breath.

Sometimes, when she was too warm, she would take off her kimono while she was already almost asleep and fling it over an armchair. As she slept I would tell myself that all her letters were in the inner pocket of this kimono, into which she always thrust them. A signature, an assignation, would have sufficed to prove a lie or to dispel a suspicion. When I could see that Albertine was sound asleep, leaving the foot of the bed where I had been standing motionless in contemplation of her, I would take a step forward, seized by a burning curiosity, feeling that the secret of this other life lay offering itself to me, flaccid and defenceless, in that armchair. Perhaps I took this step forward also because to stand perfectly still and watch her sleeping became tiring after a while. And so, on tiptoe, constantly turning round to make sure that Albertine was not waking, I would advance towards the armchair. There I would stop short, and stand for a long time gazing at the kimono, as I had stood for a long time gazing at Albertine. But (and here perhaps I was wrong) never once did I touch the kimono, put my hand in the pocket, examine the letters. In the end, realising that I would never make up my mind, I would creep back to the bedside and begin again to watch the sleeping Albertine, who would tell me nothing, whereas I could see lying across an arm of the chair that kimono which would perhaps have told me much.

And just as people pay a hundred francs a day for a room at the Grand Hotel at Balbec in order to breathe the sea air, I felt it to be quite natural that I should spend more than that on her, since I had her breath upon my cheek, between my lips which I laid half-open upon hers, through which her life flowed against my tongue.

But this pleasure of seeing her sleep, which was as sweet to me as that

The Captive

of feeling her live, was cut short by another pleasure, that of seeing her wake. It was, carried to a more profound and more mysterious degree, the same pleasure as I felt in having her under my roof. It was gratifying to me, of course, that when she alighted from the car in the afternoon, it should be to my house that she was returning. It was even more so to me that when, from the underworld of sleep, she climbed the last steps of the staircase of dreams, it was in my room that she was reborn to consciousness and life, that she wondered for an instant: "Where am I?" and, seeing the objects by which she was surrounded, and the lamp whose light scarcely made her blink her eyes, was able to assure herself that she was at home on realising that she was waking in *my* home. In that first delicious moment of uncertainty, it seemed to me that once again I was taking possession of her more completely, since, instead of her returning to her own room after an outing, it was my room that, as soon as Albertine should have recognised it, was about to enclose, to contain her, without there being any sign of misgiving in her eyes, which remained as calm as if she had never slept at all. The uncertainty of awakening, revealed by her silence, was not at all revealed in her eyes.

Then she would find her tongue and say: "My ———" or "My darling ———" followed by my Christian name, which, if we give the narrator the same name as the author of this book, would be "My Marcel," or "My darling Marcel." After this I would never allow a member of my family, by calling me "darling," to rob of their precious uniqueness the delicious words that Albertine uttered to me. As she uttered them, she pursed her lips in a little pout which she spontaneously transformed into a kiss. As quickly as she had earlier fallen asleep, she had awoken.

(*The Captive*, 84–92)

Susan Minot

I was in the woods in western Massachusetts. It was late November. Yellow and brown leaves covered the ground like a Turkish rug with the branch shadows making patterns on the light. The forest was pillared with bare white birches. I was sitting on the forest floor leaning against a tree trunk, waiting for my boyfriend. He was rock climbing on a nearby cliff with a friend. I can't remember who the friend was. I don't remember the drive getting there or what we did later when we drove away that night. But I remember the afternoon vividly. It was cold, I was smoking cigarettes. I was alone. The reason I remember it so well is that I was reading. For a college course—*The Captive* by Proust. As I read, I was keenly aware of my surroundings and yet also felt as if I were gliding on a flying carpet.

That I was so thoroughly transported to a bedroom in Paris at the turn of the century and can still remember its bed with the girl lying on it, its curtained windows and the muted sounds of the carriages in the streets, as well if not better than the setting in those woods, is just one version of the strange and unpredictable nature of memory. Why do we lodge one image in our mind when so many are sent floating down the river and forgotten?

I was reading the section near the beginning of this fifth volume when Marcel, having finally secured Albertine in a secret domestic arrangement, is looking over her sleeping body, which is "animated now only by the unconscious life of plants, of trees." She reminds him of "a long blossoming stem that had been laid there." As he watches his

Susan Minot

sleeping mistress in this relatively short section of six pages, he finds occasion to muse about love, jealousy, mistrust, self-consciousness, suffering, the unfathomability of another, sexual politics, the evolution of relationships ("At one time I had been carried away by excitement when I thought that I saw a trace of mystery in Albertine's eyes, now I was happy only . . . when I succeeded in expelling every trace of mystery"), the quality of eyes ("There are people whose faces assume an unaccustomed beauty and majesty the moment they cease to look out of their eyes"), letter writing ("[T]he letters which we receive from a person should be more or less similar to one another and combine to trace an image of the writer sufficiently different from the person we know to constitute a second personality"), and how like the sea, if not a plant, is a woman sleeping. He even describes why he *can* muse:

"[T]he faculty of dreaming, which I possessed only in her absence, I recovered at such moments in her presence, as though by falling asleep she had become a plant. In this way, her sleep realised to a certain extent the possibility of love: alone, I could think of her, but I missed her, I did not possess her; when she was present, I spoke to her, but was too absent from myself to be able to think of her; when she was asleep, I no longer had to talk, I knew that I was no longer observed by her, I no longer needed to live on the surface of myself."

We see only the outer surface. I was mesmerized by Marcel's obsession to penetrate the minds of others. I, too, spent a lot of time wondering what went on in someone else's mind. I followed his every nuance. Each sentence seemed to lift off the page with a kind of divine truth. Proust is best when you are in a state of rapt willingness to follow him wherever he takes you. His meandering, detailed sentences test the attentive reader. It's as if he's saying, "If you follow along with me, then your attention will be sharp enough to see the subtlety of what I am conveying."

Proust is unfairly maligned for being wordy. His detractors feel that he rambles. In truth, he does quite the opposite. He zeroes in. His logic

The Proust Project

may be elaborate—I think wonderfully so—but if you follow it, there is always soon a reward of stunning insight at the end.

Looking back to the fall when I read *In Search of Lost Time*, I find my memory seems to be peppered with as many images from the book as from life. In fact, the images from life are more of a blur, and those from the book remain crystal clear.

*When Albertine tells Marcel that she is going to pay a visit to Madame
Verdurin, Marcel is surprised: Albertine has never cared for the woman.
After finding out, however, that Mademoiselle Vinteuil is also expected
at Madame Verdurin's, Marcel plays along, and tells her that he will
join her. Albertine decides not to go to Madame Verdurin's after all.*

T he day after the evening when Al-
bertine had told me that she might perhaps, then that she might not, be
going to see the Verdurins, I awoke early, and, while I was still half
asleep, my joy informed me that it was a spring day interpolated in the
middle of the winter. Outside, popular themes skilfully transposed for
various instruments, from the horn of the china repairer, or the trumpet
of the chair mender, to the flute of the goatherd who seemed, on a fine
morning, to be a Sicilian drover, were lightly orchestrating the matuti-
nal air with an "Overture for a Public Holiday." Our hearing, that de-
lightful sense, brings us the company of the street, of which it traces
every line for us, sketches all the figures that pass along it, showing us
their colours. The iron shutters of the baker's shop and of the dairy,
which had been lowered last night over every possibility of feminine
bliss, were now being raised, like the canvas of a ship that is getting under way and about to set sail across the transparent sea, on to a vision of
young shopgirls. This sound of the iron shutters being raised would perhaps have been my sole pleasure in a different part of the town. In this
quarter a hundred other sounds contributed to my joy, of which I would
not have missed a single one by remaining too long asleep. It is one of the
enchantments of the old aristocratic quarters that they are at the same
time plebeian. Just as, sometimes, cathedrals used to have them within
a stone's throw of their portals (which have even preserved the name,
like the door of Rouen cathedral styled the Booksellers', because these
latter used to expose their merchandise in the open air beside it), so various minor trades, but in this case itinerant, passed in front of the noble
Hôtel de Guermantes, and made one think at times of the ecclesiastical

The Proust Project

France of long ago. For the beguiling calls which they launched at the little houses on either side had, with rare exceptions, little connexion with song. They differed from song as much as the declamation—scarcely tinged by even the most imperceptible modulation—of *Boris Godunov* and *Pelléas*; but on the other hand recalled the drone of a priest intoning his office, of which these street scenes are but the good-humoured, secular, and yet half-liturgical counterpart. Never had I so delighted in them as since Albertine had come to live with me; they seemed to me a joyous signal of her awakening, and by interesting me in the life of the world outside made me all the more conscious of the soothing virtue of a beloved presence, as constant as I could wish. Several of the foodstuffs peddled in the street, which personally I detested, were greatly to Albertine's liking, so much so that Françoise used to send her young footman out to buy them, slightly humiliated perhaps at finding himself mixing with the plebeian crowd. Very distinct in this peaceful quarter (where the noises were no longer a cause of lamentation to Françoise and had become a source of pleasure to myself), there reached my ears, each with its different modulation, recitatives declaimed by these humble folk as they would be in the music—so entirely popular—of *Boris*, where an initial tonality is barely altered by the inflexion of one note leaning upon another, music of the crowd, which is more speech than music. It was *"Winkles, winkles, a ha'porth of winkles!"* that brought people running to buy the cornets in which were sold those horrid little shellfish, which, if Albertine had not been there, would have repelled me, as did the snails which I heard being peddled at the same hour. Here again it was of the barely musical declamation of Moussorgsky that the vendor reminded me, but not of it alone. For after having almost "spoken" the refrain: *"Who'll buy my snails, fine, fresh snails?"* it was with the vague sadness of Maeterlinck, transposed into music by Debussy, that the snail vendor, in one of those mournful cadences in which the composer of *Pelléas* shows his kinship with Rameau: "If vanquished I must be, is it for thee to be my vanquisher?" added with a singsong melancholy: "Only tuppence a dozen . . ."

I have always found it difficult to understand why these perfectly sim-

The Captive

ple words were sighed in a tone so far from appropriate, as mysterious as the secret which makes everyone look sad in the old palace to which Mélisande has not succeeded in bringing joy, and as profound as one of the thoughts of the aged Arkel who seeks to utter in the simplest words the whole lore of wisdom and destiny. The very notes upon which the voice of the old King of Allemonde or that of Golaud rises with ever-increasing sweetness to say: "We do not know what is happening here. It may seem strange. Perhaps nothing that happens is in vain," or else: "You mustn't be frightened . . . she was a poor little mysterious creature, like everyone," were those which served the snail vendor to repeat in an endless cantilena: "Only tuppence a dozen . . ." But this metaphysical lamentation scarcely had time to expire upon the shore of the infinite before it was interrupted by a shrill trumpet. This time it was not a question of victuals; the words of the libretto were: "Dogs clipped, cats doctored, tails and ears docked."

It was true that the fantasy or wit of each vendor or vendress frequently introduced variations into the words of all these chants that I used to hear from my bed. And yet a ritual suspension interposing a silence in the middle of a word, especially when it was repeated a second time, constantly evoked the memory of old churches. In his little cart drawn by a she-ass which he stopped in front of each house before entering the courtyard, the old-clothes man, brandishing a whip, intoned: "Old clothes, any old clothes, old clo . . . thes" with the same pause between the final syllables as if he had been intoning in plainchant: *"Per omnia saecula saeculo . . . rum"* or *"requiescat in pa . . . ce"* although he had no reason to believe in the immortality of his clothes, nor did he offer them as cerements for the eternal rest in peace. And similarly, as the motifs, even at this early hour, were beginning to interweave with one another, a costermonger pushing her little hand-cart employed in her litany the Gregorian division:

> Tender and green,
> Artichokes tender and sweet,
> Ar . . . tichokes

The Proust Project

although she had probably never heard of the antiphonary, or of the seven tones that symbolise, four the arts of the quadrivium and three those of the trivium.

Drawing from a penny whistle, or from a bagpipe, airs of his own southern country whose sunlight harmonised well with these fine days, a man in a smock, carrying a bullwhip in his hand and wearing a Basque beret on his head, stopped before each house in turn. It was the goatherd with two dogs driving before him his string of goats. As he came from a distance, he arrived fairly late in our quarter; and the women came running out with bowls to receive the milk that was to give strength to their little ones. But with the Pyrenean airs of this benign shepherd was now blended the bell of the grinder, who cried: "Knives, scissors, razors." With him the saw-setter was unable to compete, for, lacking an instrument, he had to be content with calling: "Any saws to set? Here's the setter!" while in a gayer mood the tinker, after enumerating the pots, pans and everything else that he repaired, struck up the refrain:

> Tan, ran, tan, tan, ran, tan,
> For pots or cans, oh! I'm your man.
> I'll mend them all with a tink, tink, tink,
> And never leave a chink, chink, chink,

and little Italians carrying big iron boxes painted red, upon which the numbers—winning and losing—were marked, and flourishing their rattles, issued the invitation: "Enjoy yourselves, ladies, here's a treat."

(*The Captive*, 146–51)

Renaud Machart

Upon waking up in his Paris apartment on a winter morning uncannily touched by spring weather, Marcel is suddenly enchanted by the loud, shrill cries emanating from the street hawkers below his bedroom window. Thus begins the highly musical segment "Cris de Paris" in *The Captive.*

The French word *cri* can mean, in English, anything from *shriek, cry, squeak,* or *scream* to *slogan.* The *Dictionnaire de l'Académie française,* published in 1694, notes that it "still signifies the manner in which vendors go about peddling, in city streets, household necessities, such as fruits, herbs, etc.," adding, under the subheading "Cris de Paris," that "more than a hundred types of cries can be heard all over Paris." The once eminent nineteenth-century literary historian Victor Fournel devoted an entire, colorful chapter to the *cris de Paris* in his *What One Sees in the Streets of Paris* (1867), evoking

> [the] raucous, silvery, shrill notes . . . of a . . . symphony so monotonous
> in its variety, so varied in its monotony, that it rises incessantly from
> every street of the great capital. Lend an ear and at first you'll hear only
> the disagreeable rumble of carriages on paving stones; but soon you will

notice, beside this, the loud, discordant chant of a thousand Parisian
cries . . . One would need an entire volume to capture . . . the natural
and spontaneous technique behind the *cris* of so many little trades, each
with its own dramatic inflections, its street-wise cat calls and vivid
expressions—from the classical, staccato recitative of the cardboard seller,
to the melancholy, alluring fanfare of the clothes merchant; from the impassioned exclamations of the roaming fishwife enraptured by the beauty
of her fresh mackerels, to the resounding melody of the oyster dealer
"four *sous* the dozen."

It is very likely that Fournel's description of the *cris de Paris* was the
source for the shrill "musical score" that reaches Marcel's bedroom upstairs. Just like Fournel, Proust will distinguish in some of these street
cries a "classical recitative" and he too will hear in the lilting modulation of the snail vendor's cry ("Who'll buy my snails, fine, fresh snails?")
the echo of the famous monologue from *Armide* (by Quinault and Lully,
which Proust mistakenly attributes to Rameau). Fournel's mackerels
("Here are mackerels, fresh, new mackerels, Ladies, and a good looking mackerel this one is") indeed find their way into Proust's text, just
as his oysters will morph into Proust's snails that sell for "six *sous* the
dozen."

The change of register in Proust's text will startle every music lover.
One can hear, almost read on the printed page, a polyphony reminiscent
of those humorous Renaissance medleys called *quodlibets* and *fricas-
sées*, where musical fragments lifted from both their learned and popular contexts were woven together. Indeed, on reading these ringing
pages from *The Captive* one is reminded of the long musical tradition of
"Cris de Paris," which had been set in polyphonic form ever since the
thirteenth century. The best-known example is the polyphonic song
"Les Cris de Paris" by Clément Janequin, a model for numerous textual
and musical imitations, both in France and abroad. English equivalents
can be found in "The Cries of London" by Orlando Gibbons and by
Thomas Weelkes.

Like Caliban in Shakespeare's *The Tempest*, who hears "a thousand
twangling instruments . . . hum about [his] ears," Marcel overhears the

Renaud Machart

surrounding polyphony of cries with a distorting ear that transforms and ultimately softens every *cri* into memories of canticles, plainchant, and such beloved operas as Lully's *Armide* and Mussorgski's *Boris Godunov*. At one point, Marcel, with his strange, deranged ear, thinks he's overhearing Debussy's *Pelléas*, when instead he should have recognized the *parler popu*, the rough trade language used by Maurice Ravel in his setting of Jules Renard's *Histoires naturelles* of 1906, which was an ironic rebuttal to the highly crafted, seemingly "natural" prosody of Debussy's *Pelléas*.

It is striking that the tradition of polyphonic song in general and that of the "Cris de Paris" in particular has always retained an unmistakably domestic character. It was the sort of music meant to be played and sung in closed, intimate settings, most notably in a room around a table where the singers were also its sole listeners. Intimate music played in an intimate space, destined for the intimate few—*musica reservata*. Closet music.

So perhaps it is no accident that Proust transformed his sealed bedroom not only into a place where he could transmute his entire life into a work of literature but where he could turn that very same room into an echo chamber, a place where resonant fragments picked up here and there lie at the source of the twentieth century's most resonant work of fiction.

Even though they live under one roof, Albertine is becoming more and more elusive. When Albertine tells Marcel that she plans to spend the day at the Trocadéro with her friend Andrée, Marcel is quite sure that she will remain safe from temptation. He happens to read in the Figaro, however, that the actress Léa—a lesbian—is to be performing at the Trocadéro that day. He sends Françoise to fetch Albertine home, and Albertine returns, perfectly submissive and adoring.

Marcel visits the Verdurins one night for an evening of music, taking great care to conceal his actions from Albertine, out of fear that Mademoiselle Vinteuil would come. He is determined to keep Albertine away from all temptations to lesbianism. Once there, Marcel learns that Monsieur de Charlus's "secret" homosexuality, his love for the violinist and chauffeur Morel, has become something of a scandal. When the septet begins, the violinist is Morel, and the music he plays is none other than Mademoiselle Vinteuil's own father. But the music comes on him like a whirlwind, smothering all jealousy and suspicion and opening yet again the universe of art.

Swann, having been ill for a long time, dies.

Mme Verdurin sat alone, the twin hemispheres of her pale, slightly roseate brow magnificently bulging, her hair drawn back, partly in imitation of an eighteenth-century portrait, partly from the need for coolness of a feverish person reluctant to reveal her condition, aloof, a deity presiding over the musical rites, goddess of Wagnerism and sick-headaches, a sort of almost tragic Norn, conjured up by the spell of genius in the midst of all these "bores," in whose presence she would scorn even more than usual to express her feelings upon hearing a piece of music which she knew better than they. The concert began; I did not know what was being played; I found myself in a strange land. Where was I to place it? Who was the composer? I longed to know, and, seeing nobody near me whom I could ask, I should have liked to be a character in those *Arabian Nights* which I never tired of reading and

The Captive

in which, in moments of uncertainty, there appears a genie, or a maiden of ravishing beauty, invisible to everyone else but not to the perplexed hero to whom she reveals exactly what he wishes to learn. And indeed at that very moment I was favoured with just such a magical apparition. As when, in a stretch of country which one thinks one does not know and which in fact one has approached from a new direction, after turning a corner one finds oneself suddenly emerging on to a road every inch of which is familiar, but one had simply not been in the habit of approaching it that way, one suddenly says to oneself: "Why, this is the lane that leads to the garden gate of my friends the X——s; I'm only two minutes from their house," and there, indeed, is their daughter who has come out to greet one as one goes by; so, all of a sudden, I found myself, in the midst of this music that was new to me, right in the heart of Vinteuil's sonata; and, more marvelous than any girl, the little phrase, sheathed, harnessed in silver, glittering with brilliant sonorities, as light and soft as silken scarves, came to me, recognisable in this new guise. My joy at having rediscovered it was enhanced by the tone, so friendly and familiar, which it adopted in addressing me, so persuasive, so simple, and yet without subduing the shimmering beauty with which it glowed. Its intention, however, this time was merely to show me the way, which was not the way of the sonata, for this was an unpublished work of Vinteuil in which he had merely amused himself, by an allusion that was explained at this point by a sentence in the programme which one ought to have been reading simultaneously, by reintroducing the little phrase for a moment. No sooner was it thus recalled than it vanished, and I found myself once more in an unknown world, but I knew now, and everything that followed only confirmed my knowledge, that this world was one of those which I had never even been capable of imagining that Vinteuil could have created, for when, weary of the sonata which was to me a universe thoroughly explored, I tried to imagine others equally beautiful but different, I was merely doing what those poets do who fill their artificial paradise with meadows, flowers and streams which duplicate those existing already upon earth. What was now before me made me feel as keen a joy as the sonata would have given me if I had not already known it, and consequently, while no less beautiful, was different. Whereas the sonata opened upon a lily-white pastoral dawn, dividing its fragile purity only to hover in the delicate yet compact entanglement of a rustic bower of honeysuckle against white geraniums, it was upon flat, unbroken surfaces like those of the sea on a morning that threatens storm, in the midst of an eerie silence, in an infinite void, that this new work began, and it was into a rose-red daybreak that this unknown universe was drawn from the silence and the night to build up gradually before me. This redness, so new, so absent from the tender, pastoral unadorned sonata, tinged all the sky, as dawn does, with a mysterious hope. And a song already pierced the air, a song on seven notes, but the strangest, the most remote from anything I had ever imagined, at once ineffable and strident, no longer the cooing of a dove as in the sonata, but rending the air, as vivid as the scarlet tint in which the opening bars had been bathed, something like a mystical cock-crow, the ineffable but ear-piercing call of eternal morning. The atmosphere, cold, rain-washed, electric—of a quality so different, subject to quite other pressures, in a world so remote from the virginal, plant-strewn world of the sonata—changed continually, eclipsing the crimson promise of the dawn. At noon, however, in a burst of scorching but transitory sunlight, it seemed to reach fulfilment in a heavy, rustic, almost cloddish gaiety in which the lurching, riotous clangour of bells (like those which set the church square of Combray aglow and which Vinteuil, who must often have heard them, had perhaps discovered at that moment in his memory like a colour which a painter has at hand on his palette) seemed the material representation of the coarsest joy. Truth to tell, this joyous motif did not appeal to me aesthetically; I found it almost ugly, its rhythm was so laboriously earthbound that one could have imitated almost all its essentials simply with the noises made by rapping on a table with drumsticks in a particular way. It seemed to me that Vinteuil had been lacking, here, in inspiration, and consequently I was a little lacking also in the power of attention.

I looked at the Mistress, whose fierce immobility seemed to be a protest against the rhythmic noddings of the ignorant heads of the ladies of the Faubourg. She did not say: "You realise, of course, that I know a thing or two about this music! If I were to express all that I feel, you'd never hear the end of it!" She did not say this. But her upright motionless body, her expressionless eyes, her straying locks said it for her. They spoke also of her courage, said that the musicians could carry on, that they need not spare her nerves, that she would not flinch at the andante, would not cry out at the allegro. I looked at the musicians. The cellist was hunched over the instrument which he clutched between his knees, his head bowed forward, his coarse features assuming an involuntary expression of disgust at the more mannerist moments; another leaned over his double bass, fingering it with the same domestic patience with which he might have peeled a cabbage, while by his side the harpist, a mere child in a short skirt, framed behind the diagonal rays of her golden quadrilateral, recalling those which, in the magic chamber of a sibyl, arbitrarily denote the ether according to the traditional forms, seemed to be picking out exquisite sounds here and there at designated points, just as though, a tiny allegorical goddess poised before the golden trellis of the heavenly vault, she were gathering, one by one, its stars. As for Morel, a lock, hitherto invisible and submerged in the rest of his hair, had fallen loose and formed a curl on his forehead.

I turned my head slightly towards the audience to discover what M. de Charlus might be feeling at the sight of this curl. But my eyes encountered only Mme Verdurin's face, or rather the hands, for the former was entirely buried in the latter. Did the Mistress wish to indicate by this meditative attitude that she considered herself as though in church, and regarded this music as no different from the most sublime of prayers? Did she wish, as some people do in church, to hide from prying eyes, out of modesty or shame, their presumed fervour or their culpable inattention or an irresistible sleepiness? A regular noise which was not musical gave me momentarily to think that this last hypothesis was the correct one, but I realised later that it was produced by the snores, not of Mme Verdurin, but of her dog.

But very soon, the triumphant motif of the bells having been banished, dispersed by others, I succumbed once again to the music; and I began to realise that if, in the body of this septet, different elements presented themselves one after another to combine at the close, so also Vinteuil's sonata and, as I later discovered, his other works as well, had been no more than timid essays, exquisite but very slight, beside the triumphal and consummate masterpiece now being revealed to me. And I could not help recalling by comparison that, in the same way too, I had thought of the other worlds that Vinteuil had created as being self-enclosed as each of my loves had been; whereas in reality I was obliged to admit that just as, within the context of the last of these—my love for Albertine—my first faint stirrings of love for her (at Balbec at the very beginning, then after the game of ferret, then on the night when she slept at the hotel, then in Paris on the foggy Sunday, then on the night of the Guermantes party, then at Balbec again, and finally in Paris where my life was now closely linked to hers) had been, so, if I now considered not my love for Albertine but my whole life, my other loves too had been no more than slight and timid essays that were paving the way, appeals that were unconsciously clamouring, for this vaster love: my love for Albertine. And I ceased to follow the music, in order to ask myself once again whether Albertine had or had not seen Mlle Vinteuil during the last few days, as one interrogates anew an inner pain from which one has been distracted for a moment. For it was in myself that Albertine's possible actions were performed. Of every person we know we possess a double; but, being habitually situated on the horizon of our imagination, of our memory, it remains more or less extraneous to us, and what it has done or may have done has no greater capacity to cause us pain than an object situated at a certain distance which provides us with only the painless sensations of vision. The things that affect these people we perceive in a contemplative fashion; we are able to deplore them in appropriate language which gives other people a sense of our kindness of heart, but we do not feel them. But ever since the wound I had received at Balbec, it was deep in my heart, and very difficult to extricate, that Albertine's double was lodged. What I saw of her hurt me, as a sick man would be hurt whose senses were so seriously deranged that the sight of a colour would be felt by him internally like an incision in his living flesh. It was fortunate that I had not already yielded to the temptation to break with Albertine; the tedium of

The Captive

having to rejoin her presently, when I went home, was a trifling matter
compared with the anxiety that I should have felt if the separation had
occurred when I still had a doubt about her and before I had had time to
grow indifferent to her. And at the moment when I thus pictured her
waiting for me at home like a beloved wife, finding the time of waiting
long, perhaps having fallen asleep for a while in her room, my ears were
caressed by a passing phrase, tender, homely and domestic, of the septet.
Perhaps—everything being so interwoven and superimposed in our inner life—it had been inspired in Vinteuil by his daughter's sleep (that
daughter who was today the cause of all my distress) when it enveloped
the composer's work on peaceful evenings with its quiet sweetness, this
phrase which had so much power to calm me by virtue of the same soft
background of silence that gives a hushed serenity to certain of Schu-
mann's reveries, during which, even when "the Poet speaks," one can
tell that "the child sleeps." Asleep or awake, I should find her again this
evening, Albertine, my little child, when I choose to return home. And yet,
I said to myself, something more mysterious than Albertine's love seemed
to be promised at the outset of this work, in those first cries of dawn. I
tried to banish the thought of my mistress and to think only of the musician. Indeed, he seemed to be present. It was as though, reincarnate, the
composer lived for all time in his music; one could feel the joy with which
he chose the colour of some timbre, harmonising it with the others. For
with other and more profound gifts Vinteuil combined that which few
composers, and indeed few painters, have possessed, of using colours not
merely so lasting but so personal that, just as time has been powerless to
spoil their freshness, so the disciples who imitate their discoverer, and
even the masters who surpass him, do not dim their originality. The revolution that their apparition has effected does not see its results merge
unacknowledged in the work of subsequent generations; it is unleashed,
it explodes anew, when, and only when, the works of the once-for-all-
time innovator are performed again. Each tone was identified by a colour
which all the rules in the world could not have taught the most learned
composers to imitate, with the result that Vinteuil, although he had appeared at his appointed hour and had his appointed place in the evolu-

tion of music, would always leave that place to stand in the forefront whenever any of his compositions was performed, compositions which would owe their appearance of having originated after the works of more recent composers to this apparently paradoxical and indeed deceptive quality of permanent novelty. A page of symphonic music by Vinteuil, familiar already on the piano, revealed, when one heard it played by an orchestra—like a ray of summer sunlight which the prism of the window decomposes before it enters a dark dining-room—all the jewels of the *Arabian Nights* in unsuspected, multicoloured splendour. But how could one compare to that motionless dazzle of light what was life, perpetual and blissful motion? This Vinteuil, whom I had known so timid and sad, had been capable—when he had to choose a timbre and to blend another with it—of an audacity, and in the full sense of the word a felicity, as to which the hearing of any of his works left one in no doubt. The joy that certain sonorities had caused him, the increase of strength they had given him wherewith to discover others, led the listener on too from one discovery to another, or rather it was the creator himself who guided him, deriving, from the colours he had just hit upon, a wild joy which gave him the strength to discover, to fling himself upon others which they seemed to call for, enraptured, quivering as though from the shock of an electric spark when the sublime came spontaneously to life at the clang of the brass, panting, intoxicated, unbridled, vertiginous, while he painted his great musical fresco, like Michelangelo strapped to his scaffold and from his upside-down position hurling tumultuous brush-strokes on to the ceiling of the Sistine Chapel. Vinteuil had been dead for a number of years; but in the sound of these instruments which he had loved, it had been given him to go on living, for an unlimited time, a part at least of his life. Of his life as a man solely? If art was indeed but a prolongation of life, was it worth while to sacrifice anything to it? Was it not as unreal as life itself? The more I listened to this septet, the less I could believe this to be so. No doubt the glowing septet differed singularly from the lily-white sonata; the timid question to which the little phrase replied, from the breathless supplication to find the fulfilment of the strange promise that had resounded, so harsh, so supernatural, so brief,

The Captive

causing the still inert crimson of the morning sky above the sea to vibrate. And yet these very different phrases were composed of the same elements; for, just as there was a certain world, perceptible to us in those fragments scattered here and there, in private houses, in public galleries, which was Elstir's world, the world he saw, the world in which he lived, so too the music of Vinteuil extended, note by note, stroke by stroke, the unknown, incalculable colourings of an unsuspected world, fragmented by the gaps between the different occasions of hearing his work performed; those two very dissimilar questions that governed the very different movement of the sonata and the septet, the former interrupting a pure, continuous line with brief calls, the latter welding together into an indivisible structure a medley of scattered fragments—one so calm and shy, almost detached and as if philosophical, the other so urgent, anxious. imploring—were nevertheless the same prayer, bursting forth like different inner sunrises, and merely refracted through the different mediums of other thoughts, of artistic researches carried on through the years in which he had sought to create something new. A prayer, a hope which was at heart the same, distinguishable beneath these disguises in the various works of Vinteuil, and at the same time not to be found elsewhere than in his works. For those phrases, historians of music could no doubt find affinities and pedigrees in the works of other great composers, but only for secondary reasons, external resemblances, analogies ingeniously discovered by reasoning rather than felt as the result of a direct impression. The impression conveyed by these Vinteuil phrases was different from any other, as though, in spite of the conclusions which seem to emerge from science, the individual did exist. And it was precisely when he was striving with all his might to create something new that one recognised, beneath the apparent differences, the profound similarities and the deliberate resemblances that existed in the body of a work; when Vinteuil took up the same phrase again and again, diversified it, amused himself by altering its rhythm, by making it reappear in its original form, those deliberate resemblances, the work of his intellect, necessarily superficial, never succeeded in being as striking as the disguised, involuntary resemblances, which broke out in different colours, between the two separate masterpieces; for then Vinteuil, striving to do something new, interrogated himself, with all the power of his creative energy, reached down to his essential self at those depths where, whatever the question asked, it is in the same accent, that is to say its own, that it replies. Such an accent, the accent of Vinteuil, is separated from the accents of other composers by a difference far greater than that which we perceive between the voices of two people, even between the bellowings and the squeals of two animal species; by the real difference that exists between the thought of this or that other composer and the eternal investigations of Vinteuil, the question that he put to himself in so many forms, his habitual speculation, but as free from analytical forms of reasoning as if it were being carried out in the world of the angels, so that we can gauge its depth, but no more translate it into human speech than can disembodied spirits when, evoked by a medium, they are questioned by him about the secrets of death. And even when I bore in mind that acquired originality which had struck me that afternoon, that kinship, too, which musicologists might discover between composers, it is indeed a unique accent, an unmistakable voice, to which in spite of themselves those great singers that original composers are rise and return, and which is a proof of the irreducibly individual existence of the soul. Though Vinteuil might try to make more solemn, more grandiose, or to make more sprightly and gay, to re-create what he saw reflected in the mind of the public, in spite of himself he submerged it all beneath a ground-swell which makes his song eternal and at once recognisable. Where had he learned this song, different from those of other singers, similar to all his own, where had he heard it? Each artist seems thus to be the native of an unknown country, which he himself has forgotten, and which is different from that whence another great artist, setting sail for the earth, will eventually emerge. Certain it was that Vinteuil, in his latest works, seemed to have drawn nearer to that unknown country. The atmosphere was no longer the same as in the sonata, the questioning phrases had become more pressing, more unquiet, the answers more mysterious; the washed-out air of morning and evening seemed to affect the very strings of the instruments. Marvellously though Morel played,

The Captive

the sounds that came from his violin seemed to me singularly piercing, almost shrill. This harshness was pleasing, and, as in certain voices, one felt in it a sort of moral quality and intellectual superiority. But it could shock. When his vision of the universe is modified, purified, becomes more adapted to his memory of his inner homeland, it is only natural that this should be expressed by a musician in a general alteration of sonorities, as of colours by a painter. In any case, the more intelligent section of the public is not misled, since Vinteuil's last compositions were ultimately declared to be his most profound. And yet no programme, no subject matter, supplied any intellectual basis for judgment. One simply sensed that it was a question of the transposition of profundity into terms of sound.

Composers do not remember this lost fatherland, but each of them remains all his life unconsciously attuned to it; he is delirious with joy when he sings in harmony with his native land, betrays it at times in his thirst for fame, but then, in seeking fame, turns his back on it, and it is only by scorning fame that he finds it when he breaks out into that distinctive strain the sameness of which—for whatever its subject it remains identical with itself—proves the permanence of the elements that compose his soul. But in that case is it not true that those elements—all the residuum of reality which we are obliged to keep to ourselves, which cannot be transmitted in talk, even from friend to friend, from master to disciple, from lover to mistress, that ineffable something which differentiates qualitatively what each of us has felt and what he is obliged to leave behind at the threshold of the phrases in which he can communicate with others only by limiting himself to externals, common to all and of no interest—are brought out by art, the art of a Vinteuil like that of an Elstir, which exteriorises in the colours of the spectrum the intimate composition of those worlds which we call individuals and which, but for art, we should never know? A pair of wings, a different respiratory system, which enabled us to travel through space, would in no way help us, for if we visited Mars or Venus while keeping the same senses, they would clothe everything we could see in the same aspect as the things of Earth. The only true voyage, the only bath in the Fountain of Youth, would be not to visit strange lands but to possess other eyes, to see the universe through the eyes of another, of a hundred others, to see the hundred universes that each of them sees, that each of them is; and this we can do with an Elstir, with a Vinteuil; with men like these we do really fly from star to star.

The andante had just ended on a phrase filled with a tenderness to which I had entirely surrendered. There followed, before the next movement, a short interval during which the performers laid down their instruments and the audience exchanged impressions. A duke, in order to show that he knew what he was talking about, declared: "It's a difficult thing to play well." Other more agreeable people chatted for a moment with me. But what were their words, which like every human and external word left me so indifferent, compared with the heavenly phrase of music with which I had just been communing? I was truly like an angel who, fallen from the inebriating bliss of paradise, subsides into the most humdrum reality. And, just as certain creatures are the last surviving testimony to a form of life which nature has discarded, I wondered whether music might not be the unique example of what might have been—if the invention of language, the formation of words, the analysis of ideas had not intervened—the means of communication between souls. It is like a possibility that has come to nothing; humanity has developed along other lines, those of spoken and written language. But this return to the unanalysed was so intoxicating that, on emerging from that paradise, contact with more or less intelligent people seemed to me of an extraordinary insignificance. I had been able, while the music was playing, to remember people, to associate them with it; or rather I had associated with the music scarcely more than the memory of one person only, which was Albertine. And the phrase that ended the andante seemed to me so sublime that I told myself that it was a pity that Albertine did not know, and if she had known had not understood, what an honour it was to be associated with something so great as this which reunited us, and the heartbreaking voice of which she seemed to have assumed. But once the music was interrupted, the people who were there seemed too insipid. Refreshments were handed round. M. de Charlus hailed a footman now and then with:

The Captive

"How are you? Did you get my note? Can you come?" No doubt there was in these salutations the freedom of the great nobleman who thinks he is flattering his interlocutor and is more one of the people than the bourgeois, but there was also the cunning of the delinquent who imagines that anything one flaunts is on that account considered innocent. And he added, in the Guermantes tone of Mme de Villeparisis: "He's a good boy, a friendly soul, I often employ him at home." But his adroitness turned against the Baron, for people thought his intimate courtesies and correspondence with footmen extraordinary. The footmen themselves were not so much flattered as embarrassed in the presence of their comrades.

Meanwhile the septet, which had begun again, was moving towards its close; again and again one phrase or another from the sonata recurred, but altered each time, its rhythm and harmony different, the same and yet something else, as things recur in life; and they were phrases of the sort which, without our being able to understand what affinity assigns to them as their sole and necessary abode the past of a certain composer, are to be found only in his work, and appear constantly in his work, of which they are the spirits, the dryads, the familiar deities; I had at first distinguished in the septet two or three which reminded me of the sonata. Presently—bathed in the violet mist which was wont to rise particularly in Vinteuil's later work, so much so that, even when he introduced a dance measure, it remained captive in the heart of an opal—I caught a hint of another phrase from the sonata, still so distant that I scarcely recognised it; hesitantly it approached, vanished as though in alarm, then returned, intertwined with others that had come, as I later learned, from other works, summoned yet others which became in their turn seductive and persuasive as soon as they were tamed, and took their places in the round, the divine round that yet remained invisible to the bulk of the audience, who, having before their eyes only a dim veil through which they saw nothing, punctuated arbitrarily with admiring exclamations a continuous boredom of which they thought they would die. Then the phrases withdrew, save one which I saw reappear five times or six without being able to distinguish its features, but so caressing, so different—as no doubt the little phrase from the sonata had been for

The Proust Project

Swann—from anything that any woman had ever made me desire, that this phrase—this invisible creature whose language I did not know but whom I understood so well—which offered me in so sweet a voice a happiness that it would really have been worth the struggle to obtain, is perhaps the only Unknown Woman that it has ever been my good fortune to meet. Then this phrase broke up, was transformed, like the little phrase in the sonata, and became the mysterious call of the start. A phrase of a plaintive kind rose in answer to it, but so profound, so vague, so internal, almost so organic and visceral, that one could not tell at each of its re-entries whether it was a theme or an attack of neuralgia. Presently these two motifs were wrestling together in a close embrace in which at times one of them would disappear entirely, and then only a fragment of the other could be glimpsed. A wrestling match of disembodied energies only, to tell the truth; for if these creatures confronted one another, they did so stripped of their physical bodies, of their appearance, of their names, finding in me an inward spectator—himself indifferent, too, to names and particulars—to appreciate their immaterial and dynamic combat and follow passionately its sonorous vicissitudes. In the end the joyous motif was left triumphant; it was no longer an almost anxious appeal addressed to an empty sky, it was an ineffable joy which seemed to come from paradise, a joy as different from that of the sonata as some scarlet-clad Mantegna archangel sounding a trumpet from a grave and gentle Bellini seraph strumming a theorbo. I knew that this new tone of joy, this summons to a supraterrestrial joy, was a thing that I would never forget. But would it ever be attainable to me? This question seemed to me all the more important inasmuch as this phrase was what might have seemed most eloquently to characterise—as contrasting so sharply with all the rest of my life, with the visible world—those impressions which at remote intervals I experienced in my life as starting-points, foundation-stones for the construction of a true life: the impression I had felt at the sight of the steeples of Martinville, or of a line of trees near Balbec. In any case, to return to the particular accent of this phrase, how strange it was that the presentiment most different from what life assigns to us on earth, the boldest approximation to the bliss of the Beyond, should have materialised precisely in the melancholy, respectable little bourgeois whom we used to meet in the Month of Mary at Combray! But above all, how was it possible that this revelation, the strangest that I had yet received, of an unknown type of joy, should have come to me from him, since, it was said, when he died he had left nothing but his sonata, everything else existing only as indecipherable scribblings. Indecipherable they may have been, but they had nevertheless been in the end deciphered, by dint of patience, intelligence and respect, by the only person who had been sufficiently close to Vinteuil to understand his method of working, to interpret his orchestral indications: Mlle Vinteuil's friend. Even in the lifetime of the great composer, she had acquired from his daughter the veneration that the latter felt for her father. It was because of this veneration that, in those moments in which people run counter to their true inclinations, the two girls had been able to take an insane pleasure in the profanations which have already been narrated. (Her adoration of her father was the very condition of his daughter's sacrilege. And no doubt they ought to have forgone the voluptuous pleasure of that sacrilege, but it did not express the whole of their natures.) And, moreover, the profanations had become rarer until they disappeared altogether, as those morbidly carnal relations, that troubled, smouldering conflagration, had gradually given way to the flame of a pure and lofty friendship. Mlle Vinteuil's friend was sometimes tormented by the nagging thought that she might have hastened Vinteuil's death. At any rate, by spending years unravelling the scribblings left by him, by establishing the correct reading of those secret hieroglyphs, she had the consolation of ensuring an immortal and compensatory glory for the composer over whose last years she had cast such a shadow. Relations which are not sanctioned by the law establish bonds of kinship as manifold, as complex, and even more solid, than those which spring from marriage. Indeed, without pausing to consider relations of so special a nature, do we not find every day that adultery, when it is based on genuine love, does not weaken family feelings and the duties of kinship, but rather revivifies them? Adultery then brings the spirit into what marriage would often have left a dead letter. A good daughter who will wear mourning for her mother's second husband for reasons of propriety has not tears enough to shed for the man whom her mother singled out as her lover. In any case Mlle Vinteuil had acted only out of sadism, which did not excuse her, though it gave me a certain consolation to think so later on. No doubt she must have realised, I told myself, at the moment when she and her friend had profaned her father's photograph, that what they were doing was merely morbidity, silliness, and not the true and joyous wickedness which she would have liked to feel. This idea that it was merely a pretence of wickedness spoiled her pleasure. But if this idea recurred to her later on, since it had spoiled her pleasure so it must have diminished her grief. "It wasn't me," she must have told herself, "I was out of my mind. I can still pray for my father's soul, and not despair of his forgiveness." Only it is possible that this idea, which had certainly occurred to her in her pleasure, may not have occurred to her in her grief. I would have liked to be able to put it into her mind. I am sure that I would have done her good and that I could have re-established between her and the memory of her father a more comforting relationship.

As in the illegible note-books in which a chemist of genius, who does not know that death is at hand, jots down discoveries which will perhaps remain forever unknown, Mlle Vinteuil's friend had disentangled, from papers more illegible than strips of papyrus dotted with a cuneiform script, the formula, eternally true and for ever fertile, of this unknown joy, the mystic hope of the crimson Angel of the Dawn. And I for whom, albeit not so much, perhaps, as for Vinteuil, she had also been, had just been once more this very evening by reawakening my jealousy of Albertine, was to be above all in the future, the cause of so many sufferings, it was thanks to her, in compensation, that I had been able to apprehend the strange summons which I should henceforth never cease to hear, as the promise and proof that there existed something other, realisable no doubt through art, than the nullity that I had found in all my pleasures and in love itself, and that if my life seemed to me so futile, at least it had not yet accomplished everything.

What she had enabled us, thanks to her labour, to know of Vinteuil was to all intents and purposes the whole of Vinteuil's work. Compared

The Captive

with this septet, certain phrases from the sonata which were all that the public knew appeared so commonplace that it was difficult to understand how they could have aroused so much admiration. Similarly we are surprised that, for years past, pieces as trivial as the *Song to the Evening Star* or *Elisabeth's Prayer* can have aroused in the concert-hall fanatical worshippers who wore themselves out applauding and shouting *encore* at the end of what after all seems poor and trite to us who know *Tristan*, the *Rhinegold* and the *Mastersingers*. One must assume that those featureless melodies nevertheless already contained, in infinitesimal and for that reason perhaps more easily assimilable quantities, something of the originality of the masterpieces which alone matter to us in retrospect, but whose very perfection might perhaps have prevented them from being understood; those earlier melodies may have prepared the way for them in people's hearts. But the fact remains that, if they gave a vague presentiment of the beauties to come, they left these in complete obscurity. The same was true of Vinteuil; if at his death he had left behind him—excepting certain parts of the sonata—only what he had been able to complete, what we should have known of him would have been, in relation to his true greatness, as inconsiderable as in the case of, say, Victor Hugo if he had died after the *Pas d'Armes du Roi Jean*, the *Fiancée du Timbalier* and *Sarah la Baigneuse*, without having written a line of the *Légende des Siècles* or the *Contemplations*: what is to us his real achievement would have remained purely potential, as unknown as those universes to which our perception does not reach, of which we shall never have any idea.

Moreover this apparent contrast and profound union between genius (talent too and even virtue) and the sheath of vices in which, as had happened in the case of Vinteuil, it is so frequently contained and preserved, was detectable, as in a popular allegory, in the very assembly of the guests among whom I found myself once again when the music had come to an end. This assembly, albeit limited this time to Mme Verdurin's salon, resembled many others, the ingredients of which are unknown to the general public, and which journalist-philosophers, if they are at all well-informed, call Parisian, or Panamist, or Dreyfusard, never suspecting

The Proust Project

that they may equally well be found in Petersburg, Berlin, Madrid, and in every epoch; if as a matter of fact the Under Secretary of State for Fine Arts, an artist to his fingertips, well-born and snobby, several duchesses and three ambassadors with their wives were present this evening at Mme Verdurin's, the proximate, immediate cause of their presence lay in the relations that existed between M. de Charlus and Morel, relations which made the Baron anxious to give as wide a celebrity as possible to the artistic triumphs of his young idol, and to obtain for him the cross of the Legion of Honour; the remoter cause which had made this assembly possible was that a girl who enjoyed a relationship with Mlle Vinteuil analogous to that of Charlie and the Baron had brought to light a whole series of works of genius which had been such a revelation that before long a subscription was to be opened under the patronage of the Minister of Education, with the object of erecting a statue to Vinteuil. Moreover, these works had been assisted, no less than by Mlle Vinteuil's relations with her friend, by the Baron's relations with Charlie, a sort of short cut, as it were, thanks to which the world was enabled to catch up with these works without the detour, if not of an incomprehension which would long persist, at least of a complete ignorance which might have lasted for years. Whenever an event occurs which is within the range of the vulgar mind of the journalist-philosopher, a political event as a rule, the journalist-philosophers are convinced that there has been some great change in France, that we shall never see such evenings again, that no one will ever again admire Ibsen, Renan, Dostoievsky, D'Annunzio, Tolstoy, Wagner, Strauss. For the journalist-philosophers take their cue from the equivocal undercurrents of these official manifestations, in order to find something decadent in the art which is there celebrated and which as often as not is more austere than any other. There is not a name, among those most revered by these journalist-philosophers, which has not quite naturally given rise to some such strange gathering, although its strangeness may have been less flagrant and better concealed. In the case of this gathering, the impure elements that came together therein struck me from another aspect; true, I was as well able as anyone to dissociate them, having learned to know them separately; but those which concerned Mlle

The Captive

Vinteuil and her friend, speaking to me of Combray, spoke to me also of Albertine, that is to say of Balbec, since it was because I had long ago seen Mlle Vinteuil at Montjouvain and had learned of her friend's intimacy with Albertine that I was presently, when I returned home, to find, instead of solitude, Albertine awaiting me; and those which concerned Morel and M. de Charlus, speaking to me of Balbec, where I had seen, on the platform at Doncières, their intimacy begin, spoke to me of Combray and of its two "ways," for M. de Charlus was one of those Guermantes, Counts of Combray, inhabiting Combray without having any dwelling there, suspended in mid-air, like Gilbert the Bad in his window, while Morel was the son of that old valet who had introduced me to the lady in pink and enabled me, years after, to identify her as Mme Swann.

(*The Captive*, 342–53)

Jonathan Burnham

When Marcel hears Vinteuil's septet for the first time he is attending a Verdurin soiree, and is taken by surprise when the musicians start to play. He is expecting a work by Vinteuil, but the first notes mean nothing to him—he describes himself as being in "a strange land"—but he then recognizes the little phrase, the musical motif from Vinteuil's sonata, an earlier work, that represented the "national anthem" of Swann and Odette's love. But the atmosphere of the music has changed: what was once gentle and evocative is now fierce and charged with eroticism "so persuasive . . . shimmering."

There are several currents of tortured erotic love running alongside each other in this scene: Marcel, in the full throes of his jealous passion for Albertine, is wondering whether Albertine has been deceiving him with Vinteuil's daughter; the unfaithful Morel is playing the violin in the ensemble, watched over proudly by Charlus; the distant memory of Swann's love for Odette is conjured up by the little phrase. And in a long digression Marcel reflects that the septet has emerged from the indecipherable scraps of manuscript painstakingly pieced together by the lesbian lover of Mademoiselle Vinteuil after Vinteuil's death, in an act of atonement for the perverse games of sexual desecration the lovers used to play out in front of the composer's photograph. He recalls that their sexual relationship developed from a carnal one—a "smouldering conflagration"—into a "pure and lofty friendship," and out of this shift was born a succession of restored masterpieces. From sexual love to the deeper joy of art: The story has a shape which prefigures the transformation that is about to take place in Marcel.

Gathering up the strands of the erotic tension, the music seems to move forward in a new direction, toward a higher sphere of creative revelation. Again, Marcel refers us back to the earlier work, almost in astonishment. Where the sonata was marked by pastoral limpidity, the septet is pregnant with meaning; it is alive with "a mysterious hope" which might be love, or something more. The composer could only be Vinteuil, but the septet seems the work of a new order of artist. In a key passage Vinteuil is described as composing the septet in a state of creative frenzy that fuses the artist's energy with sexual ecstasy: "panting, intoxicated, unbridled, vertiginous, while he painted his great musical fresco"—like Michelangelo "hurling tumultuous brush-strokes" at the ceiling of the Sistine Chapel while strapped to his scaffold. The timid, sad music teacher has been transformed into a turbulent, fecund genius, channeling an erotic life force into the creation of a masterpiece.

Aware that he is about to make a significant discovery, Marcel is led away from the web of love and sexual enthrallment toward a brave new world where creative vision transfigures everything it touches. It is now that the septet triggers a rush of revelation—about art, about vocation, about truth. Marcel is struck by the new authenticity of Vinteuil's art: this is because he is being faithful to his "inner homeland," and as a result his work has attained new depths, "a transposition of profundity into terms of sound." Only music, being nonverbal and nonrepresentative, can transmit ideas, visions, directly from the artist's inner world to another human being; music is the true *communication des âmes*.

The definitive epiphany comes when Marcel hears in the music a call toward a joy that is "supraterrestrial," a transcendent happiness above and beyond the elusive rewards of love. He is now ready to move away from social life, from the torment of living with Albertine, from the toils of erotic enslavement, toward the "real life" of literature, "life at last laid bare and illuminated."

Close to the end of the novel Marcel will think back to this moment and connect it to the "extratemporal joy" caused by the taste of the madeleine or the sound of a spoon on a plate. The performance of the septet thus joins the line of sacred, time-confounding revelations which propel Marcel toward his true destiny as a writer.

Jeremy Eichler

When I go to concerts, I often bring along a colleague or a friend, but my most frequent companion, the one who always arrives just as the lights have dimmed and the silence fallen, is Marcel Proust. Indeed, ever since I first read Proust, his musical sensibilities have joined me in the concert hall, for in addition to being the poet of love, of longing, of memory, and of loss, Proust is the poet of listening.

And nowhere more so than when Marcel attends a performance of a septet by Vinteuil, a master composer of Proust's own invention. As he does with so many other experiences, Proust here brilliantly discloses the interior monologue of listening. His long spiraling sentences un-spool in the mind the way a warm sinuous melody by Brahms might un-spool in the air. Of course, the concert scene itself is also ripe for Proustian mischief. The contrast between the intensely private act of listening and the experience of doing so while surrounded by members of Parisian society, each brimming with envy and spite, allows Marcel to toggle magisterially between his two favorite roles: the social critic, who illuminates the outer world of masks; and the writer-philosopher, who spins around the searchlights, pointing them at once inward and beyond.

But the rewards of Proust's writing on music originate from some-place deeper than simply the public-private nature of a concert experi-

Jeremy Eichler

ence. They stem from the very essence of musical art. Whereas painters work on canvas, musicians work on Proust's favorite medium of all—time. They transform time by painting it with sound, and in Proust's world, if the composer is attuned to his own inner depths, then the colors he chooses will reflect those depths; his melodies and harmonies will speak in an accent that is uniquely his own, like a fingerprint of his soul. The composer's music thus becomes a summary of his memories, a distillation of a past that even he may have forgotten. It is preserved through notation and immortalized in the pages of a score. When the piece is then brought to life in a concert setting, the performance represents nothing less than the very act of time regained. In this passage, the concert enables the deceased Vinteuil to return to this earth "in the sound of these instruments which he had loved."

But as Proust shows us, the septet is more than the embodiment of a composer's lost time. For the listener, it is also a bridge to Vinteuil's interior world, a way for Marcel to glimpse the mysteries of another self that lie hopelessly beyond the reach of language. This is an essential function of great art for Proust: it permits us to bend the prison bars of our own subjectivity—"to possess other eyes"—and thereby to transcend our own limitations. A piece of music can thus become like a narrow isthmus connecting two distant islands otherwise engulfed by oceans of solitude.

Proust was indeed the ultimate cartographer of loneliness, but one need not share his radical sense of isolation to appreciate its antidote in music; powerful works can draw us blissfully away from ourselves and into another state of mind. Each music lover no doubt has his favorite routes of departure. My own include the solo violin and cello works by Bach, with their sense of somber nobility, and the late quartets of Beethoven, to which we could easily apply Proust's phrase "the transposition of profundity into terms of sound." And yet, the magic of this music is not only the journey *out* that it affords but also the journey in, the journey *back*. As Proust of all writers would appreciate, each of our most cherished pieces of music can over time become a diary into which

The Proust Project

we unconsciously inscribe a history of private moments, associations, and memories. Hearing the piece performed again can be an invitation to leaf back through its pages, and discover in its wash of sound the tokens of a past life that seem all the more precious because we never knew they had been saved.

Of course, as Marcel discovers time and again, drawing heavily on memories can leave one disappointed when faced with the thing itself; the performance in the here and now can seem pallid in comparison to those that resonate with the special depth conferred on them by memory alone. Even so, a piece as magisterial as Beethoven's Quartet Opus 132 will reveal new previously invisible details in every live performance, and one can simply sit back and relish the ways that past and present intermingle in finely woven counterpoint. Once this otherworldly music has concluded, it can be difficult, as Marcel alludes to in the original passage, to make idle conversation with a concert date. But then again, that depends on who has joined you for the program.

Monsieur and Madame Verdurin try to "explain" to Morel the motive
behind Charlus's interest in him. Morel, not without his own motives,
pretends to be shocked, and publicly humiliates Charlus in front of the
Verdurins' guests, "I'm not the first person you've tried to pervert!" It
is a stunning blow to Charlus. His humiliation is all the more spec-
tacular considering that the Verdurin crowd is far below Charlus's so-
cial station.

At this moment there stirred beneath the domed forehead of the musical goddess the one thing that certain people cannot keep to themselves, a word which it is not merely abject but imprudent to repeat. But the need to repeat it is stronger than honour or prudence. It was to this need that, after a few convulsive twitches of her spherical and sorrowful brow, the Mistress succumbed: "Someone actually told my husband that he had said 'my servant,' but for that I cannot vouch," she added. It was a similar need that had impelled M. de Charlus, shortly after he had sworn to Morel that nobody should ever know the story of his birth, to say to Mme Verdurin: "His father was a valet." A similar need again, now that the word had been said, would make it circulate from one person to another, each of whom would confide it under the seal of a secrecy which would be promised and not kept by the hearer, as by the informant himself. These words would end, as in the game called hunt-the-thimble, by being traced back to Mme Verdurin, bringing down upon her the wrath of the person concerned, who would finally have heard them. She knew this, but could not repress the word that was burning her tongue. "Servant" could not but offend Morel. She said "servant" nevertheless, and if she added that she could not vouch for the word, this was so as to appear certain of the rest, thanks to this hint of uncertainty, and to show her impartiality. She herself found this impartiality so touching that she began to speak tenderly to Charlie: "Because, don't you see, I don't blame him. He's dragging you down into his abyss, it is true, but it's not his fault since he wallows in it himself, since he wallows in it," she repeated in a louder tone, having been struck by the aptness of the image which had taken shape so quickly that her attention only now caught up with it and sought to make the most of it. "No, what I do reproach him for," she went on in a melting tone—like a woman drunk with her own success—"is a want of delilacy towards you. There are certain things that one doesn't say in public. For instance, this evening he was betting that he would make you blush with joy by telling you (stuff and nonsense, of course, for his recommendation would be enough to prevent your getting it) that you were to have the Cross of the Legion of Honour. Even that I could overlook, although I've never much liked," she went on with a delicate and dignified air, "seeing someone make a fool of his friends, but, don't you know, there are certain little things that do stick in one's gullet. Such as when he told us, with screams of laughter, that if you want the Cross it's to please your uncle and that your uncle was a flunkey."

"He told you that!" cried Charlie, believing, on the strength of this adroitly interpolated remark, in the truth of everything that Mme Verdurin had said. Mme Verdurin was overwhelmed with the joy of an old mistress who, just as her young lover is on the point of deserting her, succeeds in breaking up his marriage. And perhaps the lie had not been a calculated one, perhaps she had not even consciously lied. A sort of sentimental logic, or perhaps, more elementary still, a sort of nervous reflex, that impelled her, in order to brighten up her life and preserve her happiness, to sow discord in the little clan, may have brought impulsively to her lips, without giving her time to check their veracity, these assertions that were so diabolically effective if not strictly accurate.

"If he had only said it to us it wouldn't matter," the Mistress went on, "we know better than to pay any attention to what he says, and besides, what does a man's origin matter, you have your worth, you're what you make yourself, but that he should use it to make Mme de Portefin laugh" (Mme Verdurin named this lady on purpose because she knew that Charlie admired her) "that's what makes us sick. My husband said to me when he heard him: 'I'd sooner he had struck me in the face.' For he's as fond

of you as I am, you know, is Gustave" (it was thus that one learned that
M. Verdurin's name was Gustave). "He's really very sensitive."

"But I never told you I was fond of him," muttered M. Verdurin, acting the kind-hearted curmudgeon. "It's Charlus who's fond of him."

"Oh, no! Now I realise the difference. I was betrayed by a wretch and
you, you're good," Charlie fervently exclaimed.

"No, no," murmured Mme Verdurin, seeking to safeguard her victory
(for she felt that her Wednesdays were safe) but not to abuse it, "wretch
is too strong; he does harm, a great deal of harm, unwittingly; you know
that tale about the Legion of Honour was only a momentary squib. And
it would be painful to me to repeat all that he said about your family,"
she added, although she would have been greatly embarrassed had she
been asked to do so.

"Oh, even if it *was* only momentary, it proves that he's a traitor,"
cried Morel.

It was at this moment that we returned to the drawing-room. "Ah!"
exclaimed M. de Charlus when he saw that Morel was in the room, and,
advancing upon the musician with the alacrity of a man who has skilfully
organised a whole evening's entertainment for the purpose of an assignation with a woman, and in his excitement never imagines that he has
with his own hands set the snare in which he will be caught and publicly
thrashed by bravoes stationed in readiness by her husband, "so here
you are at last. Well, are you pleased, young hero, and presently young
knight of the Legion of Honour? For very soon you will be able to sport
your Cross," he said to Morel with a tender and triumphant air, but by
the very mention of the decoration endorsing Mme Verdurin's lies, which
appeared to Morel to be indisputable truth.

"Leave me alone. I forbid you to come near me," Morel shouted at the
Baron. "You know what I mean all right. I'm not the first person you've
tried to pervert!"

My sole consolation lay in the thought that I was about to see Morel
and the Verdurins pulverised by M. de Charlus. For a thousand times
less than that I had been visited with his furious rage; no one was safe

from it; a king would not have intimidated him. Instead of which, an extraordinary thing happened. M. de Charlus stood speechless, dumbfounded, measuring the depths of his misery without understanding its cause, unable to think of a word to say, raising his eyes to gaze at each of the company in turn, with a questioning, outraged, suppliant air, which seemed to be asking them not so much what had happened as what answer he ought to make. And yet M. de Charlus possessed all the resources, not merely of eloquence but of audacity, when, seized by a rage which had been simmering for a long time, he reduced someone to despair with the most cruel words in front of a shocked society group which had never imagined that anyone could go so far. M. de Charlus, on these occasions, almost foamed at the mouth, working himself up into a veritable frenzy which left everyone trembling. But in these instances he had the initiative, he was on the attack, he said whatever came into his head (just as Bloch was able to make fun of the Jews yet blushed if the word Jew was uttered in his hearing). These people whom he hated, he hated because he thought they looked down on him. Had they been civil to him, instead of flying into a furious rage with them he would have taken them to his bosom. Perhaps what now struck him speechless was—when he saw that M. and Mme Verdurin turned their eyes away from him and that no one was coming to his rescue—his present anguish and, still more, his dread of greater anguish to come; or else the fact that, not having worked himself up and concocted an imaginary rage in advance, having no ready-made thunderbolt at hand, he had been seized and struck down suddenly at a moment when he was unarmed (for, sensitive, neurotic, hysterical, he was genuinely impulsive but pseudo-brave—indeed, as I had always thought, and it was something that had rather endeared him to me, pseudo-cruel—and did not have the normal reactions of an outraged man of honour); or else that, in a milieu that was not his own, he felt less at ease and less courageous than he would in the Faubourg. The fact remains that, in this salon which he despised, this great nobleman (in whom superiority over commoners was no more essentially inherent than it had been in this or that ancestor of his trembling before the revolutionary tribunal) could do nothing, in the paralysis of his every limb as well as his tongue, but cast around him terror-stricken, suppliant, bewildered glances, outraged by the violence that was being done to him. In a situation so cruelly unforeseen, this great talker could do no more than stammer: "What does it all mean? What's wrong?" His question was not even heard. And the eternal pantomime of panic terror has so little changed that this elderly gentleman to whom a disagreeable incident had occurred in a Parisian drawing-room unconsciously re-enacted the basic formal attitudes in which the Greek sculptors of the earliest times symbolised the terror of nymphs pursued by the god Pan.

The disgraced ambassador, the under-secretary placed suddenly on the retired list, the man about town who finds himself cold-shouldered, the lover who has been shown the door, examine, sometimes for months on end, the event that has shattered their hopes; they turn it over and over like a projectile fired at them they know not from whence or by whom, almost as though it were a meteorite. They long to know the constituent elements of this strange missile which has burst upon them, to learn what animosities may be detected therein. Chemists have at least the means of analysis; sick men suffering from a disease the origin of which they do not know can send for the doctor; criminal mysteries are more or less unravelled by the examining magistrate. But for the disconcerting actions of our fellow-men we rarely discover the motives. Thus M. de Charlus—to anticipate the days that followed this evening to which we shall presently return—could see in Charlie's attitude one thing alone that was self-evident. Charlie, who had often threatened the Baron that he would tell people of the passion that he inspired in him, must have seized the opportunity to do so when he considered that he had now sufficiently "arrived" to be able to stand on his own feet. And he must, out of sheer ingratitude, have told Mme Verdurin everything. But how had she allowed herself to be taken in (for the Baron, having made up his mind to deny the story, had already persuaded himself that the sentiments of which he would be accused were imaginary)? Friends of Mme Verdurin's, themselves perhaps with a passion for Charlie, must have prepared the ground. Accordingly, during the next few days M. de Charlus wrote ferocious letters to a number of the faithful, who were en-

tirely innocent and concluded that he must be mad; then he went to Mme
Verdurin with a long and affecting tale, which had not at all the effect
that he had hoped. For in the first place Mme Verdurin simply said to
him: "All you need do is pay no more attention to him, treat him with
scorn, he's a mere boy." Now the Baron longed only for a reconciliation,
and to bring this about by depriving Charlie of everything he had felt assured of, he asked Mme Verdurin not to invite him again; a request which
she met with a refusal that brought her angry and sarcastic letters from
M. de Charlus. Flitting from one supposition to another, the Baron never
hit upon the truth, which was that the blow had not come from Morel. It
is true that he could have learned this by asking him if they could have a
few minutes' talk. But he felt that this would be prejudicial to his dignity
and to the interests of his love. He had been insulted; he awaited an explanation. In any case, almost invariably, attached to the idea of a talk
which might clear up a misunderstanding, there is another idea which,
for whatever reason, prevents us from agreeing to that talk. The man
who has abased himself and shown his weakness on a score of occasions
will make a show of pride on the twenty-first, the only occasion on which
it would be advisable not to persist in an arrogant attitude but to dispel
an error which is taking root in his adversary failing a denial. As for the
social side of the incident, the rumour spread abroad that M. de Charlus had been turned out of the Verdurins' house when he had attempted
to rape a young musician. The effect of this rumour was that nobody was
surprised when M. de Charlus did not appear again at the Verdurins',
and whenever he chanced to meet somewhere else one of the faithful
whom he had suspected and insulted, as this person bore a grudge
against the Baron who himself abstained from greeting him, people were
not surprised, realising that no member of the little clan would ever wish
to speak to the Baron again.

While M. de Charlus, momentarily stunned by Morel's words and by
the attitude of the Mistress, stood there in the pose of a nymph seized with
Panic terror, M. and Mme Verdurin had retired to the outer drawing-
room, as a sign of diplomatic rupture, leaving M. de Charlus by himself,
while on the platform Morel was putting his violin in its case: "Now you

must tell us exactly what happened," Mme Verdurin exclaimed avidly to her husband.

"I don't know what you can have said to him," said Ski. "He looked quite upset; there were tears in his eyes."

Pretending not to have understood, "I'm sure nothing that I said could have affected him," said Mme Verdurin, employing one of those stratagems which deceives no one, so as to force the sculptor to repeat that Charlie was in tears, tears which excited the Mistress's pride too much for her to be willing to run the risk that one or other of the faithful, who might have misheard, remained in ignorance of them.

"Oh, but it must have: I saw big tears glistening in his eyes," said the sculptor in a low voice with a smile of malicious connivance and a sidelong glance to make sure that Morel was still on the platform and could not overhear the conversation. But there was somebody who did overhear and whose presence, as soon as it was observed, would restore to Morel one of the hopes that he had forfeited. This was the Queen of Naples, who, having left her fan behind, had thought it more polite, on coming away from another party to which she had gone on, to call back for it in person. She had entered the room quietly, as though she were a little embarrassed, prepared to make apologies for her presence, and not to outstay her welcome now that the other guests had gone. But no one had heard her enter in the heat of the incident, the meaning of which she had at once gathered and which set her ablaze with indignation.

"Ski says he had tears in his eyes. Did you notice that?" said Mme Verdurin. "I didn't see any tears. Ah, yes, I remember now," she corrected herself, afraid that her denial might be believed. "As for Charlus, he's almost done in, he ought to take a chair, he's tottering on his feet, he'll be on the floor in another minute," she said with a pitiless laugh.

At that moment Morel hastened towards her: "Isn't that lady the Queen of Naples?" he asked (although he knew quite well that she was), pointing to the sovereign who was making her way towards Charlus. "After what has just happened, I can no longer, I'm afraid, ask the Baron to introduce me."

"Wait, I shall take you to her myself," said Mme Verdurin, and, followed by a few of the faithful, but not by myself and Brichot who made haste to go and collect our hats and coats, she advanced upon the Queen who was chatting to M. de Charlus. The latter had imagined that the fulfilment of his great desire that Morel should be presented to the Queen of Naples could be prevented only by the improbable demise of that lady. But we picture the future as a reflexion of the present projected into an empty space, whereas it is the result, often almost immediate, of causes which for the most part escape our notice. Not an hour had passed, and now M. de Charlus would have given anything to prevent Morel from being presented to the Queen. Mme Verdurin made the Queen a curtsey. Seeing that the other appeared not to recognise her, "I am Mme Verdurin," she said. "Your Majesty doesn't remember me."

"Quite well," said the Queen, continuing to talk to M. de Charlus so naturally and with such a casual air that Mme Verdurin doubted whether it was to herself that this "Quite well" was addressed, uttered as it was in a marvelously off-hand tone, which wrung from M. de Charlus, despite his lover's anguish, the grateful and epicurean smile of an expert in the art of rudeness. Morel, who had watched from the distance the preparations for his presentation, now approached. The Queen offered her arm to M. de Charlus. With him, too, she was vexed, but only because he did not make a more energetic stand against vile detractors. She was crimson with shame on his behalf that the Verdurins should dare to treat him in this fashion. The unaffected civility which she had shown them a few hours earlier, and the arrogant pride with which she now confronted them, had their source in the same region of her heart. The Queen was a woman of great kindness, but she conceived of kindness first and foremost in the form of an unshakeable attachment to the people she loved, to her own family, to all the princes of her race, among whom was M. de Charlus, and, after them, to all the people of the middle classes or of the humblest populace who knew how to respect those whom she loved and were well-disposed towards them. It was as to a woman endowed with these sound instincts that she had shown kindness to Mme Verdurin. And no doubt this is a narrow conception of kindness, somewhat Tory and increasingly obsolete. But this does not mean that her kindness was any

The Captive

less genuine or ardent. The ancients were no less strongly attached to the human group to which they devoted themselves because it did not go beyond the limits of their city, nor are the men of today to their country, than those who in the future will love the United States of the World. In my own immediate surroundings, I had the example of my mother, whom Mme de Cambremer and Mme de Guermantes could never persuade to take part in any philanthropic undertaking, to join any patriotic ladies' work party, to sell raffle tickets or sponsor charity shows. I do not say that she was right in acting only when her heart had first spoken, and in reserving for her own family, for her servants, for the unfortunate whom chance brought in her way, the riches of her love and generosity, but I do know that these, like those of my grandmother, were inexhaustible and exceeded by far anything that Mme de Guermantes or Mme de Cambremer ever could have done or did. The case of the Queen of Naples was altogether different, but it must be admitted that lovable people were conceived of by her not at all as in those novels of Dostoievsky which Albertine had taken from my shelves and hoarded, that is to say in the guise of wheedling parasites, thieves, drunkards, obsequious one minute, insolent the next, debauchees, even murderers. Extremes, however, meet, since the noble man, the close relative, the outraged kinsman whom the Queen sought to defend was M. de Charlus, that is to say, notwithstanding his birth and all the family ties that bound him to the Queen, a man whose virtue was hedged round by many vices. "You don't look at all well, my dear cousin," she said to M. de Charlus. "Lean on my arm. You may be sure that it will always support you. It is strong enough for that." Then, raising her eyes proudly in front of her (where, Ski later told me, Mme Verdurin and Morel were standing): "You know how in the past, at Gaeta, it held the mob at bay. It will be a shield to you." And it was thus, taking the Baron on her arm and without having allowed Morel to be presented to her, that the glorious sister of the Empress Elisabeth left the house.

(*The Captive*, 420–33)

Louis Auchincloss

That the upper middle class in Paris of the Mauve Decade should ultimately succeed in crashing the gates of the "old faubourg" (Saint-Germain) where the ancient aristocracy still held sway was clearly foreseen by as acute a social observer as Proust, and he symbolized its victory in the marriage of Madame Verdurin to the Prince de Guermantes. But the clashes along the way provided some of the most dramatic scenes of his novel, and none is finer than the one where Madame Verdurin wreaks her ultimate revenge on the Baron de Charlus.

Charlus, though almost insanely proud of his birth—he ranks his family, the Guermantes, higher than the House of France—has consented to frequent the Verdurin salon because his protégé and lover, the handsome young violinist Charles Morel, is a fixture there. And Madame Verdurin, who hides her passion to have aristocratic friends under a professed scorn of titles, hopes that the baron will provide a nucleus for his acquaintance to meet at her house. An example of the rudeness she and her husband have to endure from Charlus is shown in the latter's response to Verdurin's misguided apology for seating him at dinner below the Marquis de Cambremer, a marquis, according to the benighted host, outranking a mere baron. Charlus replies haughtily: "I am also Duc de Brabant, Damoiseau de Montargis, Prince d'Oléron, de Carency, de Viargeggio and des Dunes. However, it is not of the slightest importance. Please do not distress yourself. I could see at a glance that you were not accustomed to society."

Madame Verdurin finally hopes that she has succeeded in her objective when Charlus agrees to act as cohost at her house at a concert in which Morel will play for all his noble friends. But this time Charlus has gone too far.

"What ruined M. de Charlus that evening was the ill-breeding—so common in their class—of the people whom he had invited and who were now beginning to arrive. Having come there partly out of friendship for M. de Charlus and also out of curiosity to explore those novel surroundings, each Duchess made straight for the Baron as though it were he who was giving the party and said, within a yard of the Verdurins, who could hear every word: 'Show me which is Mother Verdurin; do you think I really need speak to her?'"

This was too much, even for so determined a social climber as Madame Verdurin. She and her husband took Morel aside after the concert and poured in his ear grossly exaggerated accounts of the public horror at Charlus's vices and warned him that any continued association of Morel with this monster of perversion would ruin his artistic career. The result of this was that when Charlus, beaming with delight at the great success of the concert, approached his beloved protégé with congratulatory arms outstretched, Morel shouted: "Leave me alone, I forbid you to come near me. You know what I mean, all right, I'm not the first young man you've tried to pervert!"

It is at this point that the deposed Queen of Naples, sister of the Empress Elisabeth, returns to the party to retrieve the fan she had left behind and which, as Charlus has already observed, the poor exile can ill afford to replace. Unobserved, she has witnessed the terrible scene and the prostration of the devastated baron. Morel, catching sight of her, recalls his great desire to be presented to her, but remarks ruefully to Madame Verdurin that he can hardly ask the baron to introduce him now.

"Wait, I shall take you to her myself," said Madame Verdurin, and she advanced upon the queen who was talking to Charlus. She made the queen a curtsey. Seeing that the other appeared not to recognize her: "I am Madame Verdurin. Your Majesty does not remember me."

"Quite well," said the queen with an air of such complete indifference that Madame Verdurin doubted that it was to herself that this "Quite well" had been addressed, uttered with a marvellously detached intonation, which wrung from Charlus, despite his broken heart, a smile of expert and delighted appreciation of the art of impertinence. The Queen offered her arm to Charlus.

"Lean upon my arm. Be sure that it will support you. It is firm enough for that." Then, raising her eyes proudly to face her adversaries: "You know that in the past, in Gaeta, it held a mob in defiance. It will be able to serve you as a rampart." And it was thus, taking the baron on her arm, and without having allowed Morel to be presented to her, that the splendid sister of the Empress Elisabeth left the house.

When Albertine tells Marcel that she plans to spend three days in Bal-
bec, and when her postcards from there arrive a week late, Marcel be-
gins to suspect trouble. When he catches her in a lie, she admits never
having gone to Balbec and having her postcards sent off by the chauf-
feur. But, she said, she had only gone to a friend's house just outside
of Paris where she spent the three days "bored to tears."

Hoping to engineer a reconciliation and bring Albertine closer to
him, Marcel tells her that they must part, never to see each other
again. In the paroxysm of tears that ensues, Marcel opens up a new
avenue: "Would you like us to try to carry on for a few weeks?" To
which Albertine responds, "Oh, it would be sweet of you!" And things
revert to normal.

Marcel goes back to brooding on the two questions that torment his
life: "What is the nature of artistic genius?" And: "Is Albertine a les-
bian?" A discussion with Albertine that runs from Vinteuil to Dos-
toyevsky addresses both.

Perhaps it was in this, I said to Al-
bertine, this unknown quality of a unique world which no other composer had ever yet revealed, that the most authentic proof of genius lies,
even more than in the content of the work itself. "Even in literature?"
Albertine inquired. "Even in literature." And thinking again of the
sameness of Vinteuil's works, I explained to Albertine that the great men
of letters have never created more than a single work, or rather have
never done more than refract through various media an identical beauty
which they bring into the world. "If it were not so late, my sweet," I said
to her, "I would show you this quality in all the writers whose works you
read while I'm asleep, I would show you the same identity as in Vinteuil.
These key-phrases, which you are beginning to recognise as I do, my little Albertine, the same in the sonata, in the septet, in the other works,
would be, say for instance in Barbey d'Aurevilly, a hidden reality revealed by a physical sign, the physiological blush of the Bewitched, of

The Proust Project

Aimèe de Spens, of old Clotte, the hand in the *Rideau cramoisi*, the old manners and customs, the old words, the ancient and peculiar trades behind which there is the Past, the oral history made by the herdsmen with their mirror, the noble Norman cities redolent of England and charming as a Scottish village, the hurler of curses against which one can do nothing, la Vellini, the Shepherd, a similar sensation of anxiety in a passage, whether it be the wife seeking her husband in *Une vieille maîtresse*, or the husband in *L'Ensorcelée* scouring the plain and the Bewitched herself coming out from mass. Another example of Vinteuil's key-phrases is that stonemason's geometry in the novels of Thomas Hardy."

Vinteuil's phrases made me think of the "little phrase" and I told Albertine that it had been as it were the national anthem of the love of Swann and Odette, "the parents of Gilberte, whom I believe you know. You told me she was a bad girl. Didn't she try to have relations with you? She spoke to me about you."

"Yes, you see, her parents used to send a carriage to fetch her from school when the weather was bad, and I seem to remember she took me home once and kissed me," she said, after a momentary pause, laughing as though it were an amusing revelation. "She asked me all of a sudden whether I was fond of women." (But if she only "seemed to remember" that Gilberte had taken her home, how could she say with such precision that Gilberte had asked her this odd question?) "In fact, I don't know what weird idea came into my head to fool her, but I told her that I was." (It was as though Albertine was afraid that Gilberte had told me this and did not want me to see that she was lying to me.) "But we did nothing at all." (It was strange, if they had exchanged these confidences, that they should have done nothing, especially as, before this, they had kissed, according to Albertine.) "She took me home like that four or five times, perhaps more, and that's all."

It cost me a great effort not to ply her with questions, but, mastering myself so as to appear not to be attaching any importance to all this, I returned to Thomas Hardy. "Do you remember the stonemasons in *Jude the Obscure* and in *The Well-Beloved* the blocks of stone which the father hews out of the island coming in boats to be piled up in the son's work-shop

The Captive

where they are turned into statues; and in *A Pair of Blue Eyes* the parallelism of the tombs, and also the parallel line of the boat and the nearby railway coaches containing the lovers and the dead woman; and the parallel between *The Well-Beloved*, where the man loves three women, and *A Pair of Blue Eyes*, where the woman loves three men, and in short all those novels which can be superimposed on one another like the houses piled up vertically on the rocky soil of the island. I can't sum up the greatest writers like this in a few moments, but you'll see in Stendhal a certain sense of altitude symbolising the life of the spirit: the lofty place in which Julien Sorel is imprisoned, the tower at the top of which Fabrice is incarcerated, the belfry in which the Abbé Blanès pores over his astrology and from which Fabrice has such a magnificent bird's-eye view. You told me you had seen some of Vermeer's pictures: you must have realised that they're fragments of an identical world, that it's always, however great the genius with which they have been re-created, the same table, the same carpet, the same woman, the same novel and unique beauty, an enigma at that period in which nothing resembles or explains it, if one doesn't try to relate it all through subject matter but to isolate the distinctive impression produced by the colour. Well, this novel beauty remains identical in all Dostoievsky's works. Isn't the Dostoievsky woman (as distinctive as a Rembrandt woman) with her mysterious face, whose engaging beauty changes abruptly, as though her apparent good nature was only play-acting, into terrible insolence (although at heart it seems that she is more good than bad), isn't she always the same, whether it's Nastasia Philipovna writing love letters to Aglaya and telling her that she hates her, or in a visit that's absolutely identical with this—as also the one where Nastasia Philipovna insults Gania's family—Grushenka, as charming in Katerina Ivanovna's house as the latter had supposed her to be terrible, then suddenly revealing her malevolence by insulting Katerina Ivanovna (although Grushenka is good at heart)? Grushenka, Nastasia—figures as original, as mysterious, not merely as Carpaccio's courtesans but as Rembrandt's Bathsheba. Mind you, he certainly didn't only know how to depict that striking dual face, with its sudden explosions of furious pride, which makes the woman seem other than she is

The Proust Project

('You are not like that,' says Myshkin to Nastasia during the visit to Gania's family, and Alyosha might have said the same to Grushenka during the visit to Katerina Ivanovna). But on the other hand when he wants 'ideas for paintings' they're always stupid and would at best result in the pictures where Munkacsy wanted to see a condemned man represented at the moment when . . . etc., or the Virgin Mary at the moment when . . . etc. But to return to the new kind of beauty that Dostoievsky brought to the world, just as, in Vermeer, there's the creation of a certain soul, of a certain colour of fabrics and places, so in Dostoievsky there's the creation not only of people but of their homes, and the house of the Murder in *Crime and Punishment*, with its janitor, isn't it as marvellous as the masterpiece of the house of Murder in *The Idiot*, that somber house of Rogozhin's, so long, and so high, and so vast, in which he kills Nastasia Philipovna. That new and terrible beauty of a house, that new and two-sided beauty of a woman's face, that is the unique thing that Dostoievsky has given to the world, and the comparisons that literary critics may make, between him and Gogol, or between him and Paul de Kock, are of no interest, being external to this secret beauty. Besides, if I've said to you that from one novel to another it's the same scene, it's in the compass of a single novel that the same scenes, the same characters reappear if the novel is at all long. I could illustrate this to you easily in *War and Peace*, and a certain scene in a carriage . . ."

"I didn't want to interrupt you, but now that I see that you're leaving Dostoievsky, I'm afraid I might forget. My sweet, what was it you meant the other day when you said: 'It's like the Dostoievsky side of Mme de Sévigné.' I must confess that I didn't understand. It seems to me so different."

"Come, little girl, let me give you a kiss to thank you for remembering so well what I say. You shall go back to the pianola afterwards. And I must admit that what I said was rather stupid. But I said it for two reasons. The first is a special reason. What I meant was that Mme de Sévigné, like Elstir, like Dostoievsky, instead of presenting things in their logical sequence, that is to say beginning with the cause, shows us first of all the effect, the illusion that strikes us. That is how Dostoievsky presents his characters. Their actions seem to us as deceptive as those effects in Elstir's pictures where the sea appears to be in the sky. We're quite surprised to find later on that some sly-looking individual is really the best of men, or vice versa."

"Yes, but give me an example in Mme de Sévigné."

"I admit," I answered her with a laugh, "that it's very far-fetched, but still I could find examples. For instance . . ."

"But did he ever murder anyone, Dostoievsky? The novels of his that I know might all be called *The Story of a Crime*. It's an obsession with him, it isn't natural that he should always be talking about it."

"I don't think so, dear Albertine. I know little about his life. It's certain that, like everyone else, he was acquainted with sin, in one form or another, and probably in a form which the laws condemn. In that sense he must have been a bit criminal, like his heroes—who in any case are not entirely criminal, who are found guilty with extenuating circumstances. And perhaps it wasn't necessary for him to be criminal himself. I'm not a novelist; it's possible that creative writers are tempted by certain forms of life of which they have no personal experience. If I come with you to Versailles as we arranged, I shall show you the portrait of an ultra-respectable man, the best of husbands, Choderlos de Laclos, who wrote the most appallingly perverse book, and just opposite it the portrait of Mme de Genlis who wrote moral tales and, not content with betraying the Duchesse d'Orléans, tortured her by turning her children against her. I admit all the same that in Dostoievsky this preoccupation with murder is something extraordinary which makes him very alien to me. I'm amazed enough when I hear Baudelaire say:

> If not yet poison, arson, rape, and stabbing . . .
> It is because our soul, alas! Lacks daring.

But I can at least assume that Baudelaire is not sincere. Whereas Dostoievsky . . . All that sort of thing seems to me as remote from myself as possible, unless there are parts of myself of which I know nothing, for we realise our own nature only in the course of time. In Dostoievsky I find the deepest wells of insight but only into certain isolated regions of the

The Proust Project

human soul. But he is a great creator. For one thing, the world which he describes does really appear to have been created by him. All those buffoons who keep on reappearing, like Lebedev, Karamazov, Ivolgin, Segrev, that incredible procession, are human types even more fantastic than those that people Rembrandt's *Night Watch*. And yet perhaps they're fantastic only in the same way, by the effect of lighting and costume, and are quite normal really. In any case the whole thing is full of profound and unique truths, which belong only to Dostoievsky. They almost suggest, those buffoons, some trade or calling that no longer exists, like certain characters in the old drama, and yet how they reveal true aspects of the human soul! What I find so tedious is the solemn manner in which people talk and write about Dostoievsky. Have you ever noticed the part that self-esteem and pride play in his characters? It's as though, for him, love and the most passionate hatred, goodness and treachery, timidity and insolence, are merely two aspects of a single nature, their self-esteem, their pride preventing Aglaya, Nastasia, the Captain whose beard Mitya pulls, Krassotkin, Alyosha's enemy-friend, from showing themselves in their true colours. But there are many other great qualities as well. I know very few of his books. But what a simple, sculptural notion it is, worthy of the most classical art, a frieze interrupted and resumed in which the theme of vengeance and expiation is unfolded in the crime of old Karamazov getting the poor simpleton with child, the mysterious, animal, unexplained impulse whereby the mother, herself unconsciously the instrument of an avenging destiny, obeying also obscurely her maternal instinct, feeling perhaps a combination of resentment and physical gratitude towards her violator, comes to give birth to her child in old Karamazov's garden. This is the first episode, mysterious, grandiose, august, like the Creation of Woman in one of the sculptures at Orvieto. And as counterpart, the second episode more than twenty years later, the murder of old Karamazov, the infamy committed against the Karamazov family by the madwoman's son, Smerdiakov, followed shortly afterwards by another act as mysteriously sculpturesque and unexplained, of a beauty as obscure and natural as the childbirth in old Karamazov's garden, Smerdiakov hanging himself, his crime ac-

The Captive

complished. Actually I wasn't straying as far from Dostoievsky as you thought when I mentioned Tolstoy, who imitated him a great deal. In Dostoievsky there's concentrated, still tense and peevish, a great deal of what was to blossom later on in Tolstoy. There's that proleptic gloom of the primitives which the disciples will brighten and dispel."

"What a bore it is that you're so lazy, my sweet. Just look at your view of literature, so much more interesting than the way we were made to study it; the essays that they used to make us write about *Esther*: 'Monsieur,'— you remember," she said with a laugh, less from a desire to make fun of her masters and herself than from the pleasure of finding in her memory, in our common memory, a recollection that was already quite venerable.

But while she was speaking, and I thought once more of Vinteuil, it was the other, the materialist hypothesis, that of there being nothing, that in turn presented itself to my mind. I began to doubt again; I told myself that after all it might be the case that, if Vinteuil's phrases seemed to be the expression of certain states of soul analogous to that which I had experienced when I tasted the madeleine soaked in tea, there was nothing to assure me that the vagueness of such states was a sign of their profundity rather than of our not having yet learned to analyse them, so that there might be nothing more real in them than in other states. And yet that happiness, that sense of certainty in happiness while I was drinking the cup of tea, or when I smelt in the Champs-Elysées a smell of mouldering wood, was not an illusion. In any case, whispered the spirit of doubt, even if these states are more profound than others that occur in life, and defy analysis for that very reason, because they bring into play too many forces of which we have hitherto been unaware, the charm of certain phrases of Vinteuil's music makes us think of them because it too defies analysis, but this does not prove that it has the same profundity; the beauty of a phrase of pure music can easily appear to be the image of or at least akin to an unintellectual impression which we have received, but simply because it is unintellectual. And why then do we suppose to be specially profound those mysterious phrases which haunt certain quartets and this septet by Vinteuil?

(*The Captive*, 505–14)

Anka Muhlstein

Marcel may believe he is analyzing the work of Dostoyevsky and Tolstoy, but in fact Proust has him discuss the *Search* itself. Though it may
be questionable that the same scenes and characters recur throughout
War and Peace, it is self-evident that they do so in the *Search*. I won't
linger over the similarities between the scenes caused by the jealousy
of Swann, Robert de Saint-Loup, or Marcel. The suffering of all three
men is enflamed by their unrelenting though unsuccessful interroga-
tions of their mistresses. So, too, their torment disappears the day they
are no longer in love. In each case, love, and therefore jealousy, vanishes as inexplicably as it had appeared. More startling still is the likeness between two characters who would each be horrified at the thought:
Oriane, the aristocratic Duchess of Guermantes, and Madame Verdurin,
who comes from completely "unknown bourgeois origins." At a quick
glance, the only characteristic they have in common is that each reigns
over a salon. The idea that they would ever exchange calling cards is in-
conceivable . . . until *Time Regained*.

Oriane's salon is frequented by her family, who represent the best of
Faubourg Saint-Germain, and certain men of prominence and distinction. Both she and her guests consider that having entrée to her salon is
a precious and much sought-after privilege. Because Madame Verdurin's origins prevent her from being on familiar terms with the up-
permost echelons of society, she concentrates on artists, scientists,

Anka Muhlstein

scholars, politicians, and a rather motley crew of regulars. While the social makeup of the two salons is completely different, their underlying principles and mode of action are identical: both are based on slavish adulation of the hostess and the necessity of arbitrary and sometimes brutal exclusion.

The husband's role is essential to cast the hostess in the most flattering light. Monsieur Verdurin repeatedly stresses his wife's musicality and artistic taste, while the Duke of Guermantes glories in Oriane's cultivation, always applauds her judgments, and is a past master at the art of circulating her latest witticism among the guests. Both ladies distrust other women—Madame Verdurin because she questions their absolute devotion; the duchess in order to apply with full rigor the principle of exclusion. It is convenient to let it be known that she doesn't like women—other than family members—which exempts her from inviting the wives of some remarkable men she would like to attract.

The duchess and Madame Verdurin each pretend to be entirely objective about the works of art they own. Passionately believing that her Elstirs are the most beautiful and her Empire furniture the finest, Madame de Guermantes praises them with an air of impartiality that leaves no room for dispute. Madame Verdurin boldly maintains that it is impossible to find furniture in Beauvais tapestry or decorative bronzes equal to hers. However, the duchess and Madame Verdurin are most alike in their cruelty and in their steely refusal to forgo pleasure on account of a friend's sorrow. Madame Verdurin relies on her husband to avoid talking about death or, worse still, postponing a dinner for that reason. It is up to him to plead his wife's oversensitive nature and forbid any mention of bereavement in her presence. When she cannot prevent the question from arising, as when her friend, Princess Sherbatoff, dies, she prefers to insist callously that she feels no sorrow, rather than cancel a reception and be forced to look sad all evening. Madame de Guermantes may be subtler, but she is no less determined to make social life her highest priority. When Charles Swann, her lifelong friend, tells her that he is going to die, rather than risk being late at a dinner by taking the time to console him, she chooses not to believe him, thereby

The Proust Project

obviating any possible conflict between friendship and frivolity. These two women, cruel in the face of death and even more cruel toward the living, unhesitatingly sacrifice those closest to them on the altar of their love of society. Thus Oriane makes Swann infinitely sad by refusing, shortly before his death, to let him introduce his daughter to her. There would be no more salons if every dying person were granted their wish, she avers; her counterpart, Madame Verdurin, enraged by the attention paid to Baron Charlus during a party he organized at her house, devastates him by turning Morel, the person he adores, against him.

Proust, at the end of the novel, as though to emphasize the interchangeability of the two women, makes Madame Verdurin become the Princess of Guermantes, therefore the duchess's cousin by marriage, and he lowers Oriane's social standing in the eyes of the younger generation by her new association with writers and actresses.

This radical transformation of his characters underlines Proust's nihilism, a quality that distinguishes him from both Tolstoy and Dostoyevsky. Society being the realm of nothingness, he wrote, the differences between the merit of this society woman or another is insignificant.

The tension between Albertine and Marcel continues to build. Still, one night, unable to sleep and feeling particularly lonely, Marcel asks Albertine to stay with him in his room a little longer. She sweetly tells him she will stay with him as long as he likes. But she will not kiss him good night.

It is early spring and they take a melancholy trip to Versailles, Albertine wearing the expensive Fortuny dressing gown that Marcel had given her. It is to be their last trip together. Soon Albertine will leave.

I rang for Françoise to ask her to buy me a guidebook and a timetable, as I had done as a boy when already I wanted to prepare in advance a journey to Venice, the fulfilment of a desire as violent as that which I felt at this moment. I forgot that, in the meantime, there was a desire which I had attained without any satisfaction—the desire for Balbec—and that Venice, being also a visible phenomenon, was probably no more able than Balbec to fulfil an ineffable dream, that of the Gothic age made actual by a springtime sea, that now teased my mind from moment to moment with an enchanted, caressing, elusive, mysterious, confused image. Françoise, having heard my ring, came into the room, rather uneasy as to how I would take what she had to say and what she had done. "I was very worried," she said to me, "that Monsieur should be so late in ringing this morning. I didn't know what I ought to do. This morning at eight o'clock Mademoiselle Albertine asked me for her boxes. I dared not refuse her, and I was afraid that Monsieur might scold me if I came and waked him. It was no use lecturing her, telling her to wait an hour because I expected all the time that Monsieur would ring; she wouldn't have it, she left this letter with me for Monsieur, and at nine o'clock off she went." Then—so ignorant can we be of what is inside us, since I was convinced of my indifference to Albertine—my breath was cut short, I gripped my heart in my hands, which were suddenly moistened by a perspiration I had not experienced since the revelation she had made to me on the little train with regard to Mlle Vinteuil's friend, and I was incapable of saying anything else but: "Ah! Very good, Françoise, you were of course quite right not to wake me. Leave me now for a moment, I shall ring for you presently."

"Mademoiselle Albertine has gone!" How much further does anguish penetrate in psychology than psychology itself! A moment before, in the process of analysing myself, I had believed that this separation without having seen each other again was precisely what I wished, and, comparing the mediocrity of the pleasures that Albertine afforded me with the richness of the desires which she prevented me from realising, I had felt that I was being subtle, had concluded that I no longer wished to see her, that I no longer loved her. But now these words: "Mademoiselle Albertine has gone," had produced in my heart an anguish such that I felt I could not endure it much longer. So what I had believed to be nothing to me was simply my entire life. How ignorant one is of oneself. My anguish must be made to end at once; tender towards myself as my mother had been towards my dying grandmother, I said to myself with that genuine wish that one has to relieve the suffering of a person one loves: "Be patient for a moment, we shall find something to take the pain away, don't fret, we're not going to allow you to suffer like this." It was in this category of ideas that my instinct of self-preservation sought for the first balms to lay upon my open wound: "None of this is of the slightest importance, because I'm going to bring her back at once. I shall have to think how, but in any case she will be here this evening. Therefore it's useless to torment myself." "None of this is of the slightest importance"—I had not been content merely with giving myself this assurance, but had tried to convey the same impression to Françoise by not allowing her to see my suffering, because, even at the moment when I was feeling it so acutely, my love did not forget how important it was that it should appear a happy love, a mutual love, especially in the eyes of Françoise, who disliked Albertine and had always doubted her sincerity.

Yes, a moment ago, before Françoise came into the room, I had be-

The Captive *and* The Fugitive

lieved that I no longer loved Albertine, I had believed that I was leaving nothing out of account, like a rigorous analyst; I had believed that I knew the state of my own heart. But our intelligence, however lucid, cannot perceive the elements that compose it and remain unsuspected so long as, from the volatile state in which they generally exist, a phenomenon capable of isolating them has not subjected them to the first stages of solidification. I had been mistaken in thinking that I could see clearly into my own heart. But this knowledge, which the shrewdest perceptions of the mind would not have given me, had now been brought to me, hard, glittering, strange, like a crystallised salt, by the abrupt reaction of pain. I was so much in the habit of having Albertine with me, and now I suddenly saw a new aspect of Habit. Hitherto I had regarded it chiefly as an annihilating force which suppresses the originality and even the awareness of one's perceptions; now I saw it as a dread deity, so riveted to one's being, its insignificant face so incrusted in one's heart, that if it detaches itself, if it turns away from one, this deity that one had barely distinguished inflicts on one sufferings more terrible than any other and is then as cruel as death itself.

(*The Captive*, 556; *The Fugitive*, 564)

Daniel Mark Epstein

Proust foreshadowed this disaster long before, in *The Guermantes Way*, when he declared that "when you come to live with a woman you will soon cease to see anything of what made you love her, though it is true that the two sundered elements can be reunited by jealousy." There the comment is a glib digression—not until *The Captive* does Marcel narrate the traumatic experience. His mistress comes to live with him in the spring; by the following spring his jealousy has made their life unendurable.

He is so suspicious of Albertine he virtually keeps her captive. Forced to prevaricate in order to steal moments of freedom, she thus becomes what he had most feared—a liar, a dissembler. Maybe she is unfaithful to him. Before, she had been honest, constant, and devoted. Even as she changes we sense that she changes as much to please him— by offering him fuel for his jealousy—as to save herself from his tyranny.

When at last he catches her in a petty lie, he decides to leave her, since his life with Albertine "was on the one hand, when [he] was not jealous, nothing but boredom, and on the other hand, when [he] was jealous, nothing but pain." She leaves him first, thus depriving him of the satisfaction.

Proust constructed his bildungsroman from the outside in—the first and final volumes were written first, then the middle of the novel was expanded to fit the love story of Marcel and Albertine. She absorbs more of his attention than does any other character. Thus the question "Who is Albertine?" begins to haunt both Marcel and the reader soon after the

Daniel Mark Epstein

beautiful girl makes her appearance in Balbec—"the dark one with the plump cheeks, who was wheeling a bicycle."

She is Marcel's "anima"—the feminine element of the psyche that Goethe called "The Eternal Feminine." Throughout the novel Marcel struggles to free his anima from what Carl Jung calls "the devouring aspect of the mother image." A man must find some "means of freeing the psychic energy attached to the mother-son relationship in order to achieve a more adult relation to woman . . ." Jung writes. And the freedom of this energy "is necessary for any true creative achievement."

Of course Albertine is first and foremost a fully realized character, and only subliminally an allegorical figure, otherwise her final escape would not be so deeply moving.

In this novel where reflection supersedes action, the reader may lose sight of Proust's powers as a "dramatist." The emphatic placement of Albertine's liberation, darkening the close of *The Captive* and illuminating the opening of *The Fugitive*, underscores Proust's artistic purpose. The seamless transition between these books constitutes a classic scene of what Aristotle calls *anagnorisis* (recognition) and *peripeteia* (sudden reversal of circumstances). Only after the tragedy of Marcel's love life has come to an end, and he has thoroughly mourned its passing in *The Fugitive*, will the aspiring writer be capable of accessing his mature psychic energies. In this singular soul's journey, the hero must renounce human love before he can assume his role in *Time Regained* as an artist, a comedian, and a critic of culture.

Life without Albertine brings desperation. Marcel's last hope is in Saint-Loup, whom he sends off to Touraine, where Albertine is now living with her aunt; his plan is for Saint-Loup to persuade Albertine's aunt to send her back to marry Marcel. Saint-Loup returns unsuccessful. Marcel, however, had already received a letter from Albertine herself, telling him that it was silly to send Saint-Loup to her aunt, that she would be only too delighted to come back if that was what he wanted. Happy with this response, Marcel writes back, telling Albertine that for the sake of her happiness and his, they must not see each other again, all the while describing in his next sentence the yacht and automobile he has ordered for her. He asks her if she would be so kind as to countermand these gifts personally, because he had ordered them in her name. "It would be madness," he writes, "for the sake of a sailing boat and a Rolls-Royce, to meet again and to jeopardize your life's happiness, since you have decided that it lies in your living apart from me."

But when Françoise saw that after writing a long letter I added the exact address of Mme Bontemps, her alarm that Albertine might return, hitherto quite vague, began to increase. It grew to the point of consternation when one morning she had to bring me with the rest of my mail a letter on the envelope of which she had recognised Albertine's handwriting. She wondered whether Albertine's departure had not been a mere sham, a supposition which distressed her twice over as finally ensuring Albertine's future presence in the house, and as constituting for me, and thereby, as I was her employer, for herself, the humiliation of having been tricked by Albertine. Impatient though I was to read the letter, I could not refrain from studying for a moment Françoise's eyes from which all hope had fled, inferring from this omen the imminence of Albertine's return, as a lover of winter sports concludes with joy that the cold weather is at hand when he sees

The Fugitive

the swallows fly south. At length Françoise left me, and when I had made sure that she had shut the door behind her, I opened, noiselessly so as not to appear anxious, the letter which ran as follows:

"Dear friend, thank you for all the nice things you wrote to me. I am at your disposal for the countermanding of the Rolls, if you think that I can help in any way, as I am sure I can. You have only to let me know the name of the agents. You would let yourself be taken for a ride by these people who are only interested in selling, and what would you do with a motor-car, you who never stir out of the house? I am deeply touched that you have kept a happy memory of our last outing. You may be sure that for my part I shall never forget that drive in a double twilight (since night was falling and we were about to part) and that it will be effaced from my thoughts only when the darkness is complete."

I felt that this last sentence was merely phrase-making and that Albertine could not possibly retain until death any such sweet memory of this drive from which she had certainly derived no pleasure since she had been impatient to leave me. But I was impressed also, when I thought of the cyclist, the golfer of Balbec, who had read nothing but *Esther* before she came to know me, to see how gifted she was and how right I had been in thinking that she had enriched herself in my house with new qualities which made her different and more complete. And thus, the words that I had said to her at Balbec: "I feel that my friendship would be of value to you, that I am just the person who could give you what you lack" (I had written by way of dedication on a photograph I gave her: "with the certainty of being providential"), words which I uttered without believing them and simply that she might derive some benefit from my society which would outweigh any possible boredom, these words turned out to have been true as well; as, for that matter, had been my remark to her that I did not wish to see her for fear of falling in love with her. I had said this because on the contrary I knew that in constant proximity my love became deadened and that separation kindled it, but in reality constant proximity had given rise to a need of her that was infinitely stronger than my love in the first weeks at Balbec, so that that remark too had proved true.

But Albertine's letter in no way advanced matters. She spoke to me only of writing to the agents. It was essential to break out of this situation, to hasten things on, and I had the following idea. I sent a letter at once to Andrée in which I told her that Albertine was at her aunt's, that I felt very lonely, that she would give me immense pleasure if she came and stayed with me for a few days and that, as I did not wish to make any mystery of it, I begged her to inform Albertine. And at the same time I wrote to Albertine as though I had not yet received her letter:

"Dear friend, forgive me for what I am sure you will understand. I have such a hatred of secrecy that I wanted you to be informed both by her and by myself. I have acquired, from having you staying so charmingly in the house with me, the bad habit of not being able to be alone. Since we have decided that you will not come back, it occurred to me that the person who would best fill your place, because she would make least change in my life, would remind me most of you, is Andrée, and I have asked her to come. So that all this should not appear too sudden, I have spoken to her only of a short visit, but between ourselves I am pretty certain that this time it will be a permanent thing. Don't you agree that I'm right? You know that your little group of girls at Balbec has always been the social unit that exerted the greatest influence upon me, in which I was most happy to be eventually included. No doubt this influence is still making itself felt. Since the fatal incompatibility of our characters and the mischances of life have decreed that my little Albertine can never be my wife, I believe that I shall nevertheless find a wife—less charming than herself but one whom greater natural affinities will enable perhaps to be happier with me—in Andrée."

But after I had sent off this letter, the suspicion occurred to me suddenly that, when Albertine had written to me to say: "I should have been only too glad to come back if you had written to me direct," she had said this only because I had not written to her, and that had I done so she

The Fugitive

would still not have come back, that she would be happy to know that Andrée was with me, and was to be my wife, provided that she herself remained free, because she could now, as already for a week past, stultifying the hourly precautions which I had taken during more than six months in Paris, abandon herself to her vices and do what, minute by minute, I had prevented her from doing. I told myself that she was probably making an improper use of her freedom down there, and no doubt this idea which I formed seemed to me sad but remained general, showing me no specific details, and, by the indefinite number of possible mistresses which it allowed me to imagine, prevented me from stopping to consider any one of them, drew my mind on in a sort of perpetual motion not untinged with pain, but with a pain which the absence of any concrete image rendered endurable. It ceased, however, to be endurable and became atrocious when Saint-Loup arrived.

(*The Fugitive*, 630–32)

Shirley Hazzard

The ever engrossing question of rendering into English Marcel Proust's *A la recherche* still turns, irresistibly, on the adjusting or supplanting of Charles Scott Moncrieff's long dominant *Remembrance*: a work that, having been the touchstone for generations of Proust's English-reading public, continues—despite necessary amplifications, commendable reworkings, and persistent criticisms—to preside, a lion in the path.

"Reworking" is the word of the late Terence Kilmartin, in his prefatory note to the three-volume edition that, revised by him, incorporates, in its final volume, the translation of *Le Temps retrouvé* by Andreas Mayor. These later translators had the benefit of the elucidated text, in the annotated Pléiade edition, of Proust's labyrinthine manuscript— dense, in its closing section, with the author's insertions and emendations as painfully indicated on his deathbed: matter that had seemed, to the eye of the layman, virtually indecipherable. Proust died in 1922; Scott Moncrieff in 1930. The "reworked" edition of *A la recherche*, revised by Kilmartin, is justly presented as "Translated by C. K. Scott Moncrieff and Terence Kilmartin," and retains its title *Remembrance of Things Past*. Working with close and sympathetic attention to Proust's words and intentions, Kilmartin made adjustments, for the most part necessary and pleasing, to Scott Moncrieff's version, paying tribute to that pioneering translation, which—as Kilmartin says in his prefatory note, has long been regarded "almost as a masterpiece in its own right."

Shirley Hazzard

Himself in ill health, Kilmartin—like Scott Moncrieff—carried his enterprise close to conclusion. That in itself marks him out among revisionists and critics of Scott Moncrieff. The road back from intended retranslations of part or all of the *Recherche* had come, over many years, to resemble those nineteenth-century paintings of the Retreat from Moscow, in which somber marshals astride drooping horses lead an exhausted multitude of putative invaders back from their aborted undertaking, through snowdrifts charged with the bodies of their fallen comrades. In the epic of retranslating Proust, considerations of time, health, finances, fatigue, and no doubt much else have contributed to withdrawals from the field. New millennial translations have as yet dealt with assigned portions, only, of the work. Whoever tackles Proust's novel is taking on the translation, from a most exigent original, of a million and a quarter words scrupulously assembled by one of the most prodigious and complex authors who ever lived. They are confronting, also, a nineteenth-century capacity for magnitude.

In 1853, Gustave Flaubert, seized with the creation of *Madame Bovary*, was already lamenting a literary decline, from the luminous power of the great masters into the troubled assiduity of contemporary writing:

> We must pile up a mass of little pebbles to build our pyramids; theirs, a hundred times greater, were hewn in monoliths.

The genius of magnitude nevertheless persisted, in its terminal phase, into the generation—to which both Proust and Scott Moncrieff belonged—that outlived the 1914–18 war: the Great War, with its everlasting debilitation of civilized conviction and sense of purpose. A reiterated commendation of Scott Moncrieff's approach to his task has logically touched on his close relation to the ambiance, atmosphere, and culture of the Proustian era. Proust's own concept of his immense endeavor had been visionary; as was the decision of his first English translator "to devote his life," in George Painter's words, "to the translation."

A dozen years or more ago, during a particular irruption of criticisms of the Scott Moncrieff rendering, I set myself the game, on summer evenings, of comparing favorite passages of the *Recherche*—spreading

The Proust Project

the original, in the Pléiade volumes, alongside the Scott Moncrieff, together with the "reworked" Kilmartin. One's lasting impression was one
of admiration for both translators; and a renewed sense not only of Scott
Moncrieff's achievement but of its importance as a precedent for every
subsequent contender. The thing had been attempted, it had been done.
It was incontrovertibly there—to be read, enjoyed, praised, patronized,
carped at, disparaged. In the realm of translation, it is a colossus—
daunting even to the most confident of its critics, since, if it is to be
challenged, it cannot merely be "redone"; it must be conspicuously
bettered.

These impressions brought to mind—with allowance for the great
discrepancies of the analogy—remarks by the nineteenth-century historian François Guizot on his successive readings of Edward Gibbon's
Decline and Fall of the Roman Empire:

> After a first rapid perusal, which allowed me to feel nothing but the in-
> terest of the narrative, always animated . . . and always perspicuous, I
> entered upon a minute examination of the details of which it is composed;
> and the opinion which I then formed was, I confess, singularly severe . . .
> I allowed some time to elapse before I reviewed the whole. A second at-
> tentive and regular perusal of the entire work . . . showed me how much
> I had exaggerated the importance of the reproaches which Gibbon really
> deserved; I was struck with the same errors . . . but I had been far from
> doing adequate justice to the immensity of his researches, the variety of
> his knowledge . . . I then felt that his book, in spite of its faults, will al-
> ways be a noble work.

Some such deference lingers with this reader toward the work of Scott
Moncrieff in relation to the persistent, and sometimes derisive, criticisms
to which it is subjected. Aside from essential inclusions of "new" material, and clearly justified modifications, the quality of the huge task—
accomplished in relatively few years and quite without the vaunted
apparatus of modern electronic innovations (which, in fact, in artistic af-
fairs, seem of little assistance when certain ineffable chips are down)—

Shirley Hazzard

still commands wonder; still gives pleasure; still dispenses beauty. Kilmartin acknowledges his fundamental debt to his predecessor. It is unlikely that any full and future rendering into our language of this great novel will not build upon and appreciate Scott Moncrieff's achievement, by now historic—and moving, also, in its evocation of a past ability to embrace the impossible single-handed, and carry it to term.

Readings of recent new translations of separate portions of the *Recherche* suggest that these most often fall below their best standard out of a wish to differ at all costs from Scott Moncrieff. Illustrations of that tendency appeared, some years past, in a lively article in *The New York Times Magazine*, where a group of prominent revisers tried their respective hands at retranslating Proust's celebrated opening sentence: *"Longtemps, je me suis couché de bonne heure"*—conveyed with faithful simplicity by Scott Moncrieff as "For a long time I used to go to bed early." This article was much discussed at the time on the New York literary scene, the verdict falling heavily—in my own experience, unanimously—in favor of Scott Moncrieff's unforced choice of words over the attempts, sometimes ingenious, sometimes desperate, merely to differ. Terence Kilmartin himself discreetly stuck with Scott Moncrieff's plain rendition.

That particular pitfall, familiar as it must be to experienced translators, inexorably lures them. Kilmartin himself is not immune, and in his "reworking" the temptation occasionally makes a significant appearance within more superficial flickerings. To my mind, it blights one of the most poignant exchanges between Proust's lovers—in the days when Albertine, ceasing to be the Prisoner, becomes the Fugitive.

On the eve of her secretly planned departure from Marcel's house, Albertine is invited by Marcel on a twilit drive out of Paris. In the carriage, in an atmosphere of dream, calm falls on their long-tormented relations. For the girl, aware that she is about to put an end to a situation grown intolerable, it is an episode of high sadness, which she invokes in her conclusion to a letter written to Marcel following their rupture:

The Proust Project

Croyez que de mon côté je n'oublierai pas cette promenade deux fois cré-
pusculaire (puisque la nuit venait et que nous allions nous quitter) et
qu'elle ne s'effacera de mon esprit qu'avec la nuit complète.

Scott Moncrieff translates this as follows:

> You may be sure that for my part I shall never forget that drive in a twofold
> twilight (since night was falling and we were about to part) and that it will
> be effaced from my memory only when the darkness is complete.

Kilmartin's version:

> You may be sure that for my part I shall never forget that doubly crepus-
> cular drive (since night was falling and we were about to part) and that it
> will be effaced from my memory only when the darkness is complete.

Kilmartin's impulse to supplant "a twofold twilight" produces an assault on the ear. "Crepuscular," written or spoken, is unnatural in English usage, and distracting. Its sound, evocative in French, is ugly in
our language—and more so, to my thinking, in its heavy-handed cou-
pling with "doubly." Since this brief passage has importance in Proust's
narrative (Marcel mean-spiritedly seizing on it as evidence of his having educated this ignorant girl) and recurs not only in the immediately
following pages but much later in the story, Kilmartin is obliged to repeat the phrase, always with unhappy effect. Scott Moncrieff's "twofold
twilight" does not jar on the ear, and is at melancholy ease with its
Proustian era. It may be criticized, but not readily replaced.

Similarly, in the same brief letter, when Albertine urges caution on
Marcel in dealing with car salesmen—*"Vous vous laisseriez monter le*
coup par ces gens"—Kilmartin's "You would let yourself be taken for a
ride" seems an unnecessary anachronistic correction to Scott Moncrieff's version, that Marcel not let himself "be taken in." Kilmartin perhaps enjoyed the double entendre of the car salesmen and the ride, but
the transatlantic note comes amiss from Albertine.

By which I suggest that Scott Moncrieff does not, as charged, always

Shirley Hazzard

overstate the case, or add to the convolutions of an intricate story; and that his best plain words have been, at times, elaborately brought up to date.

When I, at sixteen and living in Hong Kong in the postwar years, was merely aware of the *Recherche*, with no idea of what was in store, I met, at a gathering, a handsome, reserved, and pleasant person, still young, who was introduced as Miss Scott Moncrieff. I already understood the name's literary significance. It was at once explained, in her presence, that she was—the niece, was it, or a cousin?—of the great translator. She was one of a few women to hold, then, a distinguished, and beneficent, position in the colony; and it occurred to me that she possibly wearied of her reflected glory. Later, the matter being discussed in her absence, I heard, for the first time: "Of course, the whole thing will have to be redone."

Not so easy as all that.

~

Here are two later versions of what will surely be a succession of versions. The first is by D. J. Enright, who revised Scott Moncrieff's and Terence Kilmartin's translations. The second is by Peter Collier, whose translation of *The Captive/The Fugitive* has been published by Penguin as part of Terence Prendergast's team translation of Proust's novel.

"Dear friend, thank you for all the nice things you wrote to me. I am at your disposal for the countermanding of the Rolls, if you think that I can help in any way, as I am sure I can. You have only to let me know the name of the agents. You would let yourself be taken for a ride by these people who are only interested in selling, and what would you do with a motor-car, you who never stir out of the house? I am deeply touched that you have kept a happy memory of our last outing. You may be sure that for my part I shall never forget that drive in a double twilight (since night was falling and we were about to part) and that it will be effaced from my thoughts only when the darkness is complete." —*Translated by D. J. Enright*

The Proust Project

"My dear friend, thank you for all your kind remarks, I am at your disposal and shall cancel the order for the Rolls if you think that I may be of assistance, and I do think it's likely. You have only to tell me the name of your agent. You would be liable to let yourself be taken in by these people who have only one thing in mind, which is to make a sale; and what would you do with a car, since you never go out? I am very touched that you should have kept such a nice memory of our last outing. Please believe that for my part I shall never forget this excursion and its twofold twilight (since night was falling and we were destined to part) and that it will never be erased from my mind until blackest night finally invades it." —*Translated by Peter Collier*

In differing degree, these renderings strike me as suffering from what might be called translation fatigue—or, more explicitly, version fatigue. To his impassioned (or, some would say, overwrought) rendition of *La Recherche*, Scott Moncrieff brought the irreducible advantage of precedence: he was breaking new ground. He would reveal Proust's masterpiece—as far as then possible, in its entirety—to the English-reading world for the first time, in the process disclosing and developing his own interpretative powers over word and mood. He had been at work on the translation some years before being formally, and rather awkwardly, confirmed as its English translator. Every subsequent translator of Proust into English has been necessarily and monumentally aware of this precursor, and of those who followed him. Flaws have been established and corrected, revisions have been attempted. Vocabulary and syntax have been weighed for possible innovation and improvement. And consciousness of these handlings and fingerings may have elusively acted on, and dimmed, the freshness of impression that inspired Scott Moncrieff and excited his readers. Assiduity has edged out élan.

In the two later translations given above, the opening lines of the passage, dealing with the prosaic car, carry none of the tension inevitably existing between two lovers who, so recently parted in emotional exhaustion, are resuming tentative contact under a flag of truce. Awaiting word from Albertine, Marcel sees her handwriting with anxiety and expectation. In Scott Moncrieff's version, there is throughout this passage

Shirley Hazzard

a tremor of context, ineffably conveyed: the reader is aware that Albertine's remarks about the car are prelude to, and pretext, merely, for, her reversion to the poignant twilit drive and her declaration of lasting love. We ourselves, as readers, open and begin her letter sensing that something more is to come. In the latter versions, however, the shift comes abruptly, so that concern for the car appears to be given equal weight with the girl's poetic invocation of loss and remembrance.

It is hard to see how this slackening can be avoided. In the case of Proust, translators, multiplying, will naturally give attention to the work of predecessors. And, in a greater context than that of this small passage, the trend of much contemporary writing turns away from distinction: flair, style, singularity are suspect as "rhetoric." The tendency, when not infused with violence, can be rigorously poker-faced, as if a regiment of Buster Keatons were policing our once-expressive language. Marcel himself, moved by the closing words of Albertine's letter, seeks to neutralize them as hyperbole, or traces in them his own civilizing influence over her youthful ignorance. However, the words will haunt him by their generosity, as does the dignity of this farewell.

Whatever his weaknesses, Scott Moncrieff did not forget that he was dealing with greatness—already then an embattled concept in literature. Many years earlier, Gustave Flaubert, inexorable but never abstract, had himself noted—in a letter of December 1852 to Louise Colet—a new pressure on writers to move away from their fertile eccentricities toward "the modern democratic idea of equality"; citing with disdain François Charles Fourier's observation that "great men won't be needed." Distrust of stature, which leaves its reductive mark on much new writing, surely need not infect fresh renderings of past greatness.

Two letters arrive on the same day: one informing him that Albertine had been killed in a riding accident, the other from Albertine, containing the desired response: "Is it not too late for me to return to you? If you have not yet written to Andrée, would you be prepared to take me back?"

Marcel continues to investigate rumors of Albertine's lesbian assignations in the public baths until a long-desired trip to Venice with his mother diverts him from this obsession.

As often as not we would set off for St Mark's, with all the more pleasure because, since one had to take a gondola to go there, the church represented for me not simply a monument but the terminus of a voyage on these vernal, maritime waters, with which, I felt, St Mark's formed an indivisible and living whole. My mother and I would enter the baptistery, treading underfoot the marble and glass mosaics of the paving, in front of us the wide arcades whose curved pink surfaces have been slightly warped by time, thus giving the church, wherever the freshness of this colouring has been preserved, the appearance of having been built of a soft and malleable substance like the wax in a giant honeycomb, and, where on the contrary time has shrivelled and hardened the material and artists have embellished it with gold tracery, of being the precious binding, in the finest Cordoba leather, of the colossal Gospel of Venice. Seeing that I needed to spend some time in front of the mosaics representing the Baptism of Christ, and feeling the icy coolness that pervaded the baptistery, my mother threw a shawl over my shoulders. When I was with Albertine at Balbec, I felt that she was revealing one of those insubstantial illusions which clutter the minds of so many people who do not think clearly, when she used to speak of the pleasure—to my mind baseless—that she would derive from seeing works of art with me. Today I am sure that the pleasure does exist, if not of seeing, at least of having seen, a beautiful thing with a particular person. A time has now come when, remembering the baptistery of

The Fugitive

St Mark's—contemplating the waters of the Jordan in which St John immerses Christ, while the gondola awaited us at the landing-stage of the Piazzetta—it is no longer a matter of indifference to me that, beside me in that cool penumbra, there should have been a woman draped in her mourning with the respectful and enthusiastic fervour of the old woman in Carpaccio's *St Ursula* in the Accademia, and that that woman, with her red cheeks and sad eyes and in her black veils, whom nothing can ever remove from that softly lit sanctuary of St Mark's where I am always sure to find her because she has her place reserved there as immutably as a mosaic, should be my mother.

Carpaccio, as it happens, who was the painter we visited most readily when I was not working in St Mark's, almost succeeded one day in reviving my love for Albertine. I was seeing for the first time *The Patriarch of Grado exorcising a demoniac*. I looked at the marvelous rose-pink and violet sky and the tall encrusted chimneys silhouetted against it, their flared stacks, blossoming like red tulips, reminiscent of so many Whistlers of Venice. Then my eyes travelled from the old wooden Rialto to that fifteenth-century Ponte Vecchio with its marble palaces decorated with gilded capitals, and returned to the canal on which the boats are manoeuvred by adolescents in pink jackets and plumed toques, the spitting image of those avowedly inspired by Carpaccio in that dazzling *Legend of Joseph* by Sert, Strauss and Kessler. Finally, before leaving the picture, my eyes came back to the shore, swarming with the everyday Venetian life of the period. I looked at the barber wiping his razor, at the Negro humping his barrel, at the Muslims conversing, at the noblemen in wide-sleeved brocade and damask robes and hats of cerise velvet, and suddenly I felt a slight gnawing at my heart. On the back of one of the *Compagni della Calza* identifiable from the emblem, embroidered in gold and pearls on their sleeves or their collars, of the merry confraternity to which they were affiliated, I had just recognised the cloak which Albertine had put on to come with me to Versailles in an open carriage on the evening when I so little suspected that scarcely fifteen hours separated me from the moment of her departure from my house. Always ready for anything, when I had asked her to come out with me on that melancholy occasion which she was to describe in her last letter as "a double twilight since night was falling and we were about to part," she had flung over her shoulders a Fortuny cloak which she had taken away with her next day and which I had never thought of since. It was from this Carpaccio picture that that inspired son of Venice had taken it, it was from the shoulders of this *Compagno della Calza* that he had removed it in order to drape it over the shoulders of so many Parisian women who were certainly unaware, as I had been until then, that the model for it existed in a group of noblemen in the foreground of the *Patriarch of Grado* in a room in the Accademia in Venice. I had recognised it down to the last detail, and, that forgotten cloak having restored to me as I looked at it the eyes and the heart of him who had set out that evening with Albertine for Versailles, I was overcome for a few moments by a vague and soon dissipated feeling of desire and melancholy.

There were days when my mother and I were not content with visiting the museums and churches of Venice only, and once, when the weather was particularly fine, in order to see the "Virtues" and "Vices" of which M. Swann had given me reproductions that were probably still hanging on the wall of the schoolroom at Combray, we went as far afield as Padua. After walking across the garden of the Arena in the glare of the sun, I entered the Giotto chapel, the entire ceiling of which and the background of the frescoes are so blue that it seems as though the radiant daylight has crossed the threshold with the human visitor in order to give its pure sky a momentary breather in the coolness and shade, a sky merely of a slightly deeper blue now that it is rid of the glitter of the sunlight, as in those brief moments of respite when, though no cloud is to be seen, the sun has turned its gaze elsewhere and the azure, softer still, grows deeper. This sky transplanted on to the blue-washed stone was peopled with flying angels which I was seeing for the first time, for M. Swann had given me reproductions only of the Vices and Virtues and not of the frescoes depicting the life of the Virgin and of Christ. Watching the flight of these angels, I had the same impression of actual movement, literally real activity, that the gestures of Charity and Envy had given me. For all the celestial fervour, or at least the childlike obedience and application, with

The Fugitive

which their minuscule hands are joined, they are represented in the Arena chapel as winged creatures of a particular species that had really existed, that must have figured in the natural history of biblical and apostolic times. Constantly flitting about above the saints whenever the latter walk abroad, these little beings, since they are real creatures with a genuine power of flight, can be seen soaring upwards, describing curves, "looping the loop," diving earthwards head first, with the aid of wings which enable them to support themselves in positions that defy the laws of gravity, and are far more reminiscent of an extinct species of bird, or of young pupils of Garros practising gliding, than of the angels of the Renaissance and later periods whose wings have become no more than emblems and whose deportment is generally the same as that of heavenly beings who are not winged.

(*The Fugitive*, 875–78)

Louis Begley

As *The Fugitive*, the penultimate volume of the *Search*, opens, Albertine has asked for her trunks and left. Her letter of farewell, if it is to be believed, announces a definite rupture. Summoned by the distraught Marcel, who will stage-manage his every move, Robert de Saint-Loup attempts to bring her back. In vain: Albertine has been killed in a riding accident. Marcel believes he must soon follow her to the grave. However, sometime later, when his mother takes him on his long-delayed first visit to Venice, he realizes that in the meantime his indifference toward Albertine has become absolute. She has survived as a bundle of thoughts; time having changed Marcel into a new man, those thoughts have no power to move him. Love for Albertine, just as his earlier love for Gilberte, has succumbed to what Proust calls the general law of oblivion.

That the setting for this bleak and cruel discovery should be Venice is a masterstroke of irony. Ever since his father, on doctor's orders, canceled an Easter trip there, Venice has exercised a special power over Marcel's imagination—as the city of Titian and Giorgione and Gothic architecture, and also as an aquatic Baghdad in which, like a character out of the *Arabian Tales*, he would find nocturnal adventures. To go there, with Albertine, is out of the question: she would escape his surveillance in Venice more easily than in Paris. But when his jealousy slackens

Louis Begley

sufficiently for the tedium of cohabitation to be felt, he regrets wasting in her presence the time he could have spent in Venice. In fact, at the very instant Françoise tells Marcel of Albertine's sudden departure, he is preparing to go to Venice alone, without saying goodbye.

Soon after the Venetian episode, Gilberte marries Saint-Loup. Their union obliterates the geographical and class distinctions that are among Marcel's founding myths. Saint-Loup is a Guermantes. The Swann and Guermantes families being thus linked, the opposites represented by the destinations of the ritual afternoon walks undertaken in the golden age of Combray, *du côté de chez Swann* and *du côté de Guermantes,* are no longer irreconcilable. In fact, the shortcut that Gilberte shows Marcel makes the distance between Swann's property and the ducal fief negligible. The upheaval does not stop there. Saint-Loup's tender and respectful affection for Marcel and for the grandmother, since the first visit to Balbec, has been one of the happier themes of the *Search*. But Saint-Loup's marriage to Gilberte coincides with another discovery: Saint-Loup, like his uncle, Baron de Charlus, is relentlessly homosexual. Men's sexual leanings are of no concern to Marcel. However, Saint-Loup's betraying Gilberte with Charlie Morel, Charlus's tormentor and former lover, is another matter. It shows Saint-Loup to be so vilely false that Marcel is brought to the point of tears, although he tells himself that he does not believe in friendship, and did not feel any for Saint-Loup.

The passage by Proust I have chosen is a metaphor, of extraordinary power, for the universal disillusionment and devastation recorded in *The Fugitive*. As Marcel ponders the near certainty that his mother's train will pull out of the station while he, strangely paralyzed by a vulgar street song, will remain in Venice, alone with the knowledge that he has wounded his mother, the unearthly beauty of the palaces lining both sides of the Grand Canal vanishes. Stage lights illuminating a painted set have been dimmed. Marcel is no longer able to breathe life into "the lifeless heaps of marble." Only the dolorous image of the mother withstands the devastation.

In fact, Marcel will get to the station in time and rejoin his equally anguished mother. Her role is almost concluded; she will not appear in *Time Regained*, the last volume of the *Search*. Venice will. And it will do so in the great epiphany scene, when the reawakened memory of the uneven paving stones in the baptistery of St. Mark's enables Marcel to penetrate the mysteries first hinted at by the taste of a madeleine, and to confirm the reality of his literary vocation.

On his return from Venice, Marcel slowly reconciles himself to Albertine's death. During his absence, the widowed Odette Swann has become Madame de Forcheville. Taking advantage of her mother's new name, Gilberte rechristens herself Mademoiselle de Forcheville, doing away with the Jewish name of her father. But this is not to last long. Presently Marcel receives word that Gilberte has become Madame de Saint-Loup, the wife of his devoted friend Robert.

After having spent several years in a sanatorium receiving treatment for his ill health, Marcel is recently returned to Paris.

Planes drone through the night sky. The only figures moving on the deserted nighttime streets are soldiers. The war has made Paris a place of foreboding. Finding himself far from home at nightfall during a curfew, Marcel spots an inn and asks for a room. The guests are mostly soldiers, on leave from the battle. Finding his room stuffy, he leaves it and begins looking around the building. He hears, from the end of a corridor, a man screaming, and then finally a voice: "I beseech you, mercy, have pity, untie me, don't beat me so hard!" Walking toward the voice, he finds a small oval window through which he sees a man tied to a bed, receiving blows from a studded whip. It is Monsieur de Charlus.

Shortly after, Jupien, the tailor, walks in. Charlus complains to him about his tormentor; he does not hit him hard enough. But he is a real criminal! Jupien tells him. Monsieur de Charlus, however, is the one in authority here: he owns the house.

Marcel leaves Paris again, to tend to his poor health in yet another sanatorium.

When he returns years later, the war is over, and there are many changes. His best friend, Robert de Saint-Loup, has been killed and Gilberte is a widow. The Princesse de Guermantes has died, and there is now a new Princesse de Guermantes: the former Madame Verdurin. Marcel has been invited to a matinee at the home of the Duc and the Duchesse de Guermantes; it is to be his first time in society since his return to Paris.

The Proust Project

T he cab turned into the Champs-Elysées and, as I did not particularly want to hear the whole of the concert which was being given at the Guermantes party, I stopped it and was preparing to get out in order to walk a few yards when I was struck by the spectacle presented by another cab which was also stopping. A man with staring eyes and hunched figure was placed rather than seated in the back, and was making, to keep himself upright, the efforts that might have been made by a child who has been told to be good. But his straw hat failed to conceal an unruly forest of hair which was entirely white, and a white beard, like those which snow forms on the statues of river-gods in public gardens, flowed from his chin. It was—side by side with Jupien, who was unremitting in his attentions to him—M. de Charlus, now convalescent after an attack of apoplexy of which I had had no knowledge (I had only been told that he had lost his sight, but in fact this trouble had been purely temporary and he could now see quite well again) and which, unless the truth was that hitherto he had dyed his hair and that he had now been forbidden to continue so fatiguing a practice, had had the effect, as in a sort of chemical precipitation, of rendering visible and brilliant all that saturation of metal which the locks of his hair and his beard, pure silver now, shot forth like so many geysers, so that upon the old fallen prince this latest illness had conferred the Shakespearian majesty of a King Lear. His eyes had not remained unaffected by this total convulsion, this metallurgical transformation of his head, but had, by an inverse phenomenon, lost all their brightness. But what was most moving was that one felt that this lost brightness was identical with his moral pride, and that somehow the physical and even the intellectual life of M. de Charlus had survived the eclipse of that aristocratic haughtiness which had in the past seemed indissolubly linked to them. To confirm this, at the moment which I am describing, there passed in a victoria, no doubt also on her way to the reception of the Prince de Guermantes, Mme de Saint-Euverte, whom formerly the Baron had not considered elegant enough for him. Jupien, who tended him like a child, whispered in his ear that it was someone with whom he was acquainted, Mme de Saint-Euverte. And immediately, with infinite laboriousness but with all the concentration of a sick man determined to show that he is capable of all the movements which are still difficult for him, M. de Charlus lifted his hat, bowed, and greeted Mme de Saint-Euverte as respectfully as if she had been the Queen of France or as if he had been a small child coming timidly in obedience to his mother's command to say "How do you do?" to a grown-up person. For a child, but without a child's pride, was what he had once more become. Perhaps the very difficulty that M. de Charlus had in making these gestures was in itself a reason for him to make them, in the knowledge that he would create a greater effect by an action which, painful for an invalid, became thereby doubly meritorious on the part of the man who performed it and doubly flattering to the individual to whom it was addressed, invalids, like kings, practising exaggerated civility. Perhaps also there was in the movements of the Baron that lack of co-ordination which follows upon maladies of the spinal column and the brain, so that his gestures went beyond anything that he intended. What I myself saw in them was above all a sort of gentleness, an almost physical gentleness, and of detachment from the realities of life, phenomena so strikingly apparent in those whom death has already drawn within its shadow. And the exposure of the veins of silver in his hair was less indicative of profound alterations than this unconscious humility which turned all social relations upside down and abased before Mme de Saint-Euverte—as it would have abased before the most vulgar of American hostesses (who at last would have been able to congratulate herself on the hitherto unattainable politeness of the Baron)—what had seemed to be the proudest snobbishness of all. For the Baron still lived, still thought; his intellect was not impaired. And more than any chorus of Sophocles on the humbled pride of Oedipus, more than death itself or any funeral oration on the subject of death, the humble greeting, full of effort to please, which the Baron addressed to Mme de

The Proust Project

Saint-Euverte proclaimed the fragile and perishable nature of the love of earthly greatness and all human pride. M. de Charlus, who until this moment would never have consented to dine with Mme de Saint-Euverte, now bowed to the ground in her honour. To receive the homage of M. de Charlus had been, for her, the highest ambition of snobbery, just as, for the Baron, the central principle of snobbery had been to be rude to her. And now this inaccessible and precious essence which he had succeeded in making Mme de Saint-Euverte believe to be part of his nature, had at a single stroke been annihilated by M. de Charlus, by the earnest timidity, the apprehensive zeal with which he raised a hat from beneath which, all the while that his head remained deferentially uncovered, there streamed with the eloquence of a Bossuet the torrents of his silvery hair. Jupien helped the Baron to descend and I greeted him. He spoke to me very rapidly, in a voice so inaudible that I could not distinguish what he was saying, which wrung from him, when for the third time I made him repeat his remarks, a gesture of impatience that astonished me by its contrast with the impassivity which his face had at first displayed, which was no doubt an after-effect of his stroke. But when after a while I had grown accustomed to this pianissimo of whispered words, I perceived that the sick man retained the use of his intelligence absolutely intact.

There were, however, two M. de Charluses, not to mention any others. Of the two, one, the intellectual one, passed his time in complaining that he suffered from progressive aphasia, that he constantly pronounced one word, one letter by mistake for another. But as soon as he actually made such a mistake, the other M. de Charlus, the subconscious one, who was as desirous of admiration as the first was of pity and out of vanity did things that the first would have despised, immediately, like a conductor whose orchestra has blundered, checked the phrase which he had started and with infinite ingenuity made the end of his sentence follow coherently from the word which he had in fact uttered by mistake for another but which he thus appeared to have chosen. Even his memory was intact, and from it his vanity impelled him, not without the fatigue of the most laborious concentration, to drag forth this or that ancient recollection, of no importance, which concerned myself and which would

Time Regained

demonstrate to me that he had preserved or recovered all his lucidity of mind. Without moving his head or his eyes, and without varying in the slightest degree the modulation of his voice, he said to me, for instance: "Look, there's a poster on that telegraph-pole like the one which I was standing near when I saw you for the first time at Avranches—no, I am mistaken, at Balbec." And it was in fact an advertisement for the same product.

I had found it difficult at first to understand what he was saying, just as one begins by seeing absolutely nothing in a room of which all the curtains are closed. But like one's eyes in half-darkness, my ears soon accustomed themselves to this pianissimo. The sound had in any case, I think, gradually grown in volume while the Baron was speaking, perhaps because the weakness of his voice was due in part to a nervous apprehension which was dispelled when he was distracted by the presence of another person and ceased to think about it, though possibly, on the other hand, the feeble voice corresponded to the real state of his health and the momentary strength with which he spoke in conversation was the result of an artificial, transient and even dangerous excitement, which might make strangers say: "He is much better, he must stop thinking about his illness," but in fact only aggravated the illness, which lost no time in resuming its sway. Whatever the explanation may be, the Baron at this moment (even making allowances for the improvement in my own hearing) was flinging down his words with greater force, as the tide, on days of bad weather, flings down its little contorted waves. And the traces of his recent attack caused one to hear at the back of his words a noise like that of pebbles dragged by the sea. Continuing to speak to me about the past, no doubt to prove to me that he had not lost his memory, he evoked it now—in a funereal fashion but without sadness—by reciting an endless list of all the people belonging to his family or his world who were no longer alive, less, it seemed, with any emotion of grief that they were dead than with satisfaction at having survived them. He appeared indeed, as he recalled their extinction, to enjoy a clearer perception of his own return towards health and it was with an almost triumphal sternness that he repeated, in a monotonous tone, stammering slightly and

The Proust Project

with a dull sepulchral resonance: "Hannibal de Bréauté, dead! Antoine de Mouchy, dead! Charles Swann, dead! Adalbert de Montmorency, dead! Boson de Talleyrand, dead! Sosthène de Doudeauville, dead!" And every time he uttered it, the word "dead" seemed to fall upon his departed friends like a spadeful of earth each heavier than the last, thrown by a grave-digger grimly determined to immure them yet more closely within the tomb.

(*Time Regained*, 244–47)

Leslie Epstein

After many years away from Paris, and in a despondent mood, Marcel comes across the aged Monsieur de Charlus. Still recovering from a stroke, the baron is bent, nearly immobile, and though he can speak, sometimes in torrents, Marcel can hear the death rattle, like wave-tossed pebbles, at the back of his throat. He is at once majestic, almost godlike, and ruined, much like the once arrogant but ultimately fond and foolish old Lear. When Monsieur de Charlus, painfully and with "earnest timidity," removes his hat before Madame de Saint-Euverte, with whom he would never before consent to dine, the gesture has about it the aura of humbled pride with which the aged king turns to one of his subjects: "Pray you undo this button. Thank you, sir." And just as Lear has only a bemused regard for the grand social order he once fought to maintain, reducing it to the mere chatter of "who loses and who wins; who's in, who's out," so too does the baron speak with demented reck-lessness of admiration for France's chief enemy and threaten to create constant scandal by exposing those—"You know, you're just as much one as I am"—with the same tendencies as himself.

But what matters most in this wrecked nobleman is not what was overthrown but what persists. For in Charlus we see the man, the child, and even—"he is really just a big baby now"—the infant he once was. The intellect is intact. The mind is lucid. The memory thrives. What en-dures with the most force, however, is the instinctual life that has always defined him. At his most enfeebled, he had managed to pick up a ten-year-old, albeit baritone, boy. And the last Marcel sees of the baron (at first glimpse, decades before, he had admired his fine attire but did not fail to note the nearly invisible spot on his tie "like a liberty one dares not take"), he has just begun a conversation with a gardener's boy.

Proust does not paint this portrait, as moving and terrible as Shakespeare's of Lear, for its own sake but for its impact on his hero. Before this encounter, fresh from a sanatorium, he had been in a mood of "languorous boredom," indifferent to the beauty of nature and certain that "[i]f ever I thought of myself as a poet, I know now that I am not one." After this meeting, he walks on to an afternoon party at the Princesse de Guermantes's, and things begin to change. Almost at once he allows himself to be inundated by a series of sensory impressions—the feel of uneven paving stones, the touch of a starched napkin, the ring of a spoon on a plate—that revive in him the lost paradise of his past in ways that memory alone is incapable of doing. As if by magic all his doubts and dissatisfactions are replaced by a confidence and a joyousness that he had experienced only at similar, but isolated, moments of his life. He even feels stirring within him the rebirth of his "literary gifts."

Is he, then, ready to write? Not yet. First he must reexperience his meeting with the baron—that is, he must face his host and his guests, the glamorous figures from his past, all of whom seem to have disguised themselves in powdered wigs. The women are bent, as if their dresses had already become entangled on their tombstones, and the tremor on the lips of the men strikes him as the utterance of a final prayer. It is, then, with a shock that freezes his blood, that Marcel realizes that these signs of old age in others have signaled to him "the approach of my own."

Even the shock of his own mortality is not enough—quite—to propel him to set to work in search of lost time. There must first be one last encounter, this time with Mademoiselle de Saint-Loup, an encounter that will balance, enhance, and fulfill the implications of the earlier one with Monsieur de Charlus. It takes place in the single paragraph we have seen above.

What Marcel sees before him is, in a manner of speaking, the novel he wishes to write, and in referring to this vision as a masterpiece of Time, it is clear that he knows it. Charlus, an old man, carried within him his lost youth; this girl of sixteen carries within her all those Marcel had loved and who have grown old. Here is the birdlike head and piercing eyes of her father, Saint-Loup; the nose, not so much of her grandfather, Swann (Mademoiselle de Saint-Loup has been de-Judaized, while the nose of the aged Bloch, a guest at the same party, remains as Semitic as that of his most ancient ancestors), as of Gilberte, and of her grandmother, Odette. Unlike the baron, she represents not an ending but a beginning, "still rich in hopes." Indeed, we have already seen, through the collapsing telescope of time, that she will marry a mere man of letters, and in so doing end the idolatry of the social order that her grandmother's friend, Marcel, and all his friends, too, once so assiduously practiced.

And Marcel Proust himself? With these two encounters and the revelations that occurred between them, he can at last put down his pen, while simultaneously that other Marcel, having found his strength and his great idea, can pick up his and so "set to work. It was high time."

And yet, in complete contrast with these, I had the surprise of talking to men and women whom I remembered as unendurable and who had now, I found, lost almost every one of their defects, possibly because life, by disappointing or by gratifying their desires, had rid them of most of their conceit or their bitterness. A rich marriage, with the consequence that struggle and ostentation had ceased to be necessary, the influence perhaps of the wife herself, the slowly acquired knowledge of values beyond those that had formed the whole creed of a frivolous youth, had allowed them to relax the tensions in their character and to display their good qualities. Growing old, they seemed to have acquired a different personality, like those trees whose essential nature appears to be changed by the autumn which alters their colours; the essential marks of old age were manifested in them, but old age, here, was a moral phenomenon. In others, it was almost entirely physical, and so strange were its effects that a person (Mme d'Arpajon, for instance) seemed to me at the same time unknown and familiar. Unknown, for it was impossible to suspect that it was she and in spite of every effort I could not help showing signs, as I responded to her salutation, of the mental activity which made me hesitate between three or four individuals, not one of whom was Mme d'Arpajon and any one of whom I thought that I might be greeting, and greeting with a fervour which must have astonished her, for, fearing in my uncertainty to appear too chilly should she turn out to be an old and close friend, I had made up for the doubtful expression of my eyes by the warmth of my hand-shake and my smile. And yet, in a way, her new appearance was not unfamiliar to me. It was the appearance, often seen by me in the course of my life, of certain stout, eldery women, of whom at the time I had never suspected that, many years earlier, they could have looked like Mme d'Arpajon. So different was she to look at from the woman I had known that one was tempted to think of her as a creature condemned, like a character in a pantomime, to appear first as a young girl, then as a stout matron, with no doubt a final appearance still to come as a quavering, bent old crone.

Time Regained

Like a swimmer in difficulties almost out of sight of the shore, she seemed with infinite effort scarcely to move through the waves of time which beat upon her and threatened to submerge her. Yet gradually, as I studied her face, hesitant and uncertain like a failing memory which has begun to lose the images of the past, I succeeded in rediscovering something of the face which I had known, by playing a little game of eliminating the squares and the hexagons which age had added to her cheeks. For in her case the material which the years had superimposed consisted of geometrical shapes, though on the cheeks of other women it might be of quite a different character. On those, for instance, of Mme de Guermantes, in many respects so little changed and yet composite now like a bar of nougat, I could distinguish traces here and there of verdigris, a small pink patch of fragmentary shell-work, and a little growth of an indefinable character, smaller than a mistletoe berry and less transparent than a glass bead.

Some men walked with a limp, and one was aware that this was the result not of a motor accident but of a first stroke: they had already, as the saying is, one foot in the grave. There were women too whose graves were waiting open to receive them: half paralysed, they could not quite disentangle their dress from the tomb-stone in which it had got stuck, so that they were unable to stand up straight but remained bent towards the ground, with their head lowered, in a curve which seemed an apt symbol of their own position on the trajectory from life to death, with the final vertical plunge not far away. Nothing now could check the momentum of this parabola upon which they were launched; they trembled all over if they attempted to straighten themselves, and their fingers let fall whatever they tried to grasp.

Certain faces, beneath their hood of white hair, had already the rigidity, the sealed eyelids of those who are about to die, and their lips, shaken by an incessant tremor, seemed to be muttering a last prayer. A countenance of which every line was unchanged needed only the substitution of white hair for black or fair to look totally different, for, as theatrical costumiers know, a powdered wig is in itself an adequate disguise which will make its wearer unrecognisable. The Marquis de Beausergent, whom I had seen, as a young lieutenant, in Mme de Cambremer's box on the day on which Mme de Guermantes had been with her cousin in hers, still had the same perfectly regular features, indeed they had become even more regular, since the pathological rigidity brought about by arteriosclerosis had even further exaggerated the impassive rectitude of his dandy's physiognomy and given to his features the intense hardness of outline, almost grimacing in its immobility, that they might have had in a study by Mantegna or Michelangelo. His complexion, once almost ribaldly red, was now solemnly pale; silvery hair, a slight portliness, the dignity of a Doge, an air of fatigue, even of somnolence, all combined to give him a new and premonitory impression of doomed majesty. The square light brown beard had gone and in its place was a square white beard, of the same trim proportions, which so totally transformed his appearance that, noticing that the second lieutenant whom I remembered now had five bands of braid on his sleeve, my first thought was to congratulate him, not on having been promoted colonel but on looking so well in the part of colonel, a disguise for which he seemed to have borrowed, together with the uniform, the lugubrious gravity of the senior officer that his father had been. But there was another guest whose face, in spite of the substitution of a white for a fair beard, had remained lively, smiling and boyish, so that the change of beard merely made him appear more rubicund and more pugnacious and enhanced the sparkle in his eye, giving to the still youthful man about town the inspired air of a prophet.

The transformations effected, in the women particularly, by the white hair and by other new features, would not have held my attention so forcibly had they been merely changes of colour, which can be charming to behold; too often they were changes of personality, registered not by the eye but, disturbingly, by the mind. For to "recognise" someone, and, *a fortiori*, to learn someone's identity after having failed to recognise him, is to predicate two contradictory things of a single subject, it is to admit that what was here, the person whom one remembers, no longer exists, and also that what is now here is a person whom one did not know to exist; and to do this we have to apprehend a mystery almost as disturbing as that of death, of which it is, indeed, as it were the preface and

Time Regained

the harbinger. I knew what these changes meant, I knew what they were the prelude to, and that is why the white hair of these women, along with all the other changes, profoundly disquieted me. I was told a name and I was dumbfounded to think that it could be used to describe both the fair-haired girl, the marvellous waltzer, whom I had known in the past, and the massive white-haired lady making her way through the room with elephantine tread. Along with a certain rosiness of complexion, the name was perhaps the only thing common to these two women, the girl in my memory and the lady at the Guermantes party, who were more unlike one another than an *ingénue* and a dowager in a play. To have succeeded in giving to the waltzer this huge body, in encumbering and retarding her movements by the adjustment of an invisible metronome, in substituting—with perhaps as sole common factor the cheeks, larger certainly now than in youth but already in those days blotched with red—for the feather-light fair girl this ventripotent old campaigner, it must have been necessary for life to accomplish a vaster work of dismantlement and reconstruction than is involved in the replacement of a steeple by a dome, and when one considered that this work had been effected not with tractable inorganic matter but with living flesh which can only change imperceptibly, the overwhelming contrast between the apparition before me and the creature that I remembered pushed back the existence of the latter into a past that was more than remote, that was almost unimaginable. One was terrified, because it made one think of the vast periods which must have elapsed before such a revolution could be accomplished in the geology of a face, to see what erosions had taken place all the way along the nose, what huge alluvial deposits at the edge of the cheeks surrounded the whole face with their opaque and refractory masses. It was difficult to find a link between the two figures, past and present, to think of the two individuals as possessing the same name; for just as one has difficulty in thinking that a dead person was once alive or that a person who was alive is now dead, so one has difficulty, almost as great and of the same kind (for the extinction of youth, the destruction of a person full of energy and high spirits is already a kind of annihilation), in conceiving that she who was once a girl is now an old woman

The Proust Project

when the juxtaposition of the two appearances, the old and the young, seems so totally to exclude the possibility of their belonging to the same person that alternately it is the old woman and then the girl and then again the old woman who seems to one to be a dream, so that one might well refuse to believe that *this* can ever have been *that*, that the material of *that* has not taken refuge elsewhere but has itself, thanks to the subtle manipulations of Time, turned into *this*, that it is the same matter incorporated in the same body, were it not for the evidence of the similar name and the corroborative testimony of friends, to which an appearance of verisimilitude is given only by the pink upon the cheeks, once a small patch surrounded by the golden corn of fair hair, now a broad expanse beneath the snow.

(*Time Regained*, 362–67)

Diane Johnson

Jealousy is Marcel Proust's avowed subject, perhaps almost as much as memory is, an emotion that dominates his work most obviously in the lives of his creations—say, of Swann in his obsession with Odette, or Marcel himself in his obsession with Albertine. It comes in different forms. Sexual jealousy is everywhere. We know about all of it because Marcel, acutely aware of and fascinated by all the permutations of jealousy, recounts in detail the harrowed feelings of his characters and his own.

But there is another form, social jealousy, or envy, and envy is in fact in Proust the more powerful emotion. We see it in the competitive gatherings, tense dinners, and nervous changes of clothes that fill the immense novel. Proust's is a society where jealousy is an acknowledged wellspring of behavior, *bien sur*; but there is an undercurrent of this constricting emotion that perhaps Marcel is even unaware of, so organically does it color even the simplest and wittiest of his observations. Take a passage like this one, written in the last volume about a party he attended:

"I had the surprise of talking to men and women whom I remembered as unendurable and who had now, I found, lost almost every one of their defects, possibly because life, by disappointing or by gratifying their desires, had rid them of most of their conceit or their bitterness."

On the surface, this is the most genial of observations, in which Marcel seems to find his acquaintance uniformly smoothed out into acceptability after the rocky courses of their lives during the long time he has known them; but the phrase that alerts us is that he "remembered [them]

The Proust Project

as unendurable." This is Marcel's judgment alone, inadvertently revealing that he had liked neither the self-confident, whose assurance he envied, nor the bitter, though the latter, presumably, he had not envied so much then as now when he remarks on their enviable, gratified condition. He had, however, judged them harshly all along: unbearable.

Where there is envy, can malice be far behind?

For the companion and product of envy is malice, and it is both that we sense in Marcel's remarks here: the desire for what others have, hence the malice, the hint of schadenfreude with which he has tracked their progress.

But perhaps Proust the great writer, all-knowing about himself as about others, is concerned not to spare Marcel along with everybody else. Perhaps the writer's Olympian perspective obliges him to expose Marcel even as Marcel wittily indicts others. In the cork-lined room, envy and malice give way to artistic penetration.

Marcel arrives at the Guermantes home for the matinee. Crossing the courtyard, lost in thought, he does not see a car approaching him. He jumps aside just at the last moment, trips on an uneven pavement and is immediately overwhelmed by an eruption of joy. Sensations, memories he is long familiar with, course through him, but memories . . . of what? He rights himself and, to the amusement of the crowd of chauffeurs, repeats the staggering motion over and over, trying to reel out the obstinate memory to which the intensity of this joy is attached. He recalls similar moments of insight: the steeples of Martinville moving across the landscape as he rode in the carriage; the madeleine in tea he used to take with his long-dead aunt Léonie. He staggers on the paving stones, and then . . . Venice pours through him—Venice, with his mother, the baptistery of St. Mark's, his feet upon uneven stones . . .

He enters the house. Music is being performed inside; he is asked to wait in the library until the performance his finished. A butler, trying to be as silent as possible, clangs a spoon against a plate. It is the sound of a railwayman hammering the wheel of a train stopped in a forest years ago. Marcel wipes his face with a napkin, a napkin of the very same stiffness as those of the hotel at Balbec and that felt so strange on his very first, lonely day in Balbec.

He does not just feel these moments again; it is memory itself that he feels. The music finishes and he is ushered into the parlor of the Guermantes.

With everything coming together in this triple revelation, Marcel is finally ready to undertake the vocation that had been awaiting him all his life long. He will write the story of his life.

While I was asking myself these questions, it occurred to me suddenly that, if I still had the strength to accomplish my work, this afternoon—like certain days long ago at Combray which had influenced me—which in its brief compass had given me both the idea of my work and the fear of being unable to bring it to fruition, would certainly impress upon it that form of which as a child I had had a presentiment in the church at Combray but which ordinarily, throughout our lives, is invisible to us: the form of Time.

Many errors, it is true, there are, as the reader will have seen that various episodes in this story had proved to me, by which our senses falsify for us the real nature of the world. Some of these, however, it would be possible for me to avoid by the efforts which I should make to give a more exact transcription of things. In the case of sounds, for instance, I should be able to refrain from altering their place of origin, from detaching them from their cause, beside which our intelligence only succeeds in locating them after they have reached our ears—though to make the rain sing softly in the middle of one's room or, contrarily, to make the quiet boiling of one's tisane sound like a deluge in the courtyard outside should not really be more misleading than what is so often done by painters when they paint a sail or the peak of a mountain in such a way that, according to the laws of perspective, the intensity of the colours and the illusion of our first glance, they appear to us either very near or very far away, through an error which the reasoning mind subsequently corrects by, sometimes, a very large displacement. Other errors, though of a more serious kind, I might continue to commit, placing features, for instance, as we all do, upon the face of a woman seen in the street, when instead of nose, cheeks and chin there ought to be merely an empty space with nothing more upon it than a flickering reflexion of our desires. But at least, even if I had not the leisure to prepare—and here was a much more important matter—the hundred different masks which ought properly to be attached to a single face, if only because of the different eyes which look at it and the different meanings which they read into its features, not to mention, for the same eyes, the different emotions of hope and fear or on the contrary love and habit which for thirty years can conceal the changes brought about by age, and even if I did not attempt—though my love-affair with Albertine was sufficient proof to me that any other kind of representation must be artificial and untruthful—to represent some of my characters as existing not outside but within ourselves, where their slightest action can bring fatal disturbances in its train, and to vary

Time Regained

also the light of the moral sky which illumines them in accordance with the variations in pressure in our own sensibility (for an object which was so small beneath the clear sky of our certainty can be suddenly magnified many times over on the appearance of a tiny cloud of danger)—if, in my attempt to transcribe a universe which had to be totally redrawn, I could not convey these changes and many others, the needfulness of which, if one is to depict reality, has been made manifest in the course of my narrative, at least I should not fail to portray man, in this universe, as endowed with the length not of his body but of his years and as obliged—a task more and more enormous and in the end too great for his strength—to drag them with him wherever he goes.

Moreover, that we occupy a place, always growing, in Time is something everybody is conscious of, and this universality could only make me rejoice, it being the truth, the truth suspected by each of us, that I had to seek to elucidate. Not only does everybody feel that we occupy a place in Time, but the simplest of us measures this place approximately, as he would measure the one we occupy in space. People with no special perspicacity, seeing two men whom they do not know, both perhaps with black moustaches or both clean-shaven, will say that of the two one is about twenty and the other about forty years old, for the face of a young man cannot possibly be confused with that of a man of middle age, which in the eyes even of the most ignorant beholder is veiled by a sort of mist of seriousness. Of course, this evaluation of age that we make is often inaccurate, but the mere fact that we think ourselves able to make it indicates that we conceive of age as an entity which is measurable. And the second of the two men with black moustaches has, in effect, had twenty years added to his stature.

This notion of Time embodied, of years past but not separated from us, it was now my intention to emphasise as strongly as possible in my work. And at this very moment, in the house of the Prince de Guermantes, as though to strengthen me in my resolve, the noise of my parents' footsteps as they accompanied M. Swann to the door and the peal—resilient, ferruginous, interminable, fresh and shrill—of the bell on the garden gate which informed me that at last he had gone and that Mamma would presently come upstairs, these sounds rang again in my ears, yes, unmistakably I heard these very sounds, situated though they were in a remote past. And as I cast my mind over all the events which were ranged in an unbroken series between the moment of my childhood when I had first heard its sound and the Guermantes party, I was terrified to think that it was indeed this same bell which rang within me and that nothing that I could do would alter its jangling notes. On the contrary, having forgotten the exact manner in which they faded away and wanting to re-learn this, to hear them properly again, I was obliged to block my ears to the conversations which were proceeding between the masked figures all round me, for in order to get nearer to the sound of the bell and to hear it better it was into my own depths that I had to re-descend. And this could only be because its peal had always been there, inside me, and not this sound only but also, between that distant moment and the present one, unrolled in all its vast length, the whole of that past which I was not aware that I carried about within me. When the bell of the garden gate had pealed, I already existed and from that moment onwards, for me still to be able to hear that peal, there must have been no break in continuity, no single second at which I had ceased or rested from existing, from thinking, from being conscious of myself, since that moment from long ago still adhered to me and I could still find it again, could retrace my steps to it, merely by descending to a greater depth within myself. And it is because they contain thus within themselves the hours of the past that human bodies have the power to hurt so terribly those who love them, because they contain the memories of so many joys and desires already effaced for them, but still cruel for the lover who contemplates and prolongs in the dimension of Time the beloved body of which he is jealous, so jealous that he may even wish for its destruction. For after death Time withdraws from the body, and the memories, so indifferent, grown so pale, are effaced in her who no longer exists, as they soon will be in the lover whom for a while they continue to torment but in whom before long they will perish, once the desire that owed its inspiration to a living body is no longer there to sustain them. Profound Albertine, whom I saw sleeping and who was dead.

In this vast dimension which I had not known myself to possess, the

Time Regained

date on which I had heard the noise of the garden bell at Combray—that far-distant noise which nevertheless was within me—was a point from which I might start to make measurements. And I felt, as I say, a sensation of weariness and almost of terror at the thought that all this length of Time had not only, without interruption, been lived, experienced, secreted by me, that it was my life, was in fact me, but also that I was compelled so long as I was alive to keep it attached to me, that it supported me and that, perched on its giddy summit, I could not myself make a movement without displacing it. A feeling of vertigo seized me as I looked down beneath me, yet within me, as though from a height, which was my own height, of many leagues, at the long series of the years.

I understood now why it was that the Duc de Guermantes, who to my surprise, when I had seen him sitting on a chair, had seemed to me so little aged although he had so many more years beneath him than I had, had presently, when he rose to his feet and tried to stand firm upon them, swayed backwards and forwards upon legs as tottery as those of some old archbishop with nothing solid about his person but his metal crucifix, to whose support there rushes a mob of sturdy young seminarists, and had advanced with difficulty, trembling like a leaf, upon the almost unmanageable summit of his eighty-three years, as though men spend their lives perched upon living stilts which never cease to grow until sometimes they become taller than church steeples, making it in the end both difficult and perilous for them to walk and raising them to an eminence from which suddenly they fall. And I was terrified by the thought that the stilts beneath my own feet might already have reached that height; it seemed to me that quite soon now I might be too weak to maintain my hold upon a past which already went down so far. So, if I were given long enough to accomplish my work, I should not fail, even if the effect were to make them resemble monsters, to describe men as occupying so considerable a place, compared with the restricted place which is reserved for them in space, a place on the contrary prolonged past measure, for simultaneously, like giants plunged into the years, they touch the distant epochs through which they have lived, between which so many days have come to range themselves—in Time.

(*Time Regained*, 526–32)

Anne Garréta

Time? Is that the last word?

Yes, I remember, it was also the first one (almost). Many say that at this last word of the last sentence of the last volume we are meant to loop back, in memory or in effect, to the first one of the first sentence of the first volume. Then, you see, the book miraculously announced by a stumble on the cobblestones of the Guermantes's courtyard and the tinkling of a spoon against porcelain, the book finally taking shape in Marcel's mind and which he now fears he won't have time to write before his death, is in fact the book we have been reading all along. Some thus believe that the book ahead of him (and us) is the book we have just closed. The end circles back to its beginning. Eternal return.

But is it?

And how would we know for sure?

What has Marcel just told us about his future book? That its most distinctive feature would be descriptions of men standing as if on the stilts of time, higher than church steeples, their faces lost among clouds, monstrous vacillating beings, giants immersed in time . . . But besides the tottering old Duc de Guermantes, have you encountered any other of these comical creatures perilously aspiring to the celestial realm, or grotesque leviathans wallowing below?

The portrait fits Marcel, at the very least. It fits the book itself even better.

Anne Garréta

Maybe the sole hero of the book is the Book . . .

Wasn't it what the *Adoration perpétuelle* intimated? Life after all has been lived to culminate in a book, and the life of the book with which Marcel finds himself pregnant eclipses all human concerns and duties. Forget love, discount friendship. The book will be the story of a holy literary vocation: the creation shall dwarf the creatures and the creator.

Notice how the body of the work is the only true body; that is, the only body whose monstrous growth could fulfill the promise to incarnate Time. And how the "immeasurable prolongation" which Proust uses to describe men's place in Time most exactly describes the altitude of a text raised on the stilts of sentences 4.27 meters long. Besides, what could represent "those years that fell into place between the extremities" but the thousands of pages piled between origin and ending . . .

Picture this: the Great War had delayed publication of the two volumes Proust had intended after *Swann's Way*. So, from the inside, between the two set extremities or matched bookends of *Swann's Way* and *Time Regained*, grew this cathedral of a book, gaining volume, volumes prolonging, heightening (vertiginously) the body of the text.

But for that *contretemps*, time would have been regained more speedily and a measured, classical bildungsroman unfolded. *Sodom and Gomorrah*, *The Captive*, *The Fugitive* are the true expansion secreted in time. Quite literally, the time lost: lost in love and mundane pursuits, lost for publication, lost even for the narrative, since we're never told where and how (except for a few trips to Paris) Marcel spent the time (or *contretemps*) of the war.

But the entire revelation and holy promise of the *Adoration perpétuelle* is to offer the experience of "a little bit of Time in its pure form." Marcel finally sees his true calling: to capture in "the rings of a beautiful style" the short circuit of past and present allowed by reminiscence to yield "a minute freed from the order of time."

Doesn't this amount in effect to knocking down the stilts?

I have often wondered how readers are supposed to savor the *petite madeleine*. Is our imagination supposed to be strong and vivid enough that when we read of tea and cookies we might not only salivate but see

The Proust Project

Combray resurrected before our eyes in a cloud of cream? Should we start in search of our own private *petites madeleines* and then too write a book testifying to the vanity of worldly life and the true faith of Art?

Maybe the only experience available, within the book, of the transcending operation of time and memory prefigured in the taste of a madeleine, the tinkling of a spoon on a plate, or the stumble on uneven pavement, must take the form of a textual analogon. If the reader's memory is like a giant immersed in pages, in the language of the text, and simultaneously touching widely separated passages, the experience of a pure moment of time, of a freeing from time, will then proceed from a collapse of textual distances. For objects and images never occur just once in the vast expanse of Proust's book and his reader's experience of it: they return.

Thus, if we were able to dive back into our memory for those stilts, or rather if suddenly they emerged from the depth of all the time that passed since we embarked long ago upon reading *In Search of Lost Time*, we would recognize the effigies perched on them, and then truly we would see the book we just finished reading as the cathedral it is intended to be. And maybe we would worship . . .

For there they were, on the façade of Balbec church, visited hundreds of pages ago in *Within a Budding Grove*: "the tall saints' statues perched on those stilts, forming a kind of avenue."

But they were stilts only to the uninitiated, to Marcel, the disappointed narrator. It took the eye of the painter Elstir to dispel Marcel's error—and ours: "If you had looked more carefully at what seemed to you to be stilts you could have named those who were perched on them. For underneath the feet of Moses you would have recognized the Golden Calf, under the feet of Abraham the Ram, under those of Joseph, the devil advising Potiphar's wife."

Stilts are not stilts, and time is not time. The artist shows them to be allegories, the allegories of all the detours and dead ends (jealousy, idolatry, vanity . . .) that obscure and defer the true calling, the recognition of the true law of life and art handed down from prophet to prophet, from Moses and Abraham on to Marcel.

Anne Garréta

I have sometimes felt a slight suspicion that Proust's cathedral is, strangely enough, inverted. It is as if he had turned it inside out: while the masterpiece's façade (and everything we've been taught to behold in it) proclaims the transcendence of creation realized in the sign of the *petite madeleine* and its communion, the monstrous substance of Time and worldly temptations is folded *within* (in the richly detailed nave of the Sodom and Albertine cycles).

But then again, is it a cathedral?

Among the many similes proffered by the *Adoration perpétuelle*, the book stands figured as flesh and stone, child and cemetery, *boeuf en gelée* and cathedral; writing veers from an activity as profane as cuisine or couture to one as sacred as transubstantiation, resurrection, and redemption.

Who knows . . . Those stilts of time could still very well be stilts or thin threads holding together a tattered harlequin's coat; we would have mistaken for a cathedral a great circus, and the acrobat juggling the rings of style for a high priest.

Wyatt Mason

How will it end?

Whether love, plunged into willingly, or life, thrust unwittingly upon us, nothing we begin evades the question very long. And it needn't even be worded to be heard. Its empty echo is ever present, a creeping shadow, a kind of darkness through which we make our stumbling way.

Not, of course, that we believe in endings, however much we fear them, whether of life, or love, or books. For who believes in things we cannot imagine? Who believes the breath we draw will be withdrawn, the love we carry be lifted? And who—one innocent afternoon noodling in a library, or browsing a bookstore, or reclining into a bedside evening, would suspect, while sounding the iambic heartbeat of Proust's big book's first word—*Longtemps*—who would suppose that the long march through time it untethers, the last word it promises, would ever really be within reach?

We can no more suppose, beginning the *Search*, that we will finish it than, while reaching its final pages, that we truly are ending it. For how can a novel that defies the novelistic at every wide, slow, creeping turn—that chuckles at pace, that laughs at chronology, that tests the best reader's most patient attentions—a novel, in short and without argument, unlike any other, how can such a book even have an end?

What would it mean to say: "Today, I finished Proust"?

Who *finishes* Proust?

For even if we do soldier across the continents of its richly remembered world, *descending*, as Marcel says, *to a greater depth within myself*; even if we plumb those depths in his tireless company; even if we

Wyatt Mason

do reach Proust's big book's small last word; we do not finish his book as we do others.

We finish *The Great Gatsby*. We finish *The Good Soldier*. We even finish *Ulysses*. We cannot help it: every page we read brings us nearer to the end. Not so in Proust.

In Proust, even as we move forward, we grow no closer to the end than we were at the beginning. This would be a paradox were our progress measured as it is in other books.

In Proust, we quickly learn, although we move mechanically forward, we do so facing backward. On the hot backseat of the family car we kneel and stare, asleep-awake, out its rear window at the rippling distance that unfolds there to include everywhere we once were. Not in nearness to its end is our progress through Proust measured, but in our distance from its beginning:

> *In this vast dimension which I had not known myself to possess, the date on which I had heard the noise of the garden bell at Combray—that far-distant noise which nevertheless was within me—was a point from which I might start to make measurements.*

The sound of the bell was heard from what seemed a safe haven. The sound of the bell was heard, we recall, from bed. There in the childhood dark, a boy longed for a kiss, knew with animal assurance that, with the bell rung, a maternal embrace could be claimed. The march from bed begins the book just as the forward march backward leads us to its end, *a place prolonged past measure*.

And so, tucked back in, blankets to our chins, darkness kept behind us, the darkness that rests just beyond time, we, alone, in the dark, seek, as the boy in his bed at the beginning did, the bright companionship of a book too mad to read.

Holding tightly to its edges, peering nightly at its pages, we see the darkness behind us take a human shape within us. The world is rendered blank again, as unblemished as the first day of creation. The black remains, of course, but now sown neatly into our welcoming field of

The Proust Project

white in page upon page of tidy rows. And as we approach the destination for which they slowly prepare us, we may not be surprised to find one of our hands hiding the lines just past the one we are reading, lest we be tempted to skip forward, get ahead of ourselves, jump to conclusions we aren't ready for.

But, after all, truly for once *after all*, we are ready. Despite the fright of every other human end, we look forward to a book's last word as we look forward to few last things. We love a book's last word, this book's last word, a word contained in its first. We love this book's last word in equal measure and proportion to how we fear our last, forestalled, this time, in time, by *Time*.

ANDRÉ ACIMAN teaches comparative literature at the Graduate Center of the City University of New York. He is the author of *Out of Egypt: A Memoir* and *False Papers*. His essays have appeared in *The New York Times*, *The New York Review of Books*, *Commentary*, *The New Yorker*, and *The New Republic*.

LOUIS AUCHINCLOSS, a retired attorney and former president of the Academy of Arts and Letters, is the author of over sixty books, most recently *The Scarlet Letters*. He lives in New York City.

LOUIS BEGLEY is the author of seven novels, including *Wartime Lies*, *About Schmidt*, and, most recently, *Shipwreck*. He lives in New York City.

OLIVIER BERNIER, historian and translator, is the author of many books, most recently *Fireworks at Dusk: Paris in the Thirties*, *Louis the Beloved: The Life of Louis XV*, and *The World in 1800*. His lectures include the series at the Metropolitan Museum of Art in New York City, which he has delivered since 1982.

JONATHAN BURNHAM is president and editor in chief of Miramax Books. He was formerly publishing director of Chatto & Windus and the Hogarth Press in London, Proust's original English-language publisher.

MARY ANN CAWS is Distinguished Professor of English, French, and Comparative Literature at the CUNY Graduate Center and past president of the Modern Language Association and the American Comparative Literature Association. She is the author of many books on literature and art, most recently *The Surrealist Look: An Erotics of Encounter* (1997), *Picasso's Weeping Woman: The Life and Art of Dora Maar* (2000), *Virginia Woolf: An Illustrated Life* (2001), *Marcel Proust: An Illustrated Life* (2003), and *Surrealism* (2004).

Contributors

LYDIA DAVIS, a 2003 MacArthur Fellow, is the author of a novel, *The End of the Story* (Farrar, Straus & Giroux, 1995), and three books of short fiction, including *Samuel Johnson Is Indignant* (McSweeney's, 2001). Besides Proust's *Swann's Way* (Viking Penguin, 2003), she has translated works by Maurice Blanchot, Michel Leiris, Pierre Jean Jouve, and many others. Her essay on close translation of Proust appears in the April 2004 issue of the *Yale Review*.

ALAIN DE BOTTON is the award-winning author of seven books of fiction and nonfiction, including the best-seller *How Proust Can Change Your Life* and, most recently, *Status Anxiety*. Two of his books, *The Consolations of Philosophy* and *Status Anxiety*, were made into television documentaries, and his work has been translated into twenty languages.

JEREMY EICHLER is a classical music critic for *The New York Times* and a Richard Hofstadter Fellow in European History at Columbia University. His work has appeared in *The New Republic*, *The Nation*, *Vanity Fair*, *The Washington Post*, and the *Los Angeles Times*.

DANIEL MARK EPSTEIN is the author of seven books of poetry and many biographies and histories, most recently a life of Edna St. Vincent Millay and *Lincoln and Whitman: Parallel Lives in Civil War Washington, D.C.* His work has appeared in the *Atlantic*, *The New Yorker*, *The New Republic*, the *Paris Review*, and many other magazines and anthologies. For his work he has received the Rome Prize from the American Academy of Arts and Letters and a Guggenheim Fellowship.

LESLIE EPSTEIN is the author of nine books of fiction, the latest being the Proustian *San Remo Drive: A Novel from Memory*. He directs the creative writing program at Boston University.

ANNE GARRÉTA teaches at both Duke University and the University of Rennes in France. She is a member of the OULIPO, the literary group founded by Raymond Queneau, and whose best-known members were Italo Calvino and Georges Perec. She is the author of *Sphinx*, *Ciels liquides*, *La Décomposition*, a

Contributors

serial killer's take on Proust's masterpiece, and, most recently, *Pas un jour*, for which she was awarded the Prix Médicis in 2002.

SHIRLEY HAZZARD was born in Australia and lives in New York while maintaining close ties with Italy. She was married to the writer Francis Steegmuller, who died in 1994. She is the author of *The Bay of Noon*, *The Transit of Venus*, and *The Great Fire*, for which she received the National Book Award in 2003.

RICHARD HOWARD is a poet, critic, and translator. He teaches in the School of the Arts (Writing Division) of Columbia University. In October 2004, Farrar, Straus and Giroux published *Inner Voices*, a selection from his first twelve books of poetry, and *Paper Trail*, a selection of his essays.

DIANE JOHNSON, a novelist and critic, divides her time between San Francisco and France. Formerly a professor at the University of California at Davis, she is the author of *Le Divorce* and other novels, most recently *L'Affaire*.

WAYNE KOESTENBAUM has published five books of prose (*Double Talk*, *The Queen's Throat*, *Jackie Under My Skin*, *Cleavage*, and *Andy Warhol*) and three books of poetry, including *Ode to Anna Moffo and Other Poems*. In fall 2004 he will publish his first novel, *Moira Orfei in Aigues-Mortes*, and a book-length poem, *Model Homes*. He is a professor of English at the CUNY Graduate Center.

RENAUD MACHART is a classical music critic for *Le Monde*. He also hosts *Chambre d'écho*, a weekly radio show on France Musiques. He is the author of studies on Francis Poulenc and on John Adams. He has recently translated Ned Rorem's *Paris Diary*.

WYATT MASON's writing has appeared in *Harper's*, the *London Review of Books*, *The New Republic*, and other publications. In 2003 he was named a Fellow of the Dorothy and Lewis B. Cullman Center for Scholars and Writers at the New York Public Library. His most recent book is *I Promise to Be Good: The Letters of Arthur Rimbaud*.

Contributors

J. D. McCLATCHY has written five books of poems, most recently *Hazmat* (Knopf, 2003). His work in the theater includes libretti for new operas soon to open at Covent Garden, the Los Angeles Opera, and Lincoln Center. He teaches at Yale University.

SUSAN MINOT is the author of *Monkeys*, *Lust & Other Stories*, *Folly*, *Evening*, *Rapture*, and *Poems 4 A.M.* She wrote the screenplay for Bernardo Bertolucci's *Stealing Beauty*.

ANKA MUHLSTEIN lives in New York with her husband, the novelist Louis Begley. She was twice awarded the History Prize of the Académie Française and won the Goncourt Prize for biography for her book on Astolphe de Custine.

GEOFFREY O'BRIEN's books include *Dream Time*, *The Phantom Empire*, *The Browser's Ecstasy*, and, most recently, *Sonata for Jukebox*. He contributes frequently to *The New York Review of Books*, *ArtForum*, *Film Comment*, and other periodicals. He is editor in chief of The Library of America.

NOAM SCHEINDLIN's poetry has appeared in various literary journals. He lives in New York City, where he is working toward a Ph.D. in comparative literature at the CUNY Graduate Center.

ANDREW SOLOMON is the author of *The Irony Tower: Soviet Artists in a Time of Glasnost*, the novel *A Stone Boat*, and *The Noonday Demon: An Atlas of Depression*, which won the National Book Award in 2002 and was a finalist for the Pulitzer Prize in 2003. He lives in New York and London and is a graduate of Yale and Cambridge Universities. He is currently writing a book on traumatized families.

JOHN JEREMIAH SULLIVAN is the author of *Blood Horses: Notes of a Sportswriter's Son*. In 2004 he was named a Mel and Lois Tukman Fellow at the New York Public Library's Dorothy and Lewis B. Cullman Center for Scholars and Writers. He lives in Wilmington, North Carolina.

JUDITH THURMAN is the author of *Isak Dinesen: The Life of a Storyteller*, which won the 1982 National Book Award for biography, and *Secrets of*

Contributors

the Flesh: A Life of Colette (1999). Both have been translated into eleven languages. She is a staff writer and cultural critic at *The New Yorker*. Her translations of Louise Labé and Sor Juana Inés de la Cruz have appeared in *The Penguin Book of Women Poets*. She lives in New York with her son, William.

COLM TÓIBÍN is the author of five novels, including *The Blackwater Lightship*, shortlisted for the Booker Prize in 1999, and *The Master*, published in 2004. His work has been translated into twenty-two languages.

LARA VAPNYAR emigrated from Russia to New York in 1994 and published a collection of short stories, *There Are Jews in My House*, in 2003. Her work has appeared in *The New Yorker*, *The New York Times*, and *Open City*. She is pursuing a Ph.D. in comparative literature at the Graduate Center of the City University of New York.

EDMUND WHITE has written a short biography of Proust and a long one of Jean Genet, for which he won the National Book Critics Circle Award. He has written books about Paris, including *The Flâneur*, and many novels, including, most recently, *The Married Man* and *Fanny: A Fiction*. He is the director of creative writing at Princeton University.